The Pan Principle

THE PAN PRINCIPLE

Fiona Pitt-Kethley

SINCLAIR-STEVENSON

First published in Great Britain in 1994
by Sinclair-Stevenson
an imprint of Reed Consumer Books Ltd
Michelin House, 81 Fulham Road, London sw3 6rb
and Auckland, Melbourne, Singapore and Toronto

A CIP catalogue record for this book
is available at the British Library

isbn 1 85619 426 4

Typeset by Deltatype Ltd, Ellesmere Port, South Wirral
Printed in England by Clays Ltd, St Ives plc

Acknowledgements

I would like to acknowledge the help of various members of the staff and students of both the British and American Schools at Athens, most expecially Jere Wickens. I would also like to thank Don Fowles and Professor John Sullivan for useful information.

Contents

Introduction

Epitherses, the father of Aemilian the rhetorician,
sailing from Greece to Italy, in a ship freighted with
divers goods and passengers, at night the wind failed
them near the Echinades, some islands that lie between
the Morea and Tunis, and the vessel was driven near
Paxos. When they were got thither, some of the
passengers being asleep, others awake, the rest eating
and drinking, a voice was heard that called aloud,
'Thamous!' which cry surprised them all. This same
Thamous was their pilot, an Egyptian by birth, but
known by name only to some few travellers. The voice
was heard a second time, calling Thamous, in a
frightful tone; and none making answer, but trembling,
and remaining silent, the voice was heard a third time,
more dreadful than before.

   This caused Thamous to answer; 'Here am I, what
dost thou call me for? What wilt though have me do?'
Then the voice, louder than before, bid him publish,
when he should come to Paloda, that the great god Pan
was dead.

> *The Works of Rabelais*, translated by Robert Urquhart
> and P. A. Motteux

*W*hen I first decided to research the god Pan and the
places where he was worshipped, I sensed that there
was a mystery to be solved. The jigsaw pieces I had to
put together were in part literary, in part visual. There was the
Plutarch story of the god's death, various mentions of the
places where he worshipped in Pausanias, together with a host

of briefer references in the works of poets, historians, philosophers and playwrights. Then there were the objects that came from his shrines – tiny terracotta images or larger marble reliefs and statues. There were inscriptions also, naming some of his priests and worshippers. And there were the places dedicated to him – anything from tiny sordid caves to whole mountains.

I first came across the famous story of Pan's death from Plutarch's *Moralia* in Rabelais' beautifully expressed version. Thamous went on to give the message and 'deep groans, great lamentations, and doleful shrieks, not of one person, but of many together, were heard from the land'. What other God has such a story written about him? What other immortal was said to have died without resurrection?

The Emperor Tiberius heard the tale and ordered scholars to investigate. They came to the conclusion that Pan was the son of Hermes. When I went into the subject I found that there were other Pans also. There's a total of fourteen different sets of parents who may have been his progenitors. Anyone who has delved into their own family history will know the problems. In my own family, I've found that my great-grandmother lied about her age on her marriage certificate, another member of the family had no birth certificate because she was illegitimate, and most of my ancestors weren't where they should have been on the night of every census! Pan's genealogy is even more complicated. He has three possible fathers – Kronos, Zeus or Hermes – even if you discard the idea that he was the son by Penelope of all her suitors. His collection of possible mothers includes Zeus's Nanny, who was quite literally a nanny goat of monstrous size, and various nymphs.

The fact that Pan's so-called death occurred in Tiberius's reign – that is, in the time of Christ – became a fruitful source of speculation for Christians in the centuries to follow. Christian writers fell into two camps. There were those who saw Pan as a demon (their usual designation for pagan gods) and rejoiced in the death of another of Christ's rivals. Christian writers believed quite erroneously that all the old oracles failed in the time of Christ. I have already disproved this theory in my *Journeys to the Underworld*. The facts of the case are that some had closed down a lot earlier and some went on a great deal longer. The other school of Christian thought identified Christ with Pan. They were both, after all, good shepherds.

Although Pan is not considered to be a major god by most people, it's a fact that there are more dedications to him than to any other in the Greek Anthology. His lack of the obvious physical beauty of the others and his half-human, half-bestial appearance probably made him seem more approachable. There are also probably more mentions of him than other gods in our literature. Throughout the ages prose writers and poets have used his image in one way or another – adapting the truth to fit the points they make. He was an endless source of metaphysical speculation. This means that he probably also rates as the most misunderstood god of them all.

The Eleusinian Mysteries, the secret ceremonies in the worship of the goddess Demeter, are talked of as the only religious mystery in our knowledge of pagan ritual. But every cult, including that of Pan, is just as much a mystery to be solved, or, at any rate, speculated upon. Every cult – and there were many – left its scatter of objects in the places where it was practised, whether these were caves or more conventional shrines or temples. Every cult also left its clues in more artistic form. Probably the best clue to that of Pan lies in the large collection of votive tablets in Athens' National Archaeological Museum. Beyond that sort of clue there are also objects like Greek vases with their depictions of myths and religious rituals. I feel slightly mistrustful of Greek vases though – they are just a little bit too decorative. I know an artist so keen on money that property developers can persuade him to add extra persons or animals to his murals by the offer of a little extra cash. I can imagine that the same was true of vase-painters. If the ignoramus who was ordering a huge vase for his bedroom wanted two Pans instead of one in the painting, then he would certainly get it – if the money was right. At the same time, a generalised look at vases is useful. It tells you which gods and goddesses Pan was associated with. Although the caves and shrines I visited teamed him with both the nymphs and a selection of male gods – Dionysos, Zeus, Hermes and Apollo – vases quite often show him together with Artemis and Actaeon or Aphrodite.

What can be told from the appearance of Pan? The style and age of gods in images through the centuries is surprisingly similar. Most representations of the Olympians show them as exceptionally good-looking people in their twenties and thirties. It's not easy in Greek statuary to confuse them with statues of mortals. In the time of the Roman emperors it was common to have a statue of a human made to look like a god. The emperors thought nothing, too, of knocking off a head and substituting their own portrait bust. Whether they vandalised a statue or not, the end result was Caesar as Apollo, or Caesar as Zeus. I have an illustration at home of Julius Caesar's head, bald spot cunningly concealed, on a beautiful naked Hermes. It's interesting that this sort of representation didn't seem to invite ridicule in classical times. The modern equivalent would be the Queen poking her head through Titian's *Venus of Urbino* or Manet's *Olympia* to have her photo taken.

Aphrodite is usually shown naked, other goddesses rarely so. Apollo looks decidedly ambiguous sexually, Dionysos even more so. Hermes, being the messenger, looks slightly more athletic. Zeus, who is often shown naked, looks older than some of the other gods – in his thirties and at his prime. His body is thoroughly masculine and strong. His wife, Hera, is the weightiest of the goddesses and is always shown very thoroughly clothed. Athena frequently wears a helmet. All these gods are instantly recognisable in any museum across the world, even if only the head is left.

The age of the face portrayed as that of Pan is much more variable. Some are old and ugly, some young and passable if you don't mind a bloke with horns and rather large ears. (Horns are not as uncommon on humans as you might think. I possess a *Strand Magazine* with an article on the subject and pictures of a few horned Victorians.) A great many of the portraits of Pan have what I would describe as a melted look. It's as if the features were made of wax and had begun to run. It gives the impression of being halfway through metamorphosis. The nose is a slightly squashed Roman one, there are lines on either side of the thick-lipped smiling mouth and an Aboriginal-type depression of the brow between the eyes. The hair is unkempt and slightly scruffy, sometimes curly, sometimes straight, but always flattened down on the head. Sometimes the hair hides both horns and ears. Almost all the images of Pan are bearded. As gods go he looks like a bit of rough, but his expression is benign. Pan's body is short and fairly muscular, though not in perfect shape. The upper half is that of an active man, the lower that of a goat. He is always naked unless you read the lower half as goatskin breeches with the flies undone. Pan's cock is often erect – 'ithyphallic' as polite classical sources like to phrase it. But Pan is never Priapically endowed. There is no image where it stands out like a handle. You couldn't hang a thimble on it let alone your hat. If anything, his cock is rather small compared with those I've seen on humans and goats. It's in proportion to his height, which is always less than that of the other gods he's with in any relief or statuary group.

Pan, being short for a god, would still be considerably taller than most humans. Most of the gods are depicted on reliefs as fractionally under twice the height of their human worshippers. If they are round about eleven feet high, Pan still reaches eight or nine.

If you look at Pan's face alone, it would be easy to mistake him for a human when the slightly pointed ears are covered, or the horns absent or broken off. He has a lived-in face. Most of the other gods show no sign in their faces of having suffered. Some writers talk of Pan as unlucky in love compared with the other gods, but that's a delusion. Just how good was the family life of the others? Hera married Zeus (her brother in one account) after he raped her. She'd refused him for three hundred years first. He was massively unfaithful, often raping unwilling victims. A great many of his girlfriends came to sticky ends. He had bisexual and paedophile tendencies (remember Ganymede). Hera is supposed to have only been unfaithful once – she renewed her virginity yearly in a spring. Their marriage seems to have been one of incessant quarrels. Demeter was one of the other women in that marriage. Her daughter Persephone was raped and spent half the year in hell, but came home to Mummy for the other six months. Artemis and Athena were virgins. Athena, however, had lesbian tendencies. She was caught in the bath with a nymph and promptly blinded the unlucky voyeur. Hephaistos, Aphrodite's husband, had tried to rape Athena – but obviously she preferred nymphs. His marriage to Aphrodite was hardly a lucky one. She had affairs with Hermes, Poseidon, Dionysos and various mortals as well as her thoroughly public one with Mars. The guilty pair were caught in a net by Hephaistos. Most of Aphrodite's affairs resulted in children. She renewed her virginity regularly in the sea. Apollo, a bisexual bachelor, had several affairs, some by trickery. Some of those he wooed unsuccessfully came to sticky ends. Dionysos, apart from having Priapus by Venus, had a relatively sound marriage with Ariadne. Presumably she didn't mind his disappearing from time to time with a bunch of tattooed women called the

Maenads. Hermes was a bachelor with several sons. He had several successful affairs and committed a few rapes. In one case he killed the father – he might be considered the original Don Juan. Poseidon was probably one of the most stable in his love life – three kids by Amphitrite, who was persuaded not raped, as well as an affair with Scylla and one or two sea nymphs. It can be said though that all his children were monsters.

If the *News of the World* had been around in those days it could have been kept going in copy for years by that lot. Was Pan any unluckier, more unstable, less successful in his love life? The women that are associated with him are Selene (the moon), Echo, Pitys and Syrinx. Echo preferred the wimp, Narcissus. Pitys (the fir cone) and Syrinx (the reed) are as much associated with Pan as Daphne (the laurel) is with Apollo. The stories of unsuccessful affairs or attempted rapes are similar. Selene was pulled by deception. He donned a white fleece from a ram and she came down to join him in a cave on Mount Lykaion. Is that story any less successful than Zeus's metamorphosis into a bull to rape Europa? At least Selene was willing.

Christians and Jews are often horrified at the selection of gods chosen by the Greeks. But is it such a bad idea to have imperfect gods to worship? Perfect ones seem too far away, too hard to understand. If our gods have a magnified version of our faults, then we can relate to them. Could the all-male, super-perfect Trinity understand a marriage problem as well as Zeus and Hera? Personally, I find it harder to relate to a god who's had no sex as humans understand the word. The Catholic Church has at least recognised this problem and provided a vast selection of saints with very imperfect pasts for people to pray to – though none of them, I suppose, has goats' legs.

For the non-religious, Hollywood stars and supermodels are the equivalent of the pagan gods. People don't pray to them but they fantasise about sex with them, read prurient accounts of their lives and use them as role models. Most of the heroes and heroines that are chosen among stars are beautiful with perfectly fixed teeth and fit bodies. Occasionally, though, we need an anti-hero – someone who's not so beautiful that he makes us feel inferior. Someone like Rod Steiger is very ordinary-looking, but the passion in his acting puts him in the rank of shining stars. Pan is a god of this class.

Whatever his parentage, nobody seems to doubt that Pan's birthplace was Arcadia. Arcadia itself has been liable to major distortions from poets. From Theocritus to our Elizabethans it is shown as a lush, Utopian place where nymphs and shepherds live in an idyll that's forever summer. The country-side he describes is much less hard and mountainous than the reality. It is, in fact, far more like Theocritus's native Sicily in the spring to early summer before the drought of the hottest part of the year.

At the other end of the spectrum, Arcadia's hardness can also be exaggerated. A Classics professor who's a friend of mine took a long March walk there, got lost and nearly froze to death in the night. He wore out the soles of his shoes completely in that one day's walk. I have read travel-book accounts of terrible storms in summer with huge hailstones that could kill a sheep and quite possibly a man. In these books, the mountains of Arcadia are all frozen and covered with ice until the summer.

The truth, of course, is somewhere in the middle. Arcadia, historically, has not been suitable land for crops. Its original inhabitants were hard men who ate acorns and lived by herding. The area was once famous for its herds of horses. I did not see as much as one horse on my visits there. There are still many sheep and goats though. Mules take the place of horses now. In Sparta, at the top of Taÿgetos, I also saw cows.

The land is hard to farm, because parts of it are inaccessible in bad weather. Many roads are still only dirt tracks. There have always been problems with water too, ranging from drainage to drought. There are marshy basins with no outlet for the sudden accumulations of water from mountain snows and streams. When these streams dry up, later in the year, the marshes disappear. There's an unreliability about Arcadia. Survival is only possible if you're prepared to adapt and move your flocks from pasture to pasture. A shepherd has to understand his land and sense what's going to happen before disaster ensues.

Many of the legends that are Arcadian in origin, whether they concern Pan or other gods, contain an element that relates to the concept of reverting to nature in a bad sense. Though there were powerful kings and kingdoms and many temples there once, there's a sense that the people were always desperately insecure, afraid of a return to living in caves and eating human flesh. These legends often contain a metaphor of animal transformation.

Most of the temples and powerful old cities of Arcadia are no more. Yet the imagined threat of reversion to cave-dwelling cannibalism never happened. Modern Greeks, though, retain the hysteria, the fear of going back to nature. For most of them the evidence of archaeology is rejected together with the caves and the mountains. They would never understand the English idyll of retiring to grow your own vegetables and keep a few animals in a Sussex village. For almost every Greek I've met, moving to Athens and leaving behind the rural life is considered a necessity. Greeks must drive not walk. All their faith seems to be pinned on modern technology, modern housing and a rejection of everything old.

Wrong aspirations can cause the downfall of any nation. The Greek pollution problem is the greatest I've encountered in any country. It is slowly but surely damaging every outdoor work of art. Greece is years behind any other country I've visited in tackling matters relating to conservation.

In one tiny place, though, I was to find a seed of hope for the future. One village, amongst all the places I visited, had a positive policy towards the environment. Its Association was replanting trees and conserving springs. It was in one of the cleanest areas of Greece and was unadorned with the usual Greek litter of busted cars and household rubbish. That village was the highest inhabited point on Mount Lykaion, sacred to Pan and Zeus, right in the middle of Arcadia. In that place, as in few others in Greece, I had a sense that Pan and Nature were still alive.

Trivial Pursuits

By education most have been misled;
So they believe, because they so were bred.

Dryden: 'The Hind and the Panther'

*E*very cheap flight to Athens was booked solid, so I found myself grasping an inter-rail ticket in amongst students from across the world. From the moment I left the house I felt different with a pack on my back. The Hastings bus driver thought I was foreign as I went to the station, and a tramp said: 'The likes of them don't know what it's like not to have food' – pointing at some other travellers with new, unbattered suitcases.

These days, almost anyone can carry a rucksack. There was even an American of sixty or more with one on the ferry. She teetered around in gold stilettos and a dyed bouffant hairdo, trying to add height any way she could. I don't suppose anyone mistook her for a student, but mostly that's what happens when you have a pack on your back.

Taking an international train usually involves a change at Paris. Once aboard the second train, you find that each carriage, linguistically, is a law unto itself. They're like embassies. The inmates choose which language is spoken. I found myself with French Canadians, having to speak French to be understood.

In the middle of the night we were woken up by Swiss

customs officers who found it deeply suspicious that there were five Canadians there who spoke hardly a word of English. The fact that a good many Canadians are principally French-speaking doesn't seem to have reached Europe yet. Why was I, with my British passport, travelling with them? I was asked. Trains are public places and you rarely get to choose which couchette you occupy. If you don't make friends with the people you're spending anything from a night to twenty-four hours with, you could end up going mad – that is unless you've brought several good books with you. The poor Canadians had also not got Swiss visas. The fact that the train skimmed through Switzerland for perhaps half an hour on its long journey could hardly have been obvious.

Eventually things were sorted out and we were allowed to go to sleep again. This was the first time I'd booked a couchette. I'd allowed myself to be persuaded by the travel agent, just as I'd allowed myself to be persuaded on to the Sea Cat instead of a hovercraft proper or the slower ferry. The Sea Cat subjects you to a ghastly promotional film of its prowess while providing the bumpiest channel ride I've ever experienced. Even its name is a paradox – the sea and cats don't mix.

My principal mistake with the couchette was being in the top one. 'You can get a good sleep there,' the travel agent had said. 'Nobody'll climb over you to go to the lavatory.' But the trouble was, when I wanted to go to the lavatory in the morning, the ladder had been moved slightly – so slightly that it looked all right. It was loose however and, when I was about two rungs down, off it came and I went flat on my back on top of the assorted trainers of the Canadians, still clutching the ladder to my chest. Nothing was actually broken, but I could feel a bad pain in my lower back and had probably also bruised an elbow and the side of one of my feet. When I examined my back in the lavatory mirror, one of the lower vertebrae looked reddened and prominent – something seemed slightly out of place.

I had learned a little Shiatsu and luckily I remembered the right pressure points to treat the back. I sat up on my bunk and dug my fingers in either side of the Achilles tendons and the pain got a little better.

I've travelled overnight to Italy before, but never right down into its heel in one stretch. By the end of the next day, I was nearly screaming with boredom. The Adriatic coast, seen from the train, is duller than the other side. Only Apulia, with its olive groves and beehive-shaped huts, looked faintly interesting.

At Bari, there was a general rush for the ferries. For a boat that plies its trade between Bari and Patras, HMS *Tiepolo* had curiously few signs in Greek. Drachmas were not acceptable on board. Every notice was in several languages – English, German, Italian and what might have been Serbo-Croat. Only two notices were translated into Greek – the aggressive one about not putting sanitary towels down lavatories and another with a wonderful malapropism: 'The direction of the ship does not take on responsibility for all values left in the cabin or elsewhere.' The Greek version contained a similar mistake.

My night was definitely more comfortable than the previous one – there were no couchettes to fall off. At this stage, never having been to Greece, I was full of romantic illusions and went on deck early to look for Ithaca. We passed several islands but I couldn't quite decide which it was. An American girl was piously performing ballet exercises on deck – she had probably been one of the brave souls who stayed outside, with or without sleeping-bags.

When we docked at Patras I bought a large bunch of grapes, expecting them to be better than Greek grapes back home – they weren't. I also got a postcard of goats fucking for my mother – she likes goats and worries about me. Once the card was in the box, I went back to the station, determined to get on the first train out. Moving from place to place in a restless, haphazard way is the only form of travel when you're researching a god like Pan.

The train for Pyrgos came in first. I could change there and go on to Olympia and stay the night before seeing the excavations in the morning. Olympia has a slim Pan connection. There was an altar to him there. Come to think of it, there was an altar to almost every other god, major or minor, too. The altar would probably not be findable, but there might be something relevant in the museum.

I had about an hour to wait in Pyrgos so I thought I'd walk a few blocks and have a drink. Just round the corner I met Spiros who offered me the coffee I needed. Before I could get the first sip down, I found myself in the midst of a Trivial Pursuits quiz on Greek mythology. Although my knowledge of the latter is reasonable, I could not always give the answers he wanted, simply because I see things differently. 'Who is the God of Education?' he asked. The answer that was wanted was Athena. To me, Athena represents wisdom – the two things are not necessarily related.

Spiros was certainly well-educated, but perhaps a little short of wisdom. He was one of those Greeks who suffer from an insane hatred of the Turks. 'We never allow one Turk into Greece,' he said. 'They are the mice and we are the cats.' But there are buses and flights to Istanbul, not to mention crossings from various Greek islands off the Turkish coast. Can it all be one-way traffic?

So many Greeks have this irrational hatred of the Turks that I've developed a way of getting them to talk more realistically about their traditional enemies. I tell them in as much detail as I can muster about the old hatreds between the English and the Welsh. Most Europeans have a mistaken concept of all British as English, speaking only one language. I tell them that I'm English-Welsh-Scots-Irish-German-Italian by birth. This sort

4

of mongrel mixture is extremely common among the British, I say. I also speak of my Scottish name, my Welsh accent that the English hate and how I was teased for it at school. I go on to say that the accent is so slight that it's not perceivable in Wales. In fact the Welsh see me as one of the awful English, because England is where I live. Sometimes I demonstrate the enormous difference between the Celtic languages and English by quoting a few words of Welsh. This demonstrates that I'm not talking about a people who are only slightly different and who speak a dialect version of English. Sometimes, interestingly, this catalogue of the otherness and the hatreds within British society extorts a recriprocal confession. There are quite a few Greeks who'll admit to a Turkish grandfather or great-grandfather once they know that most of the so-called English are mongrels too.

Yes, of course the Turks committed atrocities – as did the Japanese and the Germans in the last war. Yet the Turks, the Japanese and the Germans that I've met have mostly been charming, kind people. What we must hate are the atrocities, the vices themselves, not any whole nation. Our energy of hate must be channelled into stamping out the things in society and in ourselves which lead to these atrocities. Without that great vice, obedience, there could have been no Nazism, no Spanish Inquisition. Children must be taught to question everything before they accept anything. It is the element of unquestioning obedience that is expected in many schools that endangers the soul. It is the element that keeps education and wisdom poles apart. Education should have a different goddess as it stands – an underworld one.

Spiros was the first Greek I'd met on Greek soil. At that stage I had not developed my method of dealing with their deep hatred of the Turks and so I just listened, taking it all with a large pinch of salt, of course. Soon Spiros was offering me his little *pied-à-terre* in the town to spent the night in – alone. We could have an evening together and he would drive me to Olympia the following morning. I took the night-alone bit with another pinch of salt, but Spiros was good-looking, so why not?

Spiros was proud of his home town and showed me round it. Half an hour is considerably too long a time to spend on seeing Pyrgos. I was asked to admire war memorials, a modern church and modern buildings. The only thing I found even faintly admirable was the old fish-market with a few mock Corinthian cornices – but Spiros found my liking for this building extremely perverse. It had been closed down years ago, he said – 'Too old-fashioned!'

We had a Greek salad, souvlaki and beer in a small café. When in doubt in Greece, that's the best meal to choose. It's very hard to bugger up, ruin or overcook. If you're led into a Greek kitchen to choose your meal and can't face anything from the greasy saucepans full of simmering ooze, you can always ask for a Greek salad.

Spiros seemed to know everybody in Pyrgos. He was an accountant and he told me how he'd done all their tax forms for them. He seemed to be showing me off. Perhaps that proved he wasn't married – but perhaps not.

We ended up at a seaside café outside Pyrgos, drinking ouzo, then walking on the beach, kissing. The beach was pitch black and I kept getting sand in my shoes and falling over ropes – but Spiros thought it romantic and admired the half-dozen or so stars that deigned to shine that night.

The *pied-à-terre* was a room in a cracking block. The rendering on the outside was falling off in large lumps. A great many houses in Pyrgos had the same problem. The ceiling of the room looked ready to fall also, and a fine flour-like dust of plaster filtered down from time to time. Outside, the courtyard was choked up with huge nettles, rubbish, yellow ragwort, a twisted orange tree, morning glory and what the Bible would describe as 'a naughty fig tree'.

6

'Can I make real love in plastic?' Spiros asked. It would make a good philosophical question, but I don't suppose he meant it that way. He chose the more precarious of the two beds for us to have sex on. It groaned and sagged with even one of us on it. Would it survive anything vigorous?

Spiros had his own condoms – a brand called STOP. Being an accountant, he was so super-cautious that he also pulled a rubber band over and slid it up to the top of his cock to hold everything firmly in place. I prayed to the infernal gods that it wouldn't catch in my pubic hair.

Some prostitutes, I suppose, would be glad of a client like Spiros. He was awfully quick about it. He'd done his foreplay miles away on the beach – so why should he bother with any more?

Before he left to go back to his family, he plugged a tiny pink lightbulb into the wall – it was supposed to deter mosquitoes. The light from it was very weak, so Spiros suggested I leave it on, which I did in order to keep a check on which bit of the ceiling looked likeliest to go first. The window didn't open and I was shut in with a noisy mosquito that didn't care a toss about any pink lights. The bed curved like a hammock beneath my bad back. I've never yet met a man who owned a nice bedroom – maybe I'd be tempted to stay longer if I did.

I am not a tidy person, but it would be hard for anyone to hit the depths of untidiness in parts of that room. There were rags, empty cartons, unwashed cutlery, a pair of tights, old calendars and coffee cups covered in mildew, or still containing half inches of various sticky liquids. They reminded me of my sixth-form common room. We had coffee-making facilities but no sinks on that side of the school. Everyone chucked their dregs out of the windows and only took the cups home to wash when things started growing in them.

Spiros' cups could have been washed quite easily in the bathroom next door. It was what I came to recognise later as

7

the average Greek bathroom – the lavatory didn't flush, but a bucket was standing by. The shower just about worked – that is if you like the odd sudden squirt of cold water.

Spiros hadn't smoked during the evening, but there were lots of empty cigarette cartons in the bedroom and spent matches. Strangest of all for a man who had claimed he was single in his thirties because he hadn't met the right woman, the whole pile was crowned with a baby's dummy. Perhaps the room didn't belong to Spiros at all, but to some chain-smoking baby.

Olympia

We are under-exercised as a nation.
We look instead of play. We ride instead of walk.

John F. Kennedy

I had been ordered not to unhook the staple on my door until Spiros did his special knock at eight the next morning. I was dressed and ready to go, but he wanted some more foreplayless sex first, STOP condom and rubber band on as usual. Luckily I'd been having sexy dreams about someone else, so I was lubricated enough for it. Spiros made us coffee afterwards with a tiny primus stove and percolator. He obviously had a system and extracted these objects, together with a jam jar of sugar, from the heap. He managed to find clean but cracked cups too. They all went back in the heap afterwards, sugar still sticking to the side of his.

Spiros' car was in a similar state to his flat – many Greek cars are. I was told that there was no Greek car industry to speak of. Consequently cars cost as much as a house, which means that owners glue them together with chewing gum and spit for twenty years rather than buy another.

The country became rather beautiful as we neared Olympia – like our moorlands, but warmer. Spiros was pleased when I admired it. Olympia itself looked sadly commercialised. Perhaps I had done better by going native and staying in a chain-smoking baby's flat. Spiros got himself free into the excavations. He had done the guard's accounts. I had a Baedeker with me so he suggested I search out the things I wanted to see from that. There's a lot left. The site has been excavated, mainly by Germans during the nineteenth century. It's still possible to trace the foundations of the *altis* (grove) or sacred precinct, the *prytaneion* where all the athletes were put up at public expense, the gymnasium where they spent the last month in training, the council-house, the temple of Zeus, the *Heraion*, several treasuries, porticoes, altars and many other buildings. But some of the remains nearest to the River Alpheios have vanished into it. When I was there the Alpheios was dry and full of rubbish. Most Greek rivers are used as dumping grounds in the summer for everything from babies' nappies to old cars that couldn't be held together any longer by chewing-gum.

The old running area for short sprints still looks pretty intact. Even the ancient marble starting line of the Stadion still exists. I enjoyed seeing that more than the rest of Olympia put together – not so much for its romantic associations, but because several elderly American ladies and gentlemen had decided to have their photos taken in what they thought was an Olympian starting position. They hadn't realised that in ancient times runners started upright, but had assumed the line was a sort of modern starting block on which they had to go down on all fours, oblivious of the pains of arthritis and gout, and in spite of the wadges of fat round their middles that kept them from bending quite that far. When one set had posed for photographs another would take its place. Someone could have had great fun videoing it – the result would have been pure Benny Hill. But tourists only produce their camcorders at cultural or boring family moments – hand-held, shaky views of the Parthenon or little Sandra splashing around. I could see more use to camcorders if people came back from their holidays with a Chaplinesque film. I don't own a camcorder, but I could have stayed and watched the activity on the starting line for hours. Curiously, none of the fit, thin tourists wanted their photographs taken there – perhaps they were too busy climbing on pedestals elsewhere.

The legendary founding of the Games dates back to the birth of Zeus, but a more specific reorganisation was made by Iphitos of Elis and Lykourgos of Sparta in the ninth century BC, after they'd taken the advice of the Delphic oracle. The Games then were a time of truce between the warring states and a national festival – an expression of Hellenic unity. The chronicle of Olympic victors dates back only to 776 BC. At the beginning of the sacred month, the Eleans who kept the sanctuary would send out heralds to proclaim universal peace and competitors would start to stream in from as far away as Sicily and Asia Minor. Though steroids weren't invented then, there were many scandals concerning bribery, mainly amongst the boxers. Olympic winners stood to gain not only their laurels (or rather their wild olive) but also great family honour and sometimes tax exemption. In Roman times athletes became professional rather than amateur – Victorian writers are appalled by this. Under Theodosius, in the fourth century, the Games were closed down.

According to my Baedeker, women weren't allowed to watch – apart, that is, from the local priestess of Demeter. But the facts as related by Pausanias seem slightly different. He mentions a ban on women entering the Olympic assembly that could result in capital punishment. One woman risked the penalty though. She entered the sacred area as a trainer with her son. Her true sex was revealed as she leapt over a fence. She escaped punishment because of her good family connections. After Kallipateira's day, trainers had to enter the area naked to avoid any confusion.

Even if they weren't allowed into the Olympic assembly, it seems that women were allowed to compete. Pausanias mentions female winners – Kyniska with her racehorses, for instance. She was the first woman winner. Spartans did better than other women – probably because of the fact that training with the men was customary in Spartan education. It would be interesting to know if Olympic-winning women competed amongst the men. It seems likely that they did, rather than in separate events, but I haven't seen any definite information on this. Perhaps different laws operated at different times.

Races in honour of Hera were held for virgin girls only. I can't help wondering if they were tested first. The virgins let their hair down and wore a rather fetching costume of a short tunic with one breast hanging out. I don't know whether there were any male spectators.

While I walked through the ruins, I caught sight of Spiros from time to time. He looked like a man with a mission. Every time he crossed the path of someone he thought was a young German tourist, he held out his hand, saying: '*Guten Morgen. Wie geht es Ihnen?*' Why was he asking how they were? I wondered. Last night he'd been slagging them off almost as much as the Turks.

All the tourists he picked on turned out to be from other nations. He changed his language accordingly, saying: '*Goede morgen*' to the Dutch or '*Buenos días*' to the Spanish. He boasted that he had even learned a little Icelandic. Eventually, by the old treasury of the Sicyonians, Spiros found some real live Germans and the mystery was revealed. He brought a huge roll of drachmas out of his pocket and tried to change as much as he could into Deutschmarks. The treasury seemed to be a good pick-up point and very soon he'd waylaid several visitors and changed a wad of notes. The Greek government, he explained, only allowed you to buy a small amount of hard currency each month.

We went to the museum next. Spiros was smiling, his pocket bulging with Deutschmarks. It's a bright, light, modern museum full of sculptures – those that did not go to Berlin or Paris from the original excavations, that is. A great many of the statues mentioned by Pausanias did not survive. There was such a wealth of statuary in his day that it took him a book or two of his guide to get round it all. One of the items that has vanished, alas, is a sculpture of a rather ugly mare with a cropped tail which got all the stallions for miles excited. Probably they shagged the image to pieces.

The museum contains much more heroic sculpture than sex dolls for horses – reliefs of lapiths and centaurs, all the labours of Hercules, and, most famous of all, the Hermes of Praxiteles. Spiros took me to look at this and asked me what I noticed that was special about it. It was another of his Trivial Pursuits questions. Well, it was obviously a major work of art (or, more probably, a good Hellenistic copy of one). It was impeccable anatomically and Hermes was a handsome chap. But what was I supposed to answer? Hermes has two expressions – one side of his face is sad, the other has a playful smile. That was what Spiros had been taught. But is it true of that statue any more than any other? Is it any more true than that the Mona Lisa's eyes follow you on stalks? It would be tempting to invent a set of legends of my own about pictures and spread it among gullible schoolchildren. Perhaps I should get them to try drawing a St Andrew's cross on a photo of a relief or painting to find its centre. It's surprising how often that centre lands on male genitals.

After his brief excursion into money-changing, everywhere we walked Spiros clung to me sweatily and romantically. By now I wanted to lose him fast. I hate people resting their armpit on my shoulder or gripping my waist like a vice. Spiros had started suggesting he come and stay with me in a hotel at my next port of call – Tripolis, or wherever. I was firm enough to offend him, but anything was better than being haunted throughout my travels by a foreplayless fucker.

Fallen Cities

All things to their decline do tend,
All falls, expires, comes to its end:
Man dies, iron rusts, wood rots away,
Towers sink, walls fall, rose has its day.
Horse stumbles, cloth wears out apace,
No work of hands leaves lasting trace.

Robert Wace: *Le Roman de Rou*
(Victorian translation)

*M*y ancient Baedeker talked of a new carriage-road being built from Olympia to Megalopolis – perhaps there would be a bus service along that route. There wasn't. The road was still in its same unfinished state, ninety years on, so I settled for a trip to Tripolis.

The bus wound past range after range of mountains. As it climbed there was almost an aerial view of the lower hills with their well-marked dirt tracks and dried-up stream beds. I felt I could have found my way anywhere on them and longed to walk for hours alone. Probably, though, if I'd been down on those roads, I'd have got lost, being unable to see the ground plan that was so obvious from above.

The bus was gradually emptying at tiny villages. Most people were not going to Tripolis. There was a seriously sick couple at the front. I don't think they were more than middle-aged, but he had eyes almost turned inside out with rheum and both of them had paper bags into which they were quietly spitting. At every major stop, they crawled off the bus, holding

15

each other up, to have a really good spit and deal with the bags of phlegm, which went flying off into various ravines. It was so disgusting that it was riveting – I couldn't take my eyes off it, although I tried to keep my face in a neutral expression not to hurt their feelings.

The couple got off at Dimitzana. From there on we were definitely in Pan country – firs and beautiful mountain peaks (part of the Mainalos range) – an area where his music could be heard in ancient times.

Tripolis itself is an underrated city. Its name – three cities – shows its origin in the amalgamation and fall of Tegea, Mantineia and Pallantio. It's supposed to have been built, originally, from their remains. There's nothing obvious left of old Pallantio, but the other two have sizeable remains. Tripolis itself is a working, non-tourist city. The hotels are often fully booked with Greeks, mostly commercial travellers. I had a hard job getting a room that day, but ended up in the nicest Greek hotel I stayed at during any of my trips – Hotel Menalon on the park, on the outskirts of the city. Unfortunately, they only had a room for one night. It had a balcony overlooking the park with a perfect view of the distant mountains.

Tripolis has a most bloody history. During the War of Independence, in 1821, the Greeks perpetrated one of the world's most bloody massacres against the Turks and the Jewish colony in the town. Ten thousand Turks were slaughtered. Those thought to be concealing money were first roasted or their arms and legs cut off. Pregnant women were slit open, decapitated and the heads of dogs put between their legs. (Presumably the dogs were decapitated too – kindness to animals has never been a Greek trait.) The Jewish colony of two thousand people was systematically tortured and killed. Two thousand women and children were stripped, then taken to a nearby valley to be exterminated. Across the summer weekend of the massacre, the town rang with screams and laughter, till Colcotronis called a halt to the killing. For weeks after, orphaned Turkish children ran about the ruins of the city, only to be shot or run through by the Greeks. Many Europeans who had joined the war for naively altruistic reasons got out at this stage.

Curiously, it's not this massacre but the Turkish reprisal that was celebrated by the artists and writers including Delacroix and Hugo. The Turkish reprisal involved the killing of a greater number as well as the enslaving of others, but it's not on record that it was perpetrated in such a fiendish fashion. Of course, it was only Muslims and Jews that the Christian Greeks killed. Such deaths are rarely considered worthy, heroic subjects by artists. It's odd, all things considered, that Tripolis doesn't have a bad atmosphere. I would not like to go there, though, on the day that the liberation from the Turks is celebrated in the form of a carnival.

My first port of call was the museum. It houses a tiny but charming collection that few people see. Objects are well set out, with photographs and plans of the excavations they came from. The museum is set in an English type of garden – apart from the grave steles that punctuate the dahlias, roses and marigolds. Most of the collection is 'unpublished' so you can't photograph there. In fact the curators prefer to confiscate your camera at the door, just to make sure.

Tucked in amongst the other finds, there's a series of small female heads, animals, a male torso and what might be a Pan figure – all terracottas, tiny as toys. The labelling told me that they were from Pan's shrine at Lycochia, near Megalopolis. It was the type of collection I was to see again and again in the museums of Greece.

Tripolis is a pleasant city to walk around in the evening and at night. The markets stay open until sunset. They sell some of the best quality fruit in Greece. I stocked up on small green pears, grapes, apples and large white peaches. Tripolis stays awake late. In the late evening, the main park is full of groups walking. Most people are in their teens or twenties. Curiously there doesn't seem to be any picking-up. All the younger people herd in groups of their own sex – women with women, men with men. It's a situation that occurs in many Greek towns. Tripolis is smarter than most though, so there seems to be a peacock element – people strutting by to show off their new outfits. I can imagine that the women, if they go on to discos later, probably dance round their handbags. Greek handbags tend to be black with the odd big buckle and large enough to carry home the kitchen sink. Probably, also, the men would herd at the other end of the disco and talk and snigger together. This separation of the sexes makes Tripolis a safe city to walk in – nobody's going to harass you. There seems to be an unwritten rule – look, but don't touch or speak.

The next morning, I had to move on. I took my pack and walked to the area where Tegea once was. I'd made a rough copy of a map in the museum. It was six kilometres along the main Sparta Road before a turning, then another two to the tiny village of Archaio Episkopi. I stopped at an old broken tower along the road to change into rougher travelling clothes and eat some of my grapes. Inside the tower there was a fig tree growing, but the figs weren't ripe, alas. Then I went on, taking the right turn for Alea over the bridge of a sort of dried-up moat containing the remains of older stonework, ending up at a church by a park. Just inside the park was an archaeological site containing extensive foundations. I asked the way to Tegea Museum but nobody seemed to have heard of it.

I walked back to Tripolis station and took the last train to Megalopolis or rather to the nearest station to it – the railway maps are marked misleadingly. Passengers share a taxi from the station, several kilometres into the town. The taxi driver charged me more than he'd quoted, so he got no tip. It was getting dark and I booked into the first hotel I came across, which happened to be the Hotel Pan.

The town of Megalopolis couldn't occupy you for more than five minutes. In Baedeker's day there was a museum, but that has long gone. The modern town consists of a square which has been built on to as new homes were needed. The small roads peter off into farmland.

Once though, as its name implies, Megalopolis was the greatest city of Arcadia. There are still some ruins outside the modern town. I started off early the next morning and walked out to the site of the Greek theatre, which dates in the main from the end of the fourth century BC. At one time the *Thersilion*, a hall named after its founder, which adjoined the theatre, was filled for meetings with ten thousand delegates from all over Arcadia. The theatre itself could hold a staggering twenty thousand – it was the largest in Greece. It's set in farmland. The turning off the Andritsaina road is clearly marked. The bottom row of the theatre is entire and several rows behind are visible in part. It doesn't compare in appearance with the much more complete Greek theatres, but the countryside setting is pleasant. There are other remains scattered amongst the nearby fields – a shrine of Zeus which once had a shrine of Pan within it and the agora – but these have become indecipherable with time.

Tracks lead on from the theatre. I followed this path for a while. I fancied taking the Karyes road that I'd seen signposted earlier. The two might meet. When they hadn't, after a mile or so, I turned back, rejoined the main road and took the other turning. According to my Baedeker, Karyes was the highest town on Mount Lykaion – the place for making an ascent.

Mount Lykaion had fascinated me since I read a few

snippets on it in Baedeker. It was there that Rhea was supposed to have given birth to Zeus, he says, although I suppose that the Cretans might disagree. It was also sacred to Pan. Human sacrifice was practised there until a late period. I determined to climb the mountain that day, or another.

The summit of Mount Lykaion looked about twenty kilometres away on my Baedeker map. If I was lucky I could get there and back in a day. I would walk for five or six hours anyway. If I turned back then I could still reach Megalopolis again by dusk.

Within a few kilometres, I met the other path – I could have got there via the theatre. Within another kilometre or two I realised that the early stages of this walk were going to be a tour through the power stations and coking plants of Arcadia. The sight of so much pollution belching out across the plain was a sad one.

After the first power station the path led me to a tiny village called Thoknea. A Classics professor told me later that this was once an important city. At Thoknea I was directed to a coal-dust covered bridge that crossed the Helisson. The signposts led to a broken, stone-covered track which looked pleasanter, but the old men of the village told me that the road was no good any longer. It may have been perfectly all right for walking – but most Greeks don't walk any longer and judge roads by whether they can manoeuvre their clapped-out cars along them.

Crossing the dusty bridge proved to be one of the world's most unpleasant walks. It reminded me of the account of Sam and Frodo's hike through Mordor in *The Lord of the Rings*. Every time a lorry passed, a cloud of black dust enveloped me. The road led through a series of coking plants. I had to go under the mouth of a large, sinister chute to find the signpost directing me back on to the old Karyes path. Almost at the beginning of the road, there was a tree with a few dark purple Turkey figs on it. I thought I'd have them on the way back. The tree didn't look as if it belonged to anybody.

Not far from all the industry, I came to the tiny village of Kalyvia Koryon. It provided a strange contrast to the modern industry I'd just walked through. The architecture wasn't ancient, but the place had a primitive air. There were asses tied up outside most of the houses. I gave the asses my rather sour Tripoli apples – they didn't seem to mind. The rest of the fruit was good, but the apples left a lot to be desired. From Kalyvia, the road wound slowly up the mountain shaded by many young oak trees. A man collecting acorns and cutting back the wood directed me upwards towards Karyes.

By three o'clock I realised I would have to turn back. The road had gone on climbing higher and higher with little change. It was too shaded by trees for me to get much idea of where I was. If my map was to be believed, I was probably only a few kilometres from Karyes. I turned back reluctantly. If I'd had my things with me rather than in the hotel in Megalopolis, I could have gone on. Next time I went on a long walk I vowed I'd have my pack on my back and keep my options open.

That was the first of many failures in getting to sites connected with Pan. On a later journey I was to reach the mountain, but I was not so successful with every other site. The lack of good Greek maps was in main responsible for this. We are lucky in Britain with our Ordinance Survey maps on which every footpath is clearly marked. It's easy also to obtain good maps for most of the rest of Europe. Greece alone, it would seem, wants to keep its paths secret. It would be understandable if the knowledge were preserved at a local level, but I doubt if it is. As people move away to Athens for jobs and whole areas of the countryside become deserted, that knowledge is lost for ever.

As I walked downhill it started to rain – a sudden thundery shower of large drops. My only protection was a silk scarf for my head. I began to worry. I had read of Arcadian storms with hailstones as big as golf balls that killed sheep. But the rain was over so quickly that I did not get wet. By Thoknea I was slightly blistered. I cursed my decision to wear espadrilles. My leather tap-dance shoes, made by a Welsh Women's Co-operative, would have carried me anywhere without trouble.

At Thoknea everyone came out to look at the tourist again – it was a phenomenon of Greek village life that I was to become used to in my later travels. I sat down at the next stream and soaked the coal dust off my feet. Cold spring water has great restorative properties.

I kept myself walking on my blistered feet by fantasising about food. But Sunday is not a good day to eat out in Greece. The only place that was open in Megalopolis that night was a rather expensive Americanised pizza restaurant. It was my first taste of Hellenic pizza. Curiously, every other time I've had pizza in Greece, it's been exactly the same. The Greeks don't seem to have any conception of changing the topping – pizza for them always contains tomato, cheese, green peppers and thin pink ham. I'm told, though, that if you're really unlucky you get raw bacon instead of pink ham.

The waiter opened my bottle of Amstel beer by clutching it phallically erect between his legs while he took the cap off. It wasn't personal – a lot of Greek waiters open bottles like that. It's hard to keep a straight face while you watch though. Maybe they know that, or maybe it's just macho instinct.

Andritsaina

Don't live in a town where there are no doctors.

(Jewish saying)

*F*rom Megalopolis, the road winds up into the mountains of Arcadia. For the average tourist, Andritsaina's just a stopping point – the nearest town to the famous temple of Apollo at Bassae. I hoped to see Bassae, but my main mission was nearer the town itself. Was there anything left of the tiny temple of Pan unearthed by the Archaeological Society early this century?

I had hoped to get a bus, but I couldn't find the unmarked stop, so I started hitching. There were plenty of cars on the road and I was soon picked up by Stephanos, a young Greek doctor. His face had an ancient quality. He reminded me of one of the melancholy saints in Byzantine paintings. He was on his way back to Andritsaina after a weekend with his people. He came from a family of doctors and talked with pride of his grandfather riding round Athens on a white horse to see his patients. Stephanos had only been working in the Peloponnese for the last two weeks, but already he missed Athens and intended to drive back there every single weekend. It was a long drive, but he kept himself awake with the odd cigarette and the thought of some strong black coffee at the end. At the moment he was in his father's car, which he hoped he'd

23

persuade him to sell. It was less of a banger than most Greek cars, so I could see why he wanted it.

We were in Andritsaina by ten. We arranged to meet that evening, his work permitting. Stephanos would be outside the coffee-shop that had tables under the tree covered in lights, he said.

Andritsaina is an exceptionally pretty town until you start to look closely. It was once prosperous – about two centuries ago. Now, it's feeling and looking its age. The houses are held together with corrugated iron. Patches of it replace parts of roofs or are slotted in where lumps of stucco have fallen from the walls. Damp ends of beams project where balconies have rotted off. The side of one of the main restaurants is patched with timber from the stair-well of a hotel that once stood at Bassae – you can still see the lettering. Next door, the Greek sign tells me it's THE COFFEE-SHOP OF EPICUREAN APOLLO, where the average age of the clients seems to be eighty. But you can't complain about the view from the town across the valley of the Alpheios to distant mountain ranges beneath the bluest of skies. The air and the water are fresh too.

Andritsaina boasts one of Greece's most remarkable stand-pipes – clear, icy water gushes from an ancient plane tree with a trunk of enormous girth and branches that stretch right across the street. A metal spout emerges from it about two feet above the ground. The tree is outside the town's restaurants and people stop to fill bottles and glasses. A grating in the road takes the residue of water away. There's no sign of other piping outside the tree. It's hard to imagine just how the whole thing works. The tree is supremely healthy, without any signs of damp or rot. Perhaps the metal piping was outside a century ago. Perhaps the great tree just got closer and closer until it grew around it. Planes are some of the thirstiest trees around. Water is meat and drink to them. You find them in every dried-up river bed, or old watercourse, their roots going down beneath the stones to secret underground sources.

The rushing water, the murmuring of the underground springs, and the rustle of the great plane tree are only part of the town's music. There's a continual tinkling of sheep and goat bells from the hill behind – loudest at dawn and dusk when the animals are moved. Then there's the place that sells bells, collars, butchers' hooks and garlic. No one seems to keep the shop – the front of the building has disappeared completely, leaving it open to the wind and rain. Only a transistor blaring Greek music day and night proclaims ownership of a sort. At night, on the outskirts of the town, the cold air comes alive with the sound of Greece's loudest cicadas.

There's a shop selling blankets – hand-woven for tourist tastes – and a woman spinning local wool in the window of the crafts co-operative further into the town. But there's very little fresh food to be had. No one seems to stock bread. There's only a greengrocer's full of wilting vegetables and several emporiums that sell dried beans, sugar, olive oil and other basics – if you can find them under the heaps of ironmongery and plastic containers of paraffin and Johnson's baby shampoo. These shops seem to be exceptionally well-stocked in dustpans and brushes – all sizes of brushes, some obviously handmade – in deference to the dustiness of Greece. There are also two hotels. Foolishly I chose the one with the petrol pump outside. I couldn't resist it because it was yet another 'Hotel Pan'. The inside was harmless enough apart from a bed that sagged nearly as much as the ones owned by Spiros and a large dead moth in the bath.

After I'd booked in I went up the hill behind the town to look for the temple. I scoured the area, but there was only a chapel and houses, some of which were ruined and deserted. If there were no remains of columns on this hill, perhaps the few lines in Baedeker referred to the larger hill or the small mountain, part of the Minthi range, that lay behind the town. I set out resolutely.

What looked vaguely like the bases of Doric columns from a distance turned out to be a ring of old car tyres that had been whitewashed many moons ago. Near these a dog was tied up. He fawned over me as I shared my muesli bar with him. He had worn a perfect circle in the ground by running round on the end of his chain. The chain was tied to a stake. He could just about reach the shade of a nearby tree. His task was guarding the sheep or goat pen nearby. It had a formless quality like a 'bash' from cardboard city. From under the asymmetric mess of rusty corrugated iron sheeting and odd pieces of plywood a wild bearded face with slanting eyes peeped out. Most of his friends were on the hillside. They had just been sheared within a fence – more of the corrugated sheeting – that stood at one end of the pen. A mass of beige and steel-grey lanky tufts lay on the grass like pensioners' hair.

Nearby there was a donkey tied up. I still had an apple or two left. He turned out to be a most delicate donkey. Instead of seizing the whole between his teeth as any other would, he demanded personal attention. I had to hold the apple and turn it while he took gentle, lady's-bite-sized nibbles from its sides. He took a long time to finish. If men can ever be changed into animals, he was certainly a case. Like Apuleius's *Golden Ass*, he had kept his human sensibilities within a different shape.

I had done the easy part of the climb. The steeper parts were to follow. Most Greek mountains have paths or roads to the top, but, as you climb higher, these are not always easy to find. It was my first experience of the Greek equivalent of fell-walking. I devised a technique that has since stood me in good stead – following animal droppings. On the easy early roads you'll come across a trail of mule droppings like brown lumps of coke. That means the road's easy enough for any fool to follow. As you get higher it'll be down to goat and sheep droppings and tiny, almost invisible, paths or ways up dried-out watercourses. At this stage you need to be a bit athletic; having cloven hoofs also might help. When these run out and there's only bird lime, you're in deep shit so to speak.

My last hundred feet or so was minus all goat droppings and through a patch of Kermes oak – one of the most vicious plants known to man. It's a pest that's spreading unchecked across the tops of most Greek mountains. Superficially, it looks like a scrubby bush of small-leaved holly, but the acorns here and there tell you it's from the oak family. Kermes oak was once prized for a crimson dye that could be made from its galls. These days the only crimson comes from the blood of those unfortunate enough to get caught by it. The stuff has a life of its own. If you attempt to tread it down like a bramble, it fights back. It's springy enough to unbalance you or fly back and catch you in revenge.

When I reached the top of the mountain, the last stretch mostly on all fours, picking my way from stone to stone amongst the prickles, I found no temple remains, but only the foreleg of a goat, cloven hoof still intact, with a bluebottle buzzing round it. I felt a shiver go through me. Perhaps it was the height I was looking down from, or the appropriateness of that hoof on a spot that might once have been dedicated to Pan.

Most Greek mountain tops have a chapel. This one was a dreary moulded concrete job with a few chairs and a bench. Quite how any parishioners made it up there I couldn't visualise, but I'm told that some chapels are only used on their Saints' days, once a year. I searched for a sign of whom the chapel was dedicated to – the reproduction icons were unlabelled and ambiguous. Eventually I found out by looking at carved letters on the back of some of the chairs. The chapel belonged to Saint Nicholas.

I didn't expect to have a date with eight Greeks that night. It was about quarter past eight when Stephanos turned up. I'd given him up and gone inside the café for a coffee as it was cold outside, now the sun had gone down. Stephanos came in and found me, then took me across to introduce me to his friends. The professional people of Andritsaina, all reluctant exiles from Athens, got together every evening to complain about the locals. Apart from the telephone-exchange manager and the bank manager, the others all worked at the health centre. While we sat drinking coffee, a man came up to have an insect bite examined. It was no more than the average mosquito one – even I could have told him that – but he seemed worried. He was told he'd live. Stephanos commented that you couldn't have a drink in peace without something like that happening. Usually though, they showed you a worse wound or mentioned some sickening symptoms while you were trying to eat lunch. Such is the life of a doctor.

After talking about Athens and England, Stephanos decided to take me to Bassae which was supposed to look wonderful by moonlight – we would rejoin the others later. Pausanias says that the Phigalians built Apollo this temple, employing Iktinos, the architect responsible for the Parthenon, in gratitude for being saved from a plague in the fifth century BC. Stephanos drove carefully – it was a slow ride along a steep, winding road strewn with the boulders of occasional land-slides. By moonlight, the imposing temple is supposed to be a romantic sight and has probably gladdened the heart of generations of Andritsaina's lovers. But that night there was no moon. Worse still, the authorities had clapped a four-gabled tarpaulin over the whole thing. We could dimly make it out by the light of the stars and with the aid of a torch.

We drove back into Andritsaina and threaded our way on foot through a maze of streets below the main one. When we got to his friend's house, where we had arranged to meet the others, I felt I was in the middle of a scene from *M.A.S.H.*, with a group of chain-smoking, whisky-drinking doctors and dentists.

The Greek government, in its wisdom, is in the process of setting up large health centres with advanced technology in towns and villages with small populations – 'It's politics!' Andritsaina's centre was staffed by the doctors and dentists I'd met, who were all in their twenties and mostly from Athens. A year's exile in the mountains, though boring, had seemed infinitely preferable to more conventional military service, or, worse still, prison. But after only two weeks they were all itching to get away. Andritsaina isn't exactly big on night-life. The locals had asked all about them, they complained, but had stopped talking once they'd found out everything they felt they needed to know. Of course, the fact that they'd asked the townspeople why on earth they stayed in a place like Andritsaina might also have had something to do with the cessation of friendly relations.

We sat and played cards for a while. We were all hungry by now and someone suggested we get some pizza in. I assumed they meant from a takeaway until the hospital was mentioned. Stephanos was elected to go. He said he was always put upon because he came from a family of brothers, all older than himself. He had always been the errand boy and now his friends treated him the same way. He was the butt of various jokes, too. One of the doctors told me he'd been known as *Strategos* in the army (he'd done some conventional military service too). In the days when I learned ancient Greek, *strategos* only meant 'a general' in the military sense. These days, it's slang for bisexual. Stephanos refused grumpily to go for pizzas after his sexual mores had been exposed, but gave in when I agreed to go along with him. After the stories I'd been listening to, I wanted to be sure exactly what sort of fridge the pizza was kept in. An anaesthetist who'd left the party earlier had boasted that he'd cooked a chicken in with the medical instruments during an operation. Doctors always seem to be remarkably fond of sick jokes and usually relay them at meal times. We had Challenger Shuttle ones, followed by concentration camp stories – the latter, especially, I could have done without.

Andritsaina feels like a healthy place – far too healthy to need an enormous health centre. All the local pensioners seem to have is smoker's cough and the sort of hip trouble that afflicts elderly German Shepherd dogs. Yet, in a way, it's strangely right that there should be a health centre on the way to the temple at Bassae. Epicurean Apollo was the health-giving aspect of the god.

That night, my sleep was broken by the sound of cars and lorries stopping for petrol. The bed was also deteriorating by the minute. By the early hours my bottom had dropped through it on to the floor. I got up and tried to find out what was wrong. The mattress had only been held by four loose slats. I disposed them at regular intervals and the bed felt a little better. Perhaps a night in the health centre would have been more peaceful – the doctors had offered it if I could rustle up an interesting condition – but all I had was a bruised back after falling off the international couchette, and a blistered foot from my tour of the coking plants and power stations of Arcadia the day before. It hardly rated my risking Greek medicine which has, I am told, declined since the days of Galen and Hippocrates.

The next afternoon I visited the temple by daylight. Only a few kilometres along the way, the road was already beginning to get the precipitous look I'd only half seen in the dark. A German couple with a Volkswagen dormobile offered me a lift as I strode uphill. The husband said that they spent a month in Greece each summer or autumn, seeing all the sights they knew and loved. The temple at Bassae was one of their favourites – a lone, impressive monument set 3,705 feet up in wild mountain country, almost complete apart from the twenty-three tablets bought by the British. They'd been coming back for years. Perhaps I should have warned him along the way about the tarpaulin . . .

Passengers

The proper study of mankind is Man.

Pope: 'An Essay on Man'

I had only eight days to spend in Greece on this first brief trip before making my way back via Italy, so I bussed to Tripolis where I picked up a train to Argos. I decided to put off visiting the Pan cave which has been converted into a chapel at Kephalári until the spring. My Baedeker hinted at a Dionysiac festival there. I contented myself with a brief look at Argos museum which was full of pots and interesting mosaics but nothing that bore any relation to Pan. If the cave at Kephalári had been excavated before it became a chapel, nothing of interest had been brought there.

Argos is out on a limb as far as the Greek railway is concerned –few trains go there. While I had my inter-rail ticket it made sense to see as much of the Peloponnese country as I could. I decided to take the train to Athens, spend an hour or two there then take another train along the coast to Kyparissia. I could swim there. It seemed a waste to leave Greece without having tested its waters. That would still leave me time to return to Patras for my boat by the following evening.

While I was standing looking at the train times, two men came up. The first, who looked like a Greek version of Roman Polanski, covered in bristles, offered me the use of his villa by the sea – he'd drive me there. The second told me he had

33

learned his English in Basingstoke and asked if I'd heard of 'The Sike' – at least that was what it sounded like. Had he read Dickens and did he mean Bill Sykes? A few sentences on, I realised that he thought that we pronounced psyche that way. A few sentences more and I realised he was a keen scientologist. I did my utmost to convince him that I was a completely materialistic pagan with no interest whatsoever in my spiritual welfare.

I find that the devotees of strange sects are surprised if I say I believe in many gods. A young Mormon doing market research had no space for polytheism on his form. He offered to come round to talk further about it. I said yes, blithely, knowing I'd be away and that my mother would be at my place cat-sitting. She likes a good religious argument and can quote the Bible as effectively as a Jehovah's Witness. There's something to be said for a Plymouth Brethren upbringing.

Greek trains are packed and smell of diesel. The only way to take your mind off the bumpy ride is by chatting to the other passengers. A strange Greek who looked like a guru, with long grizzled locks and horny-toed feet in sandals, got talking to me. He knew no English so I had to function in my poor modern Greek. I loved Ancient Greek at school, although I've forgotten much of what I learned. I assumed it would help when I started to learn modern, but it didn't. I have had less pleasure in trying to learn modern Greek than with any other language. Having experienced the ancient version I developed a strong dislike of what has been done to it – a dislike that almost amounts to a mental block. I can't think of any changes in it that have been for the better. It must be impossible to take dictation in modern Greek – so many vowels and vowel combinations come out as an 'ee' sound. All of these are transliterated to 'i' when Greeks try to write in our script. It's nonsensical, considering we already have long-established spellings for place names, heroes, gods, etc. If we adopted their system it would mean spelling the name of the goddess Hera as 'IRA' and Hebe as 'IVI'.

When the guru went off to buy himself a cup of coffee, the other men in the carriage told me that he was a famous film star. He had good diction, so it was just about possible. I'll never know if they were joking or not. I've managed to avoid seeing Greek films.

When we reached Athens, the guru walked me up to Omonoia Square – it was about all I had time to see. I have no idea why the Greeks love this square so much – it's a bit like Piccadilly without Eros. There is a central sculpture, it's true – a futuristic work of a man moving. It seems to be constructed of a lot of slates, or thin metal plates in a sort of piled effect to show that speed blurs the outline. It's neither dislikeable nor memorable. The chief virtue of Omonoia Square, I was to learn on later visits, is that it's the main pick-up point in Athens.

I caught the night train to Kyparassia and achieved my early swim. I undressed in the dark. The sea was pleasantly warm and fragrant and I was in it to see the sun rise.

The train was to skirt Phigaleia on the way back – one of the areas where there were caves sacred to Pan. I assumed wrongly that such caves would be near the sea. I wasn't used to the mountain caves of Greece, though I became so in later journeys.

The two old men sitting opposite started talking to me. They asked me first if I was German. When I said I wasn't they started to insult the Germans liberally. Nobody had forgiven them the last war, they said. They told me also something I don't believe – that Germans hate the English. If I were German, I wonder what they'd have said about the English.

The two men were Americanised Greeks. Their village had died when everybody migrated, mostly to America. Once a year, everyone who could afford it came back for a sort of month-long party and every house was opened up. This has been the fate of many villages since the last war.

Further up the carriage there was a mentally handicapped girl. She ate six bags of crisps and several small packs of biscuits with that pious look that fat people have if they've been indoctrinated by their mothers into believing that there's something morally good about clearing what's on their plate. If she'd brought all the junk food with her I'd simply have written her off as greedy, but there was something about the way she went to the buffet for each packet, having pulled out wads of notes and counted them as if she'd never seen money before. In between eating, she picked her nose ostentatiously, pulled her dress up and held her knicker elastic out so that she (and probably those next to her) could have a good look inside. The Greeks are much kinder to the mentally handicapped or, for that matter, the insane, than most nations. Where the British would have avoided sitting next to her and glared across muttering things like, 'Shouldn't be allowed out on her own!', the Greeks treated her like an ordinary human being, handing back her money whenever she dropped it, or leaving it on her seat while she went to the buffet.

A tall young man got on at one of the tiny village stops past Kyparissia. I noticed that the ticket collector didn't seem to like him and got him to give up his seat to somebody who didn't really look old enough or sick enough to need it. I was in the process of clearing my back-pack off the seat by me to make room – the train was getting full now – but the conductor gestured to me to stop. I found myself trying to work out why he disliked the man. Was he Greek or some other nationality? I decided I didn't particularly like his looks either – he had a petulant expression combined with eyes that searched for a direct contact as they looked at you. Anyway, there was now a free seat next to me which I felt he was entitled to, whether the conductor agreed or not.

36

Con soon started talking in perfect Australian English. I commented on how good his English was. It had been his only language until recently, he said, although he was one hundred per cent Greek. His parents emigrated to Australia when he was just out of nappies. He learned his English from Australians as he grew up, while his parents continued to speak only Greek. Consequently there was a slight communication problem, not to mention an identity crisis. To Australians he was always 'The Greek' – a nickname that irritated him. He then told me how he hated Greeks. I could see the old men opposite bristling with indignation, so I attempted a feeble defence mentioning past culture, etc.

Con's hatred was understandable once I had heard his life story. When he was just starting drama school and had secured a minor part in a film, his parents decided that Australia was not for them and yanked him back to Greece. Athens he could have stood, he said, but not their ancestral, half-empty, one-horse town of a village. As he was a few months under eighteen, he had no choice but to go, although he begged and pleaded to stay. They spoke so little English and he spoke so little Greek that most of his objections were not even understood. When his parents saw how unhappy he was in Greece, they suggested a compromise. If he could save the fare back to Australia, once he was eighteen he was free to go his own way. He saved like crazy, working all hours on the tomato plantations, and scraped together enough money in a few months. He bought his ticket, then his call-up papers came through. Being Greek by birth there was no getting out of a spell in the army. He couldn't get more than a partial refund on the ticket so, once he was out of the army, he would have to start saving again.

The only good thing about his military service was that he now knew Greek thoroughly – all kinds of Greek. The other men saw to that. But it was a time of his life he hated. He described vividly being forced to hold back desperate

Bulgarian refugees along the borders at gunpoint. He'd have loved to let them through, but it would have meant a prison sentence if he'd disobeyed orders. He described the scene so vividly, throwing in odd words of Bulgarian and Greek, that I felt I was there. Con had told me of his script-writing as well as acting ambitions. Why didn't he make a play of that? I said.

Con was so desperately depressed that I felt it was my duty to make positive suggestions about what to do with his life. If someone's only slightly depressed, I try to find out where they want to go with their lives rather than imposing my own ideas. But Con seemed nearer the edge than that. He could do nothing right, where he lived. Although he'd reached a better understanding with his parents now that he knew Greek, he couldn't bear village life. If he just spoke to a girl, marriage was immediately talked about. Every now and again he'd go to Omonoia Square in Athens for a bit of life, or, if he couldn't afford such a long trip, to Patras. He was going to Patras today. Once he got out of the village, he'd slip his earring on and start to be himself, without anyone to talk or speculate about him. I think Con was gay or bisexual – like many Greek men – and that was part of the problem in a tiny village.

Con was impressed that I was a writer and I tried to give him advice in that capacity. I told him that the lesson I've learned from life is that misfortunes make exceptionally good copy. There can come a time when you can see them retrospectively as good fortune instead. If he could use his experiences in the army and his feelings of being an outsider, then these would become something positive. If he went back to Australia, he feared that he would now be years behind those with whom he'd been at drama school. I suggested that he could bullshit producers that he'd been making a study of Greek drama in the country where it all came from. He could pretend, at any rate, to be proud of his Greekness. You can't change the nationality you are, I said. You can only come to terms with it – the good as well as the bad side.

When I come to think about it, I don't suppose for one minute that I would choose to be English. But then there's no point in my being ashamed of my English quarter or so. They have, after all, produced the world's best literature. I have to admit that, even if I hate everything else about Englishness. Con seemed a little cheered by my suggestions – I'd done my good deed for the day.

I had a few hours to kill in Patras before catching the boat. I stocked up on the sweet dessert wines that are produced there – *mavrodaphne* is a very good substitute for port. I tried the local water also and found it absolutely filthy. This was a bit galling as I'd climbed the immensely long flight of steps that leads you up above the town to get to the only water fountain.

Patras is a bustling, fashionable town. All the restaurants along the waterfront offered tourist menus in several languages. I could see that Con would find some life there – perhaps meeting up with other Australians. In the streets that led away from the waterfront and its untidy modern docks, it was more pleasant, more of an ordinary Greek town.

Return Through Italy

La terra dei fiori, dei suoni, dei carmi.
The land of flowers, of music and of lays.

Mercantini: *Inno di Guerra di Garibaldi*

*I*taly is a country where there are more straight men than gay, so I hoped my sex life would pick up once I'd shaken the dust of Greece off my feet. I'm far more at ease speaking Italian than Greek. I like Latin better than Italian, but still see the latter as a beautiful language, unlike modern Greek.

In Greece, as in England, the men are predominantly homosexual by inclination. Homosexual friends of mine have told me that Athens and Mykonos are wonderful places to find a Greek sugar daddy. They are not so good for a straight woman. The wealth of hard porn I'd walked by in my brief look at Omonoia Square in Athens showed that Greek tastes are decidedly anal.

I had decided to waive my usual rule about not fucking smokers, otherwise I'd have had even less sex in Greece. But Greek smokers have a rather unattractive habit of spitting, both out on the road and at home. Every hotel I'd stayed at, I'd been woken in the small hours by a bronchitic symphony: 'Chu. . .kerr. . .pah!' You could actually hear the gouts of phlegm landing.

Though there are plenty of good-looking men in Athens, on

the Peloponnese I had seen very few that I fancied. The faces were all right, but there was something wrong with the bodies. If a Greek hasn't eaten himself into a Sumo shape, his body is wasted and without muscles – I put that down to the nicotine-addiction in part. It's also aggravated by lack of exercise. Most Greeks think it's a positive perversion to walk anywhere and showed horror at my desire to do so. A man who rides in a car all day and smokes like a chimney ends up with atrophied legs. Any Greeks who don't have atrophied legs get put in the Greek Guard. I can't fancy men with atrophied legs, but then neither can I fancy men with short skirts and woolly stockings who go about doing the goose step all day.

After landing at Brindisi I decided to get a night train to Naples from Bari. I slept fitfully on the train. In the early hours, at one of the larger stops, I was woken by the loudest voice I've ever heard. It was only a drinks-and-sandwiches man with the usual patter of 'Acqua, panini, Coca, Fanta . . .' Although I wasn't thrilled at being woken at three, I couldn't help marvelling at the sheer power of the voice. He could have won any town criers' championship hands down, or filled the Albert Hall. He was definitely wasted in his current position.

As I left the train at Naples I noticed armed police at the platform end. Perhaps it was a mail train that needed guarding. I had to spend time in Naples when I was researching *Journeys to the Underworld*. It's one of the world's most sinister cities. On this visit, I was determined to go straight to the museum and get a train northwards by the afternoon.

It was so early that I had to wait an hour or two until the shops and museums opened. I was so bored in the waiting room that I started scribbling a picture of a cat on the back of an envelope. A tiny old man with the look of a bantam fighting cock appeared to be watching me. His hair was swept up into a sort of quiff and delicately tinted with Lord Grecian (or perhaps the Italians call it *Il Duce Greco*). Nino wanted to know if I was an artist. I told him I'd been to art school but was now a writer. That was a cue for him to tell me that he was a poet. Nino, who was from Palermo, proceeded to prove it by unzipping his hold-all and pulling out a large cup he'd won. That was followed by a profusion of cuttings, some forty years old, that I was supposed to read and admire. He told me I had a beautiful soul, pointing at my breasts, and we talked about poetry and love. I shocked him with my cynicism. He of course was totally in favour of romantic love. Short old men always are.

When the buffet opened we got coffee. He took me to one of the platforms so that he could recite – not, thankfully, for anything else. Various passers-by stopped in amazement. Though not quite as loud as the soft-drinks seller in the night, he was loud enough. Every few lines, he would stop to explain a *double entendre* and tell me how clever it was, or to comment on how much feeling was in a line. I found his Italian highly understandable because it was so slow and ponderous. I was issued with a few photocopies of his reviews and one poem before I left.

I got to the Archaeological Museum shortly after opening time. I had seen it all on a previous trip. But it's a big museum that needs more than one visit. This time I hoped to penetrate the secret collection. I knew from the postcards sold in the shop downstairs that there was a statue of Pan fucking a goat and several Priapuses as well as other goodies. I had another mission too. I wanted to use a painting of Polyphemus and Galatea for the cover of my *Literary Companion to Sex*. My publisher had got no response from the museum by writing.

As I walked through the sculpture halls downstairs, I was waylaid by an attractive museum guard who proceeded to take me on a touch tour of the statues by way of showing me the differences in musculature between Roman and Greek types. Eventually, the comparing of Aphrodite's breasts from statue to statue, not to mention Apollo's buttocks, started to involve the odd touch on my own – just by way of demonstration, of course. Giovanni took me to a closed wing (though not, alas, to the secret collection) for a further anatomy lesson.

If you've never had sex on a marble floor, don't try it. The coolness on a hot day is fine – the problem is that whoever is underneath goes flying if the marble's well polished. The floor of the closed wing was like glass. By the time we'd finished with it, it was even better polished. I used up two of some samples I'd been given by Jiffy. Jiffy had offered to send a large batch to Molly Parkin who'd written the first sex column in *City Magazine*'s pages. I wrote the next column on that subject. By then, the condoms had arrived, but Molly had declined them, so the magazine's office telephoned to ask whether I wanted them. They began reading out the different kinds. 'How about mocha flavoured?' I couldn't resist quibbling – 'Is it decaffeinated?' – so I never got that one. In the end they were passed around City Magazine's office and I only got a handful of luminous ones, which I saved for Greece – shocking pink, orange and green.

Giovanni didn't bat an eyelid at the pink and orange ones. I didn't have the heart to put the green one on him. I knew I'd laugh if I saw that on anybody. I ended up leaving it to disintegrate at home.

Maybe they only shine in complete darkness. The museum room was merely murky. I had expected something dramatic like Lear's 'Dong with the luminous nose' but they just looked coloured when they were on.

Mercifully, Giovanni preferred being underneath on the slippery floor, for the second time. He liked a slightly unusual position with me on top, seated with my back to him. My back is fairly muscular and that was obviously to his taste, judging

44

by all the statues he'd felt and by his parting gift – two postcards of the statue known as 'Venus of the beautiful buttocks'.

After our interlude in the locked wing, Giovanni took me to the Director's office to enquire about using the painting on the cover of my book and also about seeing the secret collection. Only the Director had a key to that. Apparently he also had keys to the closed wing and could have come in at any minute. He was away, but two secretaries were holding the fort. Seeing the secret collection requires a lot of advance notice, so I wasn't going to get there on that visit. To do so, in due course I would have to write a long letter in Italian, explaining my motives, and then await my permit.

I ended up having to sit down and write a letter on the spot in Italian to ask for permission to use the painting of Polyphemus and Galatea. Eventually, I got a brief reply. I was given permission, but only to reproduce from the postcard. Neither I nor the publisher could get an adequate transparency, so the idea was dropped.

That painting was from the secret collection. The nearest I got to it that day was a peep through the keyhole of a pair of locked doors. Inside, I could see a statue of a couple fucking, the woman in the man's lap. Painted panels were propped all around the walls.

It's a curious anomaly. The museum makes a lot of money from selling erotic postcards of items from this collection, but won't let the public see them without an immense amount of hassle. Giovanni explained their reasons. A German photographer had been allowed in years before and published the lot in a book without permission. The authorities were so angry that they closed the collection. Probably, the German photographer's book is the one that's now a hot seller in among the postcards.

It's a silly reason for closing a section of a museum. Erotic art and literature represent a large and important part of Roman culture. Any survey that does not take them on board is producing a warped view of Roman society. Victorian translators bowdlerised Roman and Greek texts widely. Many were not translated in their entirety until recently. Some are still to be found only in the original language. Okay, you might say that scholars should have to work for their fun. But classical dictionaries can be decidedly prudish when it comes to certain words. It's unlikely that any obscenities will appear in the smaller volumes. You'll have to go to the library and pull out the largest dictionaries before you get any explanation for those very ordinary words for everyday activities like fucking. Worse still, some poems are not even available in texts printed in this country. The body of work known as the *Carmina Priapea*, most of which is decidedly more innocuous than the title would suggest, is only available in a German-edited version of the original texts.

As so much has been withheld from us, our view of the classical has become distorted. Surely now it's time for all the museums of the world to put *everything* on view? The keyhole in the huge barred doors seemed a symbol of the faint glimpse of the underside of Roman society that education allows us.

One day I'll write that letter and go back and see the collection. Or perhaps I'll take an easier path. An academic I know has offered to put me in touch with 'Il Colosso di Napoli' – a very short Neapolitan with friends in high places. I'm told he can fix anything.

The Sacred Way

To see the desolation spread,
Pan drops a tear, and hangs his head.

Gay's Fables: 'Pan and Fortune: To a
Young Heir'

*I*n the cause of cheapness, on my second visit, I had booked a charter flight that got me to Athens in the small hours. I took the airport bus to Syntagma Square and, with hours to waste before anything would be open, I walked through the drizzling rain up to the closed gates of the Acropolis. Greek museum officials are always on sites an hour early at least, but they have a tradition of keeping the queue outside waiting for ten minutes after opening time.

While the few early-bird tourists queued, gnashing their teeth, the Greek Guard were let in and out. Perhaps it was the rain, but I felt a certain disappointment at the Acropolis. There seemed little to lift my soul above the weather. About half the buildings on the Acropolis were roped off – the Erectheon, for instance – and the Parthenon was full of scaffolding and large cement blocks.

Though there had only been six at the door, by the time I got to the museum on the Acropolis, the hordes had entered. I've returned more than once since, but I still felt that same sense of disappointment. On other occasions, later in the day, the whole area was one surging multinational crowd. There's a positive babel of languages as one guide shouts down another

47

in yet another language. Every tenth person in the groups flourishes a camcorder. The film that results is probably just a mass of elbows and shoulders with the odd pillar as the camera reels skyward.

On my way down from the Acropolis I took in the small Byzantine Museum. Again, it was slightly disappointing. I've seen more impressive icons outside Greece. The museum in Venice is much better, with good natural light and a generous array of pictures.

Once off the Acropolis, I trailed across the city through the street market around the tourist Plaka area. It was here that I first encountered the common male Greek habit of walking into passers-by at full tilt. By the end of the street, both arms were hanging off my plastic mac.

Every Greek man who offers to take you out threatens to take you around the Plaka. It has been offered so many times that I feel like saying I'll only go out if they promise not to take me anywhere near the bloody Plaka. It's a bit like offering Trafalgar Square as an inducement to a visitor to Britain – there's every likelihood they've seen it before. The Plaka's not unattractive – it's certainly no worse than Omonoia Square – but enough is enough. The traders in the shops are boringly pushy. Most are out on the pavement to lure you in, offering T-shirts, porno postcards and loathsome Greek art reproductions. You can buy everything from mini Parthenons to a helmet. Reproduction helmets are not quite as loathsome as the rest, but it would be hard to find the right place to wear one and it wouldn't fit snugly into the average suitcase.

Shortly after I'd cleared the Plaka, I found a cheap hotel near the Sacred Way. I had wanted to stay in that area so that I could perform a sort of pilgrimage to Eleusis the following morning. *Iera odhos*, the Sacred Way, runs all the way from Athens to the ruins at Eleusis. In ancient times, would-be initiates walked along this road to the secret ceremonies. I had

48

seen the walk done on television by the historian, Michael Wood, and knew that most of it would be unpleasant. The distance is not great – fourteen miles or so – but almost all of it is along a main road with lorries roaring past. Still, the map showed sea for the last few miles, so surely that couldn't be so bad?

In the first century BC there was a strange inscription – long lost – near the beginning of the Sacred Way. It was cut on three bricks and placed to form the inner rim of a well by the Dipylon Gate and near the Sanctuary of Hecate, just round the corner from my tatty hotel. The inscription has been translated as 'Oh Pan, O Mên' (a Phrygian moon god), 'Hail, O beautiful nymphs. Rain, conceive, flood.' A prayer for rain and fertility in the earth was an element in the known part of the Eleusinian Mysteries.

I started out early the following morning. The first few miles out of Athens were what I expected them to be – noisy and polluted, relieved only by the botanical gardens on the left. The road begins to climb steadily through dull, modern suburbs. There are few food shops along the road, but a surprising number devoted to car repairs. They all add to the oily smell. About halfway, just before the road veers to the left, there's the tiny monastery of Daphne. The main church and the cloisters are open, but the antiquities are safely locked away in a side room with a dusty window. The church is dark and slightly ruinous. It's obviously not a working monastery. You can just make out some Byzantine saints glaring down from behind the scaffolding inside. It's a welcome diversion, a pocket of quietness before you return to the main road.

The kilometre either side of the monastery is the only bit of the walk that could be termed pleasant, by any stretch of the imagination. After the monastery, there's hilly land on the left. Some blocks of stone there are supposed to have once belonged to a temple of Aphrodite. There are little paths leading to an array of beehives on a small hill. Soon, the land runs down to the sea. The part along the coast is, surprisingly, the most unpleasant part of the walk.

What Michael Wood's pilgrimage could not convey on TV was the disgusting cocktail of smells and the grit in the wind. I put on my sunglasses to keep some of it out and cautiously opened just one eye at a time as I walked. When that eye began to stream, I'd open the other. The last few kilometres to Eleusis contain some of the most noxious chemical plants I've had the misfortune to pass. Even the beach, if it can be called a beach, is obviously polluted with oil in several slimy shades – black, rust and poison green. Here and there it's held back by tiny booms. The oil refinery probably smells worst – hot metal, oil and bad eggs – but there's strong competition from all the other plants. I found myself breathing as shallowly as I could and trying to walk faster and faster at the same time. I did most of the last few kilometres at a trot.

The area is so seriously polluted that breathing that air not only gave me hay fever and streaming eyes but made my nose bleed afterwards. A Canadian friend of mine noticed a similar effect when he lived in Hamilton. The body rebels and bleeds when hit by anything noxious enough. On my previous trip to Greece I passed through Eleusis by train. Now I understood the haste of all the Greek passengers to close every window, even on a raging hot day.

When you reach the town of Eleusis, or rather, Elefsina, the smells get a little better. The archaeological site is a clue to how beautiful that area once was. There are curious additions to the ruins though, in the shape of a twentieth-century clock tower on the hill at the top and several factory chimneys to the right, lower down – but from a distance they look like classical pillars.

When I came to the gates of the site, I found everything closed. Monday is a day off for many museums and sites in Greece. I had done my long walk for nothing and would have to return next day. Fortunately there were buses to and from Plateia Eleftherias, near where I was staying.

I thought I'd have a good lunch to cheer myself up before returning. I stopped at a little café on the outskirts of the town. Looking at the dishes by the counter I began to have doubts. Surely they couldn't taste as awful as they looked? Perhaps I should have a salad instead. But no – they were also ready prepared and full of wilted wisps of lettuce. I opted for *bifteki* – a sort of rissole – and spinach. It looked the most harmless thing there. But the *bifteki* was cold and tasted as if it had been dead a long, long time. Eleusis was first inhabited in the Middle Helladic period – 1900 to 1600 BC – perhaps it had been left over from then. The spinach needed to be wound up on a fork like spaghetti, it was so long and stringy.

The dyspeptic-looking proprietor was eating tomato soup in the corner. Perhaps I should have opted for the soup. This restaurant had a woman cook – a rarity. Women, I'm told, do most of the home cooking, but commercially it's an almost exclusively male business. Conversely to what you might expect in Greece, though most cooks are male most of the high-powered jobs in archaeology and museums are held by women.

The next day I was back for the ruins (but not the food) of Eleusis. I walked up the broad path from the entrance gate. Once inside, I searched unsuccessfully for the Pan shrine that was once amongst the other buildings. The huge cave-shaped structure visible from the outside had looked like a possibility but it turned out to be dedicated to Pluto. I asked the gatekeeper where the Pan shrine was, but he didn't know and told me to try the German visitors. Germans always have good guide books. Most of the best archaeological books are in German, a reason why I'm starting to learn the language. The Germans were able to tell me that there had been a cave nearby but that it had been lost by quarrying. From other sources, I found out later that there had also been a shrine on the acropolis, but that had been destroyed too.

There's still a collection of objects from the shrine in the museum. I'm told that the collection also includes objects from the tiny Pan cave at Daphne, which I was to visit later. It's wrong, I think, that the museum should mix together collections in this way without labelling them separately. The Daphne cave is several miles away and different essentially from the shrine that once existed in Eleusis. It was dedicated solely to Pan, whereas the one on Eleusis was a sort of sideline, you might say, for those who came to worship Demeter.

The trees on the highest parts of the site, above the museum, are half dead from the effects of pollution. This is the area where Pan's shrine once stood. Most of the agricultural land around the area has been swallowed up by industry. Yet the Greeks seek to put the blame for their dying land at our doors. The fact that Demeter's head is now in England is sometimes cited as being the reason for the death of nature in this area. I sketched that head, when I was seventeen or so, in the Fitzwilliam Museum in Cambridge. I was drawn to it, but completely unaware of its history.

Eleusis is, of course, most famous for its temple of Demeter and the Mysteries celebrated there. The first temple is supposed to have been built in the fifteenth century BC. But the festival and fullest institution of the Mysteries wasn't until 760 BC. A famine had frightened the Greeks into a new fit of religious dedication. In the time of Solon, 600 BC, the Eleusinian Mysteries became, by law, one of the sacred festivals of Athens. There were various fluctuations in its fortunes, but the worship of Demeter continued until the sanctuary was destroyed by Alaric's Visigoths in AD 395. In the time of Justinian, the walls alone were repaired. Eleusis lay low in history until it was used as a military camp by the Greeks during the War of

Independence. After their liberation from the Turks, the Greeks used material from the sanctuary to build a settlement on the east hill. As in most sacred spots, the Greeks have done at least as much, if not more than everybody else, to wipe out their own heritage.

The great problem with finding out anything more about the Mysteries than the public ceremonial bits springs from the fact that initiates were sworn to secrecy. I remember when a friend of mine decided to take up Transcendental Meditation. She had promised to tell me her secret mantra after the first meeting, but didn't. Suddenly it all became too sacred. About the only clues to the Mysteries come in the shape of hints dropped by Clement of Alexandria, an ex-initiate turned Christian.

Persephone's visit to Hell may involve darker mysteries than those we know of. There's a hint of this in the speech of the cannibal witch, Erictho, in Lucan's *Pharsalia*. In order to conjure back a spirit into a fallen soldier's body, Erictho blackmails the underworld deities. She compels Persephone's aid by threatening to reveal what she really ate while in Pluto's domain. If it was anything like Eleusinian *bifteki*, no wonder she couldn't wait to get back to Earth.

I finished the day with a brief trip to Salamis. The ferry runs from Perama, a bus ride from my hotel. The boat passes two islands, either of which could be Psyttaleia, an island sacred to Pan where wooden images of him were worshipped. These images were rough enough to look like found objects – driftwood perhaps. When the Persians were defeated at Salamis, those who had landed on Psyttaleia were left behind by the rest of the troops. They were all slaughtered by a band of armed citizens, women included, who took advantage of the situation. Peter Levi, in his notes to Pausanias, seems convinced that the old Psyttaleia is now St George's Island, but Baedeker mentions that island separately – in his day it was a quarantine station.

Hymettos

Bees work for man, and yet they never bruise
Their Master's flower, but leave it, having done,
As fair as ever and as fit to use;
So both the flower doth stay, and honey run.

George Herbert: 'Providence'

*T*he next day was sunny – an early foretaste of the summer to come. It seemed perfect for going out into the country near Athens.

Mount Hymettos was once the site of many temples and sacred spots. Zeus was worshipped on its summit – a statue and his altar were there in ancient times. Now it's capped with radar. There were also altars to Demeter and Persephone, Artemis and Apollo. Hymettos is even claimed as the rival to Delos as the birthplace of Apollo. There was also a grotto of Pan – legend has it that Plato's parents offered sacrifice there and bees clustered on the lips of their baby – an omen of his eloquence of course.

Mount Hymettos is on the outskirts of Athens. It's very visible from the suburbs on the eastern and southern sides. I took the trolley bus to Kaisariani and walked uphill from there, cutting across the campus of Athens University to take me away from the main road. All the signposts there were for different subjects – 'Philosophia', 'Theologia' etc. There was a kind of Bunyanesque feel to naming routes in this fashion. At the top, where the main road turned away from the mountain,

I asked a fruit-seller the way and was directed up the side-road via Kaisariani Monastery.

It was on this road that I first heard and saw the famous Hymettos bees. There were only about twenty crate-like wooden hives – perhaps the bulk of what is labelled 'Honey of Hymettos' doesn't really come from the area. There were plenty of bees out loose on the mountain, though. The air vibrated with their constant buzzing.

There are rosemary and lavender and other herbs growing near the monastery and acres of wild thyme higher up. In the monastery itself, a few old fragments of masonry give a clue that there were once temples in the area. The church is of the eleventh century, its paintings of the sixteenth. It once had a wonderful library that included the most ancient manuscripts. Luckily the monks sold some of its treasures to European travellers. Those that weren't sold were taken 'for safekeeping' to Athens, together with the library of the Penteli Monastery. There, they were deliberately turned into cartridges for the defence of Greece in the last century.

In ancient times, the mountain was a place of pilgrimage for its healing springs. It was also a refuge for philosophers. Timon the Misanthrope retired to a cave there and placed on its entrance the inscription: 'Go your way. You may curse me if you wish, only leave me alone.' It beats 'Chez nous'.

The men on the bookstall in the monastery gave me excellent instructions for walking up the mountain and also for getting to the caves at Paiania which I followed later. They believed that they were the only open caves on the mountain, although a book that they were selling mentioned the Vari grotto.

From the monastery, I walked up the gentle path to the summit of the lesser Hymettos. Very soon I came upon water –the spring that's the source of the Ilissos river which once ran through the earliest part of Athens. The path wound on gently upwards through banks of wild thyme and the greatest number of other plants I've ever seen on any Greek mountainside. A few snips with the secateurs on some dry flower-heads and the whole thing could have won hands down in the Chelsea Flower Show. The lower slopes were covered with several dozen species of vetch. Most were tiny versions of British wild flowers, but often of a different colour. A plant similar to our bird's foot trefoil was not yellow, but brilliant vermilion. There were no animals around – perhaps that's why the flora is so good. Neither was there anything prickly to spoil my walk. Somewhere, halfway up, someone had constructed a little house with two beds built into the fabric of rendered breeze blocks and covered with a Greek blanket apiece. By the fireplace was a frying-pan, blacker than those at the National Museum from the excavations at Mycenae.

On the highest slope, past a mountain hut on stilts, I came upon the best floral display of all. The peak was covered with stunted creamy yellow irises, early spotted orchises and several other types of orchid including those whose flowers are the shapes and colours of various insects. The view from the top was dull – I was only at the top of the lower part of the mountain. All I could see was a crater connecting the part where I stood with a larger barren peak with radar along the top. A great many Greek mountain peaks are now covered with radar apparatus, which means that if you do climb them you can't get right to the top because of the security fences and warning notices.

My water bottle broke at the top when I dropped it on a stone. That reminded me that I must always divide my water between two large bottles. I managed to save a little in a tiny flask, but it was a hot day and I knew I would soon feel dehydrated. The slope of the mountain had been gentle so I speeded my descent by walking down in a straight line, avoiding the meandering path on my return. I came down at a point slightly west of the monastery and found the fountain,

Kilou Pira (the Cripple's Wallet), mentioned in Baedeker as being a certain cure for the barrenness of women. It now had a Greek health warning to boot, but I was too dehydrated to care. The spring was also once used to cure cripples, hence the name. There was a homoeopathic reasoning behind this – it was near a sanctuary of Hephaistos, the lame god. Its anti-barrenness properties probably came from its proximity to the temple of Aphrodite, nothing of which is left. I drank deeply and walked down through the campus area again. When I was almost at my bus stop I met Nick, a physics lecturer at the university. We went for a coffee nearby and arranged to meet that evening.

Nick was late. I had not really learned that Greek time wasn't English time at that stage. Just as I was about to give up on him, I saw him standing disconsolately on the wrong corner just out of Omonoia Square. He had brought his cousin Kostas on the date, because he was convinced (quite wrongly) that his English wasn't good enough to cope. Nick was badly lacking in confidence. Even his trick of managing to stand in the wrong place seemed to tell me that he expected to lose out. I went to a restaurant with Nick and Kostas and we shared a pizza.

Kostas had learned his English in America and had a tendency to say 'You bet!' with annoying frequency. When we'd thoroughly exhausted the subjects of English politics and English sexuality, we moved on to the subject of Macedonia. It was the first time I'd heard about that particular problem. I was asked what the English thought of the question. I had to say that they didn't – it wasn't big news in the English papers in March 1992. Yugoslavia had been at war for several months, but it was not the centre of world news at that stage.

Kostas was a little surprised that all England wasn't talking about the Macedonian problem and asked for my opinion. I said, as I thought diplomatically, that there was an easy solution. The Greeks should find out what the Skopjen area of land was called in antiquity, then suggest they revive the old name instead. It sounded like a good solution to me and I couldn't understand the puzzlement on Kostas' face. My vague memories of ancient geography hadn't told me precisely where Macedonia was in the old days.

Although Kostas was more travelled and therefore not quite so prejudiced against the surrounding nations as Spiros, I found myself coming up against what seems to be the prevalent twentieth-century Greek myth: racial purity equals control over your destiny. Forget all minor battles that were lost and the subsequent merging of conquering and conquered peoples, forget where your grandfather really came from – *say* you're one-hundred-per-cent Greek and that makes you one-hundred-per-cent Greek. The attitude seems remarkably like that in Nazi Germany fifty-five years ago. If the Greeks were competent at organising anything, the world would have much to fear.

Kostas was extremely good-looking. He boasted that his looks came from having been born in Delphi. 'Apollo', Nick said, pointing proudly at his cousin's profile. It's curious how even a good-looking man can become awfully unattractive when he's talking a load of bullshit.

I ended up at Nick's place – another Greek *pied-à-terre*. Nick often ate with his relatives and slept in their house, because he hated being on his own. Being on your own is something that almost no Greek is willing to come to terms with. Perhaps that's why they've all given up walking. If a Greek leaves his family down south, or up north (Nick was from Thessaloniki), there'll be relatives for him to stay with in Athens. So that Grandad, his aunt, or his distant cousins aren't shocked by his goings-on, he'll keep a separate bedsit to bring women back to – but he won't live in it.

Kostas left, saying he'd have loved to have stayed, but the woman he was living with was jealous. Nick didn't seem to know what to say or do when his cousin was gone, so he had a cigarette to help him think. I'll say one thing about Greek men – they're less apt to have a post-coital fag than the British. By that stage they've fallen into a stupor. But they do, unfortunately, need a quick smoke to get up courage to kiss you, unaware that someone who's not a nicotine addict doesn't really appreciate the flavour on their tongues.

Nick's room for his other life was bare apart from a bed, chairs and religious pictures. It was tidy, unlike Spiros'. Nick had sex very quickly on the bed below a smirking reproduction of Jesus. Nick had once been a singer in the Orthodox Church and was still too religious to do anything without his icons. He had slightly more staying power than Spiros, but not a lot. Soon he was fast asleep, with his limbs locked tightly over mine. I had explained before that I could not stay the night, as I'd arranged to leave early for Corinth the next morning and had to be back at the hotel to pack my bag. After a while, I had to wake Nick to remind him. He begged and pleaded with me to stay. I didn't get the feeling there'd be any more sex if I did. Nick just said that he couldn't bear sleeping alone and clamped legs and arms round me again like the old man of the sea, and fell back to snoring. Why someone can't bear sleeping alone, I can't understand. They're on their own, or not, in their dreams, anyway. Eventually, I got Nick awake, prising him off me, and persuaded him I was serious about being back at my hotel and leaving early in the morning. He got a taxi for me as his car was in for repair – the other reason he'd brought Kostas along on the date.

I had no particular wish to see either of them again but, on the other hand, when I mentioned my long-term project of writing a book on all the red-light districts of the world, Kostas had volunteered their services as guides and interpreters. Nick spoke Greek like Democritus, he said; consequently he might not be so good on the vulgar terms as Kostas himself was. I

60

promised to send them a book of my poetry and stay in touch, which I did.

Kephalári

Pan ovium custos
(Pan, guardian of sheep)

  Virgil: *Georgics*

Pan is my name; the herds on yonder plains,
My herbage fattens and my care sustains;
To me the woodland empire is decreed.

  Gay: 'The Story of Cephisa'

*C*orinth is not a well-signposted town. I meandered through a street or two then started asking for old Corinth – I knew that it was several kilometres out of the centre. I caught a bus near the main square. It was crowded with tourists carrying back-packs like myself and talking in a variety of languages.

I hoped to fill up my bottle with water from the Peirene spring in old Corinth – it had been famous in antiquity – but it was too well-hidden in its well-house to be got at. I even squelched up one of its exits, torch in hand, but could find no water, only mud. A conga of tourists followed me in, wearing less sensible shoes than mine, so I beat a hasty retreat before they started blaming me.

I had just finished exploring the museum and most of the main areas of the site when a frantic blowing of whistles announced its closure. There was a strike and all museums were closing at twelve that day. Some people were turned away at the entrance. Others had had their ticket money taken for only about five minutes' worth of sightseeing. They were all grumbling in their different languages outside. The museum had proved slightly disappointing. Not only were there no Pan-related objects, but virtually every statue had its head missing. Still, it does contain some good comic items from the shrine of Asklepios – a pair of breasts and two penises, one of which is erect. Presumably these were donated in gratitude for a cure.

All that was left to see was Akrocorinth. The guards who were closing up the site said it was about two kilometres away – but even by eye it looked further. After I'd walked the first half-kilometre, some French tourists offered me a lift in their camper. We stopped at an arch which led to the last bit of the road which could only be climbed on foot. The French gave up and sat down in the restaurant instead. By the arch, I met an English girl I'd talked to briefly at the bottom. She had been fortunate with a lift also. We walked to the top together. Charlotte was about to become a Classics student at Durham University. She was spending most of the summer months in Greece. Her purpose was to learn everything she could about Ancient Greek music. If money ran low she was going to busk with one of the family of recorders she'd brought with her.

Akrocorinth is a steeper climb than most Greek mountains, with slippery limestone flags underfoot. It must be lethal when it rains. Akrocorinth is dry now, but it once contained the Upper Peirene spring. According to one legend, it gushed forth where the hoof of Pegasus had struck. Now, there was not even as much as a patch of mud left to tell where it had once flowed. The whole area of Akrocorinth is covered with insubstantial remains of ruins. Some are ancient, but most are medieval fortifications, gutted houses and chapels from the last couple of centuries. Though the ruins aren't exactly imposing, it's worth making the stiff ascent for the views alone – they are some of the best in Greece. At every turn, in the higher stages, there's a new vista of distant blue mountains. To the west, the Arcadian ranges stretch into the far distance. To the north and the east, you can see out to sea. Athens was once visible from this point, but presumably pollution has put paid to the city ever being seen from there again.

On our way down we stopped at a café which sold souvenirs. There was a thriving trade in Greek vases, painted to order. Most were in high colour. How (or why) anyone would take one home amazes me. A great many of them were two feet six high, and broad to match.

Back in modern Corinth, Charlotte went to her lodgings and I continued to Argos. I decided to get a local bus straight on to Kephalári and hope there were some rooms there. My Greek Tourist Office leaflet waxed lyrical about the restaurants and the beauty of the place – so surely there must be a hotel?

The bus dropped me at the Kephalári turning and I walked into the village. It is indeed a strangely beautiful place. Mount Chaon, sacred to Dionysos, provides a sinister craggy back-drop for a tiny chapel and bridge across a stream. The stream sounds so powerful that it's hard not to think of it as a river. The Kephalóvrysis was known as the Erasinos in ancient times. Most of its waters come from the outflow of the Stymphalian Lake. They were powerful enough to drive twelve mills in the time of Baedeker. The village is full of the sound of ducks quacking, but there's not a bird in sight.

Several people came out to watch me and ask my business. There was no hotel, I learned. One of the restaurants let rooms – but only in the height of the season. An elderly priest who did not speak a word of English and whose Greek was particularly hard to understand due to an unusual accent insisted on escorting me from door to door, asking for rooms. I was obviously on to a loser there, and the endless flow of questions about what I was up to from the priest didn't help. The

65

villagers suggested I walk back to Argos where there were plenty of hotels. The priest suggested I stay and have a meal at one of the restaurants, then walk back – not a very clever idea as there were no street lamps along the few kilometres of country road. The light was failing, so I walked fast once I was shot of the village.

Next morning, I returned and quickly found the cave and chapel. They were up steps to the left of the Kephalóvrysis stream as you face the mountain. A huge mass of wisteria with lilacy-blue flowers hung over the cave's mouth. Inside, the cave was decorated with icons for Holy Week. A cable punctuated by electric light bulbs ran around its walls. Presumably, these illuminated the place at night, or during services. In front, in more traditional style, there were oil lamps. Amongst the twenty or so icons there were three of Saint Marina with the devil. Perhaps that's the nearest the village gets to celebrating the existence of Pan these days.

According to my Baedeker, the cave was sacred to Dionysos, while the chapel next door is built in what was once another cave – that of Pan. The Baedeker also mentions a festival, the *Panegyris*, celebrated on 18 August. It's the equivalent of the old *Tyrbe*, the festival of disorder, sacred to Dionysos. The Blue Guide, while following Baedeker in other details, places the festival on 18 April. I had come there on that day, just in case – but nothing seemed to be happening.

The booklet sold in the church was vaguer than my guides on which cave was which, and mentioned no festival. Interestingly, it gave a slightly unusual definition of Pan's role. He was billed as the god of woods and forests. Every area has its own type of Pan, I was to discover.

The large cave was about twenty-five metres deep and divided into two. In the back, there was a layer of gravel on the ground. The paintings were mostly modern primitives, a bit like inn signs. The older ones were of a reasonable standard,

66

but very flaky, thanks to the damp atmosphere. Inside the cave, a picture of the Virgin on a sort of easel-like stand made of brick and metal concealed the spring. The water was excellent. I drank deeply. Round the edge of the picture people had stuffed in scraps of paper. I thought they might be prayers like those thrust into the Western Wall in Jerusalem. I pulled one out to look – it had no message, only a name on it. Perhaps this Virgin is known for her cures. On the left of the picture there was an eye of thin metal plate, on the right, a hand.

The chapel next door was mostly lined with marble – all semblance of its cave-like structure had gone. It's known as the Chapel of the Spring of Living Water. It is an attractive nineteenth-century building, with a bell-tower built on at the side. Inside, there were more icons, some of which were draped with bridal veils. In the half-darkness, their slightly grubby unusedness reminded me of Miss Havisham in *Great Expectations*.

I went and sat on a bench outside, still hoping some festival might be about to happen. Where were all the Dionysiac revellers? An elderly man crept past me carrying a basket of communion bread into the church. I decided that Baedeker had probably got the date right, not the Blue Guide, unless things have quietened down a lot lately.

While I sat jotting down notes and the numbers of the photographs I'd taken, an old woman came up to see me, determined to talk. Once she'd found out why I was there, she used a word about me that I didn't understand. Her arms were covered in soap suds to the elbows and she seized my notebook to write it down for me. The top two sheets of paper puckered with the damp. Writing was obviously a bit difficult for her, and nobody has ever been able to decipher the word she called me since. Once she'd found out my profession, how many of my family were still living and shown horror at my travelling alone, she decided to go through my bag. I told her I only had maps there but she checked for herself, amongst the debris of food, books and paper hankies. Then it was the turn of my handbag. What did I use on my skin? She had to see for herself and inspected my tube of Nivea cream. Did I pluck hairs from my face? And those were the questions I could understand . . . When she left, I began to feel faintly paranoid about the hairs bit and pulled out my mirror to see if a bushy beard had sprung up in the night. But no, of course, she was simply wondering why I didn't have a moustache like the rest of her friends.

Walking out of the village back towards Argos I discovered the reason for the quacking noise. Kephalári does a primitive line in battery farming. The sounds were coming from small boxes scattered in the fields. You could see the odd duck's bill trying to poke through the breathing holes.

About halfway back to Argos I met a flock of itinerant sheep. They were popping in and out of gardens and fields on their own, tasting anything and everything from roses to cabbages. I made friends with several of them and gave them a bunch of grass to show them what they should be eating. It's the only time in my life I've been able to stroke sheep's noses. Greek sheep must be a lot bolder than ours. British lambs that have been kept as pets are anybody's, but adult sheep never.

Delphi

A little learning is a dangerous thing;
Drink deep, or taste not the Pierian Spring:
There shallow draughts intoxicate the brain,
And drinking largely sobers us again.

Pope: 'Essay on Criticism'

I took the coach into Athens, crossed to the other bus station and headed out to Delphi. I was there by nightfall.

There's no doubt that the Delphinians have become more than a little corrupted since the time of Apollo. The minute you get off the bus there are offers of 'Cheap hotel, cheap food!' You can be absolutely sure that they are not going to be cheap, either, when the touts come out offering them to you. Several restaurants are given over to the coach-party business and specialise in tourist menus – hamburgers or moussaka and chips followed by ice cream, with the occasional wilting Greek salad thrown in for authenticity. It's all at double Greek prices, of course . . . You won't do much better if you try to picnic with food bought from the main shopping streets either. Oranges are at British prices and the cheeses on offer have strange names like 'Processed Chester'. If you want cheaper shops there are one or two, including a good baker's, if you climb a great many steps into the little village above the town.

The shops that are not selling food have signs across the front saying GREEK ART GALLERIES. Greek art, Delphi-style, consists of luridly coloured amphorae. Unlike the Corinthian ones, these often contain erotic scenes of nymphs and satyrs in Kama Sutra positions. Erotica sells. Even the Delphic post-cards are thoroughly phallic. As in Olympia, the Greeks have realised that their Priapic statues are something to be cashed in on.

I must have been the only tourist to stay three nights in Delphi. I could hear all the others complaining it was cold. (It's about 1,800 feet above sea level.) Some were also disappointed that there was no beach to lie on. There is no doubt that Delphi is a damp place. If you wash your underwear there it won't be dry for a week. If you go out early enough, you might even see a cloud blow down the street.

If 'Greek Art' is not your style, Delphi runs an unashamed fur trade, with everything from the sort of hats worn by Davy Crockett and Fergie to full-length coats. British tourists are either too mean or realise that they'd be lynched if they took one back home; but the French and Italians were definitely looking interested.

The most Philistine travellers to Delphi are disappointed even by the ruins. How could something described as the 'Treasure House of the Athenians' be nothing but foundations with no gold or silver left lying about? The only place the average tourist appreciates is the temple of Apollo – it's complete enough for a good photo-opportunity.

The problem is that Delphi, like the Acropolis in Athens, has become a must on the itinerary of every tourist, whether he or she likes archaeology or not. The site and museum need only take you a morning, so some people do the whole thing in a day trip – three hours each way by bus from Athens. Proprietors are amazed if you want to stay more than one night in their hotels.

In ancient times, Delphi was filled with marble friezes, gold tripods and bronze statues by the thousand. Some impressive remains from the friezes that adorned various temples have been removed to the museum for safekeeping. Most of the gold and the bronze was looted by a succession of invaders and thieves. What happened to the gold eagles, for instance, that were attached to either side of the *omphalos*, the sacred image of a navel that marked Delphi as the centre of the earth? Nero, who never did things by halves, nicked five hundred different images of gods and men. There were also a great many animal images – including a bronze nanny-goat from Crete and a wolf from a town on Parnassus. The wolf was an animal sacred to Apollo in this area. Although much was melted down and lost for ever, a few items have turned up in other parts of Europe – the horses on St Mark's came from here, as did the bronze serpent in the courtyard of Hagia Sophia in Istanbul.

I love archaeological sites, even if there's nothing obviously valuable and even if a great exercise in imagination is needed to reconstruct walls, temples and the way of life in my mind's eye. While others complained at the lack of obvious treasures, my disappointments lay in other directions. I had been determined to see the Kastalian Spring, named after Kastalia, a daughter of the river god Acheloos, who's often lumped with Pan in dedications of shrines and altars. But when I got there, I found it sheathed in unromantic corrugated iron because of rockfalls. Fortunately, there was water left to drink – a stone channel at the side provided a plentiful supply which ran out over fallen leaves and mud to the road. I was determined to drink deeply of it, being mindful of poetic cautions on that subject, and made three trips across on the days I spent in Delphi, filling up litre bottles two at a time. It was this spring that Pope was referring to under the title 'Pierian' – just a highfalutin word for anything to do with the Muses. I would certainly have to say that the water has a marked effect – you start to talk in iambic pentameters, have vivid nightmares and pee gallons.

Then there was my trouble trying to get to the Korykian Cave – a cavern full of stalagmites, sacred to Pan and Dionysos. Both my Edwardian Baedeker and the modern Greek Tourist Office leaflet had said that it could be reached by walking across mountain ridges from the archaeological site. The Tourist Office leaflet had specified a two-and-a-half-hour walk. I was wearing what my mother terms my 'lesbian walking boots', so I figured I was good for the five-hour round trip. But where, oh where, was the path? I tried at first to find it up where it ought to have been in the left-hand corner of the ruins, by the stadium. There was what looked like a grassy path, but it was on the other side of a high wire fence and locked gates. I asked the guards by the site's main entrance, but they denied that there was any path leading from there. There was a dirt track, they said, but that started from the village. I must ask there. I did – in fact I asked a great many people. Most of them had never heard of the cave and therefore didn't believe that it existed. Some recommended me to the main road which gets there eventually as it meanders up towards the ski centres.

At last, when I had begun to feel like giving up asking, I found someone who had heard of the track and took me to the beginning of it – a tiny path about a foot wide on waste land opposite the King Niahos Hotel in the village area of Delphi. My helper had never walked that way himself and thought it might take one and a half hours, but he didn't know anyone who'd actually tried it. The beginning of the road was only the beginning of my troubles. Greeks never signpost footpaths and have little respect for them. A few zigzags up the hill and there was a choice of ways. Every choice I took confronted me with more choices. Paths that went to the right usually ran to a dead halt beside a fence, the one I'd seen from the site. Sometimes paths ran out where people had planted a few fruit trees or – worse – at the foot of a landslide. Feeling thoroughly lost while still in sight of the hotel I'd started from, I started to cross from path to path, taking any way of getting up the first mountain ridge that I could. Eventually, when one of my paths ran out at the foot of a landslide, I took to climbing. It didn't look such a long way up from the bottom.

Unfortunately, the particular landslide I'd chosen was full of wiggles and bends which concealed its real length. About fifty feet up, balancing from rock to rock, I began to realise I might have made an awful mistake. Should I admit defeat and go back down or might I find the real path again at the top? Going on seemed like a preferable option. I should be able to see paths more clearly from the top, I decided. There would obviously be a better path to lead me either on, or back, if time was getting short. I climbed and climbed. Every time I got round a bend, the way behind vanished and the way up looked even longer. I told myself that what can be climbed up can be climbed down – a general truth. On the other hand, when you're dealing with stones that are balanced precariously rather than rooted in the earth with plants around them, down can be a lot more slippery than up.

Either side of my chosen landslide was the dreaded Kermes oak. When you're on your own on a mountain for several hours you tend to go slightly mad and talk to things. It wasn't long before I heard myself snarling: 'Bugger off!' at a particularly troublesome branch of the stuff. I set myself a time limit before turning back. It was something I was going to have to do again and again each time I searched for a Pan cave. By three o'clock I had made it to the top of the landslide, but not, alas, to the top of the first ridge where I found ten feet of sheer limestone to defeat me. There was absolutely nothing for it but to begin the long descent. Every time I made it to a large flat stable stone I sat down, drank some water and contemplated my folly.

When you're faced with thousands of odd loose stones, you begin to see them differently. Every stone in front of me, I realised, had distinct characteristics – almost a personality.

73

And each one had to be negotiated with. Like people, some looked all right, but turned out to be very unsteady and landed me on my bum. Fortunately, I was wearing a tough pair of culottes that have stood me in good stead for everything from camel-riding to mountain-climbing.

Halfway down, my morale, which was at rock bottom, was suddenly lifted by the sight of a wild tortoise. He was as surprised as I was. Probably it had taken him a year to get up there, away from the tourists of Delphi. I stroked his head, but he nearly fainted and toddled off painfully into the thickets of prickly oak. I continued my descent using muscles I'd never explored in years of weight-training. Sometimes the most comfortable way (not that comfort had a *lot* to do with it) was walking on hands and feet like a spider, with my back to the earth, resting my bottom occasionally on the steadier stones. By half past five I was back on terra firma among the dried-out scratchy little thyme bushes on the tiny goat paths that led back to the hotel. Above me, I heard the tinkling of goat bells as a sure-footed local shepherd led his flock high up across my landslide on tiny paths that only he knew. Now, if only he'd been within asking distance . . .

The following morning, after the weekend, the Tourist Office was open again and I went to try to find the solution to my problems. The woman in Delphi's Tourist Office is remarkably good at not giving information in several languages. Her windows are plastered with all the things any decent tourist could possibly want to know – hotels, times of opening for the site and the museum, etc. Tourists are also ordered to ask the bus station, not her, for the times of buses.

Those in Greek information offices, or on the street, for that matter, always seem proud that they don't know where something is. The woman in charge had recognised me as English and rapped out happily and proudly, 'I don't know it – I've never been there!' the minute I asked her about the cave.

I have never yet heard any expression of regret for Greek ignorance. In English, or in most other languages that I know anything of, it's customary to say something like: 'I'm sorry, I don't know.' Such an expression of regret does not seem to exist in Greek, or if it does, it's never used. Any phrase book will give you *Sygnomi* for 'excuse me' or 'I'm sorry', but I've only ever heard this used by Greeks as a prelude to barging past me or into me at full tilt, never as an apology.

My tourist brochure had said that the Korykian Cave was reachable from Arachova by the road leading to the ski centres. I pointed this out, but to no avail. I was simply given another copy of the leaflet I'd shown containing the false information about the path from the site. Perhaps someone in the village might be prepared to sell me a map, the woman suggested. Should I go to Arachova instead and try from there, I asked. Oh no, she said, Arachova was impossibly far away. I'd never get there that way.

And so it was that I decided to opt for one more try along the path opposite the hotel. I had all day – this time, though, I was going to avoid any short cuts up landslides. I had to make numerous peeing stops thanks to the Kastalian effect. I suppose I must be the only poet who can claim to have washed her private parts in water from the Pierian spring – it seemed a better alternative to leaving toilet paper strewn around Parnassus. Usually, when I drop my knickers a rustic appears from nowhere, even if I haven't seen anyone for hours. But I was out of luck. Although I normally dread such interruptions, in this case I could at least have asked the way.

I got a lot further along the slopes of Parnassus that day, but on lower levels. I even got round the first mountain ridge, rather than over it and down into a sort of disused rubbish dump. When I got back on to the main road I found that I had only progressed about two miles from Delphi as the crow flies.

The Korykian Cave

There, in the cool of a cleft sat he – majestical Pan!
Ivy drooped wanton, kissed his head, moss cushioned
his hoof . . .

Robert Browning: 'Pheidippides'

*T*he following morning, I caught the seven-thirty bus to
Arachova with my pack on my back. It turned out to be
only about eight kilometres away. Even walking both
ways would certainly have been easier than climbing a
landslide, and there were several buses a day – a fact that
Madame of the Tourist Office hadn't thought fit to tell me.
One day I shall return to see her, dressed in a 'Macedonia is
Macedonian' T-shirt, and ask for some directions in Turkish.

The road that climbs Parnassus starts just before Arachova.
I went into Arachova first for a coffee to warm me. I could
already feel the cold of the higher slopes of Parnassus, having
come ill-equipped without a coat, jersey or even tights. I had
donned instead two silk T-shirts, the serviceable culottes and a
couple of men's shirts which just about kept me this side of
hypothermia.

Arachova is a base for skiing holidays. The shops are full of
souvenirs of a more practical kind than those of Delphi – chunky
hand-knitted jumpers, fur hats and gloves. There's still the odd
luridly painted amphora or reproduction statue, but mercifully
these are in a minority. The prices too seem more normal.

The road from Arachova to the Korykian Cave is about

fifteen kilometres. I walked the first few uphill before a Greek couple stopped and offered me a lift in the open back of their van. Clinging to the red metal sides as the wind whistled by I could feel myself turning blue. The road ran through a sort of dull plateau with the odd restaurant and some new houses in the process of being built. By a piece of good fortune the couple were going to pick mushrooms beneath the pines above the cave. The road climbed gently, winding its way up through pine trees with red and blue anemones at their feet. The couple dropped me at the top of the road and pointed out the cave above me. The footpath leads between limestone boulders to a flat piece of grass in front of the cave's opening.

From the edge there's a splendid view of distant peaks and mile upon empty mile stretched out below. Inside, the cave is almost as wonderful as on the outside. You can see most of it by daylight. It's only at the back that you really need a torch. Surprisingly, the sides of the cave and some of the largest stalagmites have recent graffiti about Pan in Greek. It's as if his worshippers still come here equipped with felt pens or pieces of chalk. Most of the graffiti is illegible. The constant dripping calcifies into a crust over anything carved or written, forming new shapes in the darkness. Just here and there, the name of Pan and the beginning of a prayer seem to be all that's left.

The Korykian Cave was named after one of Apollo's lovers, the nymph Korykia. The mountain path to it – the one I had tried and failed to follow on previous days – has always been a difficult and secret one. Its Greek name is *Kaki Skala* – 'bad ladder'. On one occasion, secret knowledge of this way saved some of Delphi's most prized treasures from being looted by invaders. The priests carried them up to the cave and concealed them until all danger had passed. It's not surprising that any locals who do know the right route want to keep it to themselves. Nowadays, though, the cave is too well signposted by the other road to provide any concealment.

I walked back into the murky depths of the cave. Most of the largest stalagmites are in its furthermost recesses. The foremost of these, labelled 'Pan' in Greek letters in felt pen, is a little like a seven-foot standing figure, halfway between a goat and a hare. Others are squatter and more convoluted in form. My torch kept going out and I could only take photos in the blinding blackness at the back of the cave, marvelling later at the strange shapes like solid clouds of white or yellow stone thrown up by the camera's flash.

The floor of the cave is mostly dirt with odd fragments of limestone. It has been excavated. There's a strange little row of Silenuses with erect penises in Delphi's museum. The museum doesn't say where they came from, but the postcards in local shops do. The French excavation team turned up a good many other fragments as well as a couple of interesting small statues but this material's not on show. I've only seen a photograph of the Pan figure that came from the cave, but it's rather different from other representations of him. The upper torso is in much better shape. He doesn't have the slightly protuberant stomach of other versions. It's basically an athlete's torso. The face too is different. Although the profile has the usual flattening, both the beard and the nose are much longer than usual. Both this and the small statue of a satyr found there are in marble. They are not the usual terracottas found in Pan caves. They must have been given by rich worshippers.

Part of the floor is covered in goat pellets. Presumably the cave is a good place to shelter from the rain as well as to worship the god of your species. There's evidence of a great many other types of animal having used the cave or having been eaten there. The French excavation analysed the bone fragments and recorded a long list of different types of animals, both wild and domestic, that had met their end in the cave or on the flat terrace in front of it.

On my way down, I met a coachload of German pensioners.

They had all been turned out to walk the last couple of kilometres as the road was too narrow for their coach to turn at the top. I was glad that I'd had the cave all to myself. It was worth the long walk back.

As I waited for the bus in Arachova one of the local men offered me a lift with his friend who had been skiing. I could have gone as far as Athens, but I decided to stop at Lebadea briefly and take the other road to Thebes. Lebadea, the home of the old oracle of Trophonios, is a bustling modern town with signposts to the place where the oracle used to be. Actually nobody's too sure exactly where it was, but if you ask in the restaurant that straddles the stream from several niches carved in the rock, they'll tell you it was there.

The Oracle of Trophonios was a rather sinister affair. According to Graves, it involved being whacked on the head and dragged through a hole. Enquirers drank the waters of Lethe and Mnemosyne first. Lethe was to make them forget their previous life, Mnemosyne to make them remember the oracle given to them. Interestingly, the spring near the niches and the water below are marked as unfit for human consumption. I did not feel tempted to try either.

Lebadea's stream is attractive, but the area has suffered very badly from graffiti – most of it English and Satanist in character. It's odd that the place should have been blitzed like this. It's not what you would think of as a tourist town.

From Lebadea I took the bus to Thebes. You can't forget the ancient city in Thebes. Old Thebes must have been on much the same level as the modern streets. There are small, locked sites, full of old foundations, sprinkled through the town. Archaeologists tend to say that the only thing worth seeing in Thebes is the museum. It's true in a way, although the town is pleasant enough. There must be barracks nearby as it's filled with young soldiers. Most Greeks I've spoken to hate Thebes because it brings back memories of their military service.

I visited the museum next day. It has a good collection of Boeotian antiquities. I can't help wondering what the Boeotians were like. I first came across their name as a toddler hearing 'I'm the King of the Boeotians' sung on the radio. I presume that the song must be by Offenbach, but I'm not sure. Ancient Boeotian artefacts have something of that same jokiness. Everything they produced seems to have a toy-like cartoon quality. It's the combination of naïve form and primitive painting. Perhaps Walt Disney had a drop or two of Boeotian blood in his veins.

Thebes was once connected with the worship of Pan – mainly because of Pindar who had a house on its outskirts. Pan was heard singing a paean by Pindar, so the poet rewarded him for his good taste by writing a hymn to him. He also built him and the Mother a shared shrine near his house. The whereabouts of the house and shrine are not known now.

That afternoon I returned to Athens by train and checked into the same seedy hotel. The proprietor looked slightly surprised to see me back. Probably all the other tourists only gave Athens a couple of days. This time I got a better room with a balcony. The view wasn't marvellous – a nearby building site – but it was good to be able to walk out into the sun for a few minutes if I felt like it. Also, usefully, I had a double bed . . .

I finished the day by going to search for a relief of Pan that lies on a wall beside the little church of St Photini, in the Ilissos area where the earliest parts of the city lay. It's a little hard to find, or rather to see, because the wall is so badly weathered. I visited the church itself, before I found the relief. St Photini's contains a series of desperately unattractive modern frescoes of saints on its walls. Someone taught the painter how to do shadows and he used this technique in exactly the same way on every face. There's an ugly grey blob below every mouth, giving every saint a discontented, pouting expression. All the upper lips have a grey moustachioed look, irrespective of the sex of their owners.

Outside, a film crew were busy making a commercial. I slipped to the right of the church, behind a tree, and found the subtle Pan relief. It's so damaged that it will soon disappear completely. Curiously, it came out more plainly in my photographs. The goat legs are unmistakable. There's a crack running across the figure. A sturdy bunch of yellow stonecrop has sprouted from Pan's groin like pubic hair.

Marathon

The mountains look on Marathon,
And Marathon looks on the sea

Byron: 'The Isles of Greece'

*T*he next day I set out for Marathon. Unaware that there was a direct bus from Victory Square, I took the tube to Kephisia – a spot that sounded attractive in my guide. Athenians are supposed to love Kephisia and buy houses there if they have enough money. Perhaps, a hundred years ago, it was attractive, but these days it's just an expensive suburb composed of a series of overpriced shopping malls above a park.

There were no buses going in the right direction from the station, so I walked up further into the town and then turned left along what I took to be the modern Marathon road. A few kilometres on, I picked up a bus to Stamata – a spot that was on the old road to Marathon before the new highway was built. The bonus of operating with an out-of-date Baedeker is that you get to travel by deserted country roads and see the sort of scenery that is missed by those on the orthodox route. The negative side to this is that you usually add a few kilometres to your walk and suffer from the Greek lack of signposting. I hadn't travelled more than half a kilometre along the old Marathon road before the turnings started. I asked at the first two, but had to cross fields and hold complicated conversations to get any answers. I made a mental note how to direct foreigners in my own country. I shall remember to put a clear direction at the start of my information – a 'yes' or a 'no', 'right' or 'left', and not to say (as I suppose was said to me): 'Oh God, it's a hell of a way. Are you sure you really want to go there? Why didn't you take a bus from Athens? There's not a lot to see there, anyway. Well, as you're on the road in the middle of nowhere, I suppose you might as well continue . . . You just keep on going straight ahead over the next few hills, and eventually, a few kilometres on, you turn right along the main road . . .'

In the end I realised that all the future turnings had to be decided on without help – there was no one around and my map was a little vague. I began to look carefully at the way the road was made. The key to keeping on the right track in Greece lies in this – find out which road is joined to the main one and don't take it. The road may look like a T or a Y junction – but one or other branch belongs to the main stem and the other doesn't.

The wooded hills between Stamata and Marathon make infinitely more pleasant walking than the main road. I still had a long way to go, though, so I accepted a lift in a small van from two boys – they hardly looked old enough to be driving. It wasn't long before the one who wasn't driving had his hands all over me. As I removed them, saying '*Ochi*' ('No!'), the driver kept putting his right hand on my thigh. I'd have liked to look at the scenery – we were passing Marathon Lake. A tiny road turns off down to the village, eight kilometres away. The main bus routes and motoring roads avoid this area entirely, missing the wonderful view. Everyone I know who's approached Marathon by the modern route has hated it. From below you only see the plain and two tumuli mixed up with the farmland near the village.

Shortly after the view of the lake, the two boys turfed me out.

If they weren't going to get a fuck, I should have to walk the last few kilometres. I kept thinking what nice men they were going to grow up into. Although I do have a taste for younger men, these two had more spots than years between them, so I wasn't tempted. There's nothing less erotic than a dose of acne.

Over on the right I could see a tower which had to be the Frankish one marked on the Baedeker map as near the cave of Pan. But there were no turnings, and a lot of fenced farmland and a stream lay between me and it. I walked on to the village and asked in the supermarket about the cave, but the man didn't know it. The woman in the agricultural supply shop did, though. She had been there years ago, but, since then, it had been blocked by a landslide. There was no way she'd ever go near there alone, she said. She wouldn't give me directions either. She suggested instead that I come back on a day when the museum was open and get someone to take me from there. That sounded like a reasonable idea, so I gave up my search for the day and waited at the cigarette kiosk in the town for the bus back to Athens. Curiously, that kiosk stocked some of the hardest porn I'd seen outside Athens. The titles were all in English – *Teenage Sex*, *Anal Sex* and so on – and yet few tourists penetrate to the village. I was certainly the only one around that day. But perhaps the magazines were only pictures. Photographs are the same in any language.

Looking back at that trip, I realise that I should not have heeded sensible advice. I should have legged it across the fields to the tower and found the cave of Pan alone. Being sensible never gets you to a cave of Pan.

The next morning I went to Marathon again, taking my back-pack in case I decided to book into one of the hotels there. It was a bad decision. Carrying it round all day wore me down. This time, I asked the conductor for the museum, but he'd never heard of it; nor had the driver. An old lady who spoke

French told them where it was and got them to stop the bus at the right turning, a few kilometres or so before the village.

It's a pleasant walk of two or three kilometres along a winding road through farmland to the new museum by the tomb of the Plataeans. The mound that covers them was only excavated recently. Most people only bother with the tomb of the Athenians. The Plataeans were only slaves after all.

The museum is so new that you can't take photographs – everything is 'unpublished'. Case sixteen is full of small objects from the local cave of Pan. The tiny terracottas are supposed to date back to the sixth to fifth century BC. Most of them are women's heads, but there are also a few heads of Hermes, four Pan figures and a headless figure with a lion in its lap.

I asked the curator about the cave of Pan, but he'd never visited it and only knew vaguely where it was. There was a map in the museum, but it was almost as vague on detail. The cave was at Ninoi, I learned, formerly Oinoe. According to a minor writer called Araithos, Pan's mother was the nymph Oinoe. This genealogy makes his father Aither, or the air – virtually the same as Kronos, as Aither is called the father of Zeus.

I got back to the main road and walked towards Marathon. Just before the village, a parallel road went towards the cave. There was even a coloured map there to prove it. Motorists might be misled into thinking that the cave was a huge cavern from the painted board. What's left is hardly a tourist attraction.

The side road led past houses. Now and again I asked the way just to make sure. Eventually, several kilometres on, the road petered out and divided into three tracks past a tomato farm and a rather sumptuous villa complete with its own tennis court. I asked the way at the tomato farm. I was told that the cave was near a *piscina*. The man was speaking Greek, but I don't believe that's the Greek word for a pool. Looking back on it, I think he must have been South American and giving me the Spanish word for a fish-pond, pronounced softly. At the time, I registered it as being near to the Italian for a swimming-bath and searched for a pool of the wrong size.

I felt, from the first, that the track nearest the dried-up stream would be the one to the cave. It bent to the right of the Frankish tower. The tower was described differently on every map I'd seen – Frankish, Turkish, Byzantine. It was sharply square with a hole blasted in its front side. Behind it, to the left, there was an old deserted factory with various disconnected pipes. Below the ground you could hear the pulse of a strong force of water.

There was a pool along my chosen track. I bathed my feet in it and unclogged the leaves from the area where the water was welling up. Immediately it looked fresher. There were a few old stones at the edge to sit on.

I kept making forays off the road to the left looking for the cave, which should have been near. There were several deserted farmhouses and many broken walls. Everything had been allowed to run riot. I eventually found what looked like a landslide of stones up on the left. This was all that remained of the cave, although I did not realise it at the time. My maps were confusing me. The Victorians identified another site, further along the stream bank, as the cave of Pan. Only recently was it proved, by the ritual objects found within, that the true cave was much nearer the pool. After excavation, the cave became unsafe. Nobody can now crawl through the three openings in the hill to see the flocks of goat- and sheep-like stalagmites. These exits and entrances have been thoroughly blocked with dry-stone walls and the waste material from the excavation. It has been done so effectively that it takes a lot of imagination to believe that there was ever a cave there at all.

I learned all this much later from archaeologists and Greek records of the excavation. At the time, I believed I had found nothing and went back to the nearest house to ask my way. An

Albanian was painting the gates. It was a searingly hot day and he offered me a cigar, a deckchair and a Heineken. The chair and Heineken were gratefully accepted. We conversed in pigeon Greek. He hadn't been there long enough – just a few weeks – and so did not know the local sights. He offered to mind my pack while I walked the other two roads.

The left one petered out behind the old factory. The middle one was obviously a path to somewhere – Kapandriti, perhaps. I walked it for two or three kilometres, but it ran across flattish, heath-like ground, all wrong for caves. The path by the stream had obviously been the right one.

I retrieved my pack and gave up for the day. Back in Marathon I caught a bus to Athens. There was no point in staying in a hotel there – they were all miles away by the sea. Marathon is a vast area. I was just beginning to realise this after the miles in different directions that I'd clocked up on two visits. 'The mountains look on Marathon and Marathon looks on the sea' has to be one of the most misleading descriptions ever. The mountains, or, more probably, hills, may look down on to Marathon, but, from most of the many miles that comprise that area, you won't get a whiff or a sight of the sea.

Curiously, every time I visited Marathon, then and later, my legs bled copiously. On this occasion it was the brambles; on others, it was Kermes oak as I climbed other hills searching in the wrong place for the cave. Another time, I trod on a bamboo spike in the stream. Although the place has a good enough atmosphere, a battle marks a place permanently. I joked to people that I must have been present there in a previous incarnation.

Demetrios

The sailor goes home singing; the lamplit lovers
Make private moments in a public place.

Paul Dehn: 'At the Dark Hour'

T hat evening, after my trip to Marathon, I meandered
through the full market of Odhos Athenas and talked to
Paulos, an insurance agent I met there. I was bored, so
I accepted his offer of coffee. As we talked, I realised that he
was balder than I'd thought. He'd had his hand on his head,
casually, when we first met. Occasionally, he remembered and
clapped it to the naked bit up front. Worse still, Paulos was a
terrible bore. He went on and on and on about the need for
insurance – anybody would have thought he was trying to sell
me a policy. He asked several times for a date. He couldn't
seem to believe my excuse about having already arranged to
spend time with someone else.

After Paulos had been despatched, I made my way up to
Omonoia Square, half hoping for a better pick-up. First, I was
accosted by an immensely fat man with a belly like a barrel and
an auburn wig set rakishly on one side. He circulates there
constantly telling every English woman who passes that he
knows Blackpool. I thought my luck was out that day when my
next encounter was with a rather worn-looking man with an
over-prominent Adam's apple. I took my sunglasses off to get a
better look at him in the hope that, without that murky amber

89

tint, he might seem younger, less worn and less covered in bristles. But he didn't.

Most Greeks who chat up English girls give jolly mono-syllabic versions of their names that don't sound a bit Greek. There's a fear that our tongues won't make their way round anything foreign. My pest said he was called Bill and seemed determined to discuss, or rather come out with his opinions on, the Irish question. When the Irish question had been thoroughly exhausted to his satisfaction, Bill found out that I was a writer working on a book about Pan. As I half expected by then, he was equally opinionated on that subject. I mustn't write about or believe in evil spirits, he said. They were all dead – there were only good spirits. By then, I was getting a little sick of Bill. Although he was definitely more entertaining than Paulos, I wanted to get rid of him and pick up something better, or go for dinner alone. But Bill was not easy to get rid of. He kept telling me I needed protection. Revolting men always tell me that. Well, perhaps I do – from people like them.

A few feet away, I saw a handsome stranger. I cursed my ill luck at seeming to be with Bill and wondered if there was any chance of extricating myself and any hope of meeting the other man. It has often been my ill luck, because I'm too polite not to reply to strangers, to be caught with someone loathsome by a man I'd have much preferred. I shall never forget the time a loony with a forked beard that almost reached the ground and horny bare feet insisted on joining me in a health-food restaurant and a handsome man came in and looked at the couple we made with the utmost disgust.

Bill kept putting his hands on me – not indecently, just taking my elbow or shoulder. It was annoying, yet he did not take the hint every time I backed away from his touch. Eventually I told him I was going to meet someone – an excuse that even a pest usually takes as final – and he shook hands, tried to kiss me, and went off. At that moment, on cue, the

90

handsome man I had been looking at came up and started talking with all the usual questions such as 'Are you English?' I don't actually feel English, but it's a useful enough cover story abroad.

Demetrios told me that Bill must have been an Albanian – Greeks always say that of anyone who's being a nuisance. Demetrios was the handsomest man I'd seen for a long time. I wanted him madly the minute I saw him. So often I've had sex with a man not because there was that level of attraction, but because they've been better than average, some rapport has been established and I've felt that sex would be fun – a nice end to the evening. Demetrios wanted to take me for a coffee, which was a good sign. So seldom is coffee given without intent that it almost ought to go down as a synonym for sex in every language.

I had been longing to feel a strong attraction again. Most relationships are a bit like office jobs – better than nothing, a way of passing the time and looking useful – but they lack passion or purpose. Demetrios was a lot younger than me – straight out of university. I was nervous that he might only be practising his English and would soon disappear into the night.

We had coffee in a small café below the Acropolis. The subject kept skirting around sex and his right hand occasionally brushed my left thigh. I left my hand lying there and soon we were holding hands. He asked me if the British liked to fantasise while having sex. I told him that many did – particularly those stuck with unattractive partners or people they were bored with. We were both firmly convinced that fantasy was a bad thing. Probably a lot of people indulge in it, but I think they're missing out on the real situation. It's a kind of betrayal of your partner too.

Demetrios told me that when he had felt less happy with himself he used to indulge in all sorts of positions, oral sex and so on. But now that he felt more secure, ordinary sex was enough. Great, I thought, it looks as if I'm going to get a night, or at least an evening, of ordinary, straightforward sex with someone very good-looking. That'll make a change.

We kissed occasionally as we sat talking and soon moved off under the trees for more privacy. I was wearing a grey silk flying suit which men love to stroke, seemingly by accident, but which had to be about the worst possible garment for casual sex.

Jump-suits and flying-suits are wonderfully becoming if you've got a reasonable figure. Most of the time they are also very practical. Problems only arise when calls of nature are involved – either peeing or sex. I have learned never to wear them on aeroplanes – there's never enough room in those lavatories to take anything much down. Nobody had passed us in our secluded spot and it seemed safe to drop my flying suit to my ankles – Demetrios had undone most of the buttons anyway. It only remained to remove my nurse's belt and slide everything down. Not being a devotee of the standing fuck, I chose a marble bench to recline on. I was feeling the cold slightly on an April night, but figured that passion would soon warm me up. Then the passers-by turned up – a whole party of them – and all determined to have a bloody good look. Demetrios, who was sitting on the bench, clasped me to his chest and dropped his leather jacket over my shoulders until they passed. In typical male fashion he had managed to remain fully dressed and fully buttoned otherwise. The cold and the passers-by didn't suit me and the murkiness didn't suit Demetrios. He had been complaining that he couldn't see enough – it hadn't seemed to be a problem for the passers-by. I figured he must be a broad daylight or electric-light man.

It was back in my hotel bedroom that I found out precisely what Demetrios wanted to see clearly. He was absolutely mesmerised by my cunt. When I was very young, no lover ever paid my cunt a compliment. Curiously, though, from the age of thirty-five onwards, the compliments for that part seemed to come thick and fast. Obviously there's something to be said for experience, although it is slightly worrying that, these days, I get more compliments paid to it than my face.

From time to time, I've quizzed some of these cunt-loving men on what was special about a good cunt as opposed to a bad one. As I haven't had a long, hard, close-up look at that part since I was at school, I have begun to forget the niceties of the differences between them. They all seem pretty much the same to me – like nasty, predatory, salivating, toothless mouths, surrounded by hair. The lips of some bearded men remind me of them. The answers I get from connoisseurs of cunts vary – some men are keen to see clitorises clearly, some not, but all agree that tightness, depth and lubricity are important.

Some men have a lifelong obsession with cunts. A friend showed me a medical dictionary with pages of tracings made from the imprints of dozens of them. Women patients had been asked to sit astride a small plate of glass. The disturbed doctor responsible had used all these ragged little drawings to illustrate his theories. Most of the illustrations were titled with notes complaining that various parts had been enlarged by lesbian practices. They all looked perfectly average to me – but then I did go to a girls' school.

One of my fans also has a cunt obsession – he sent me some photographs of elderly whores with their legs spread wide apart. Did I agree they were beautiful? he asked. Interestingly, he is still a virgin in middle age.

At the moment, 'cunt' is the only really taboo word on British television. I have been taken aside by the producers of two late-night programmes and told I could say 'fuck' – they could okay that with their bosses – but not 'cunt'. I put it to both of them that this was sexism, considering I was allowed to say 'prick' – but they didn't take my point.

If you can't call a cunt a cunt, what words are you left with?

There's the coy, mispronounced medical Latin *vagina* which just meant sheath; 'pussy'; or one of the twee Victorian women's names like 'Fanny' or 'Mary-Jane'.

Greek has no equivalent of the male and female names we give to genitals. There's a word that's near in meaning to our 'pussy' – *'gatoula'* – more of a kitty, actually. Old people sometimes call it *'pragma'* – thing. They are also known as *'evee'* – youth. (In old Greek, Hebe, the older form of the word, was the name of the Goddess of Youth.) But mostly the Greeks call them *'mouni'* – cunt. As with English, it is also an insult you can use. For an even stronger insult you can call someone the word for pubic hair. The Greeks have separate words for male and female pubic hair – *'mounotricha'*, literally 'cunt-hair', is the one that gets used as an insult. It would be, wouldn't it?

Demetrios's fascination with my cunt seemed to be leading us into all sorts of strange positions. 'So this is your definition of "ordinary sex"?' I thought, as I found myself in a shoulder stand with my legs round his neck, not because he was attempting cunnilingus, but simply because he wanted a better look.

Position-wise, Demetrios seemed to be shying away from what I would define as ordinary sex. He didn't seem to want to be masturbated either. My hand was gently removed when I put it on his cock. As a lover, he was all give and no take – something I'd never come across before. Any other man I'd met who was settling for masturbation instead of sex would want some reciprocity. Demetrios didn't seem to. He was very skilled with his fingers – always gentle and seeming to sense telepathically what movements I'd like. Although I do believe in telepathy, I also believe that this effect can be achieved by a man who watches tiny bodily responses, analyses them at speed and then decides whether to continue or change whatever type of touch he's using at that moment. Some men like to blame their lack of skill on their partner not telling them verbally what she likes. They're unsubtle if they can only operate in that way. The sort of instructions she could give are at best vague and would lead to misunderstandings – 'harder' could mean very much harder or only slightly harder. By the same token every other word usable in this context – gentler, slower, faster, etc. – has a whole range of meaning possible within it. The instructing partner would have to continue modifying the other's activity by issuing further commands. The process of verbalising what she wants, even if she is not embarrassed by it, could shift sensation away from the area that's being stimulated.

Curiously, when lovemaking consists of clitoral stimulation rather than going for the old-fashioned vaginal orgasm, verbalising is more destructive to pleasure. The clitoral orgasm has a sense of being located very precisely in the genital region. The process involved in analysing sensation in your head then reporting back in usable instructions involves a shift from head and genitals to head and mouth. The ability to come from clitoral stimulation seems to involve a mental concentration on that part that is shattered by articulate speech. A man who demands instructions in that situation, rather than before or after, is setting up a cycle of frustration. As he interprets these instructions, sometimes wrongly, his partner will have to issue further clarification. While she does this her mind will be diverted from her own sensations. She'll therefore start to analyse them wrongly. He'll be frustrated that she's not coming – for which he'll either blame her or blame himself. The whole thing's a trip to nowhere. At the end of it, both parties will certainly decide that they could have done better by themselves.

It's often said that we can give ourselves the best orgasms because we know exactly what we want without having to put it into words. It's not a concept I agree with. For one thing, as I once wrote in a poem, 'the foreplay's rather short on fun'. For years, though, I tended to believe that the best masturbatory, rather than penetrative, orgasms were to be had alone. Demetrios taught me that's not true. By using complex positions, he was achieving something essentially different from anything I could do alone.

But while Demetrios was a master with his hands – the best I've experienced – he had one grievous fault as a lover. He would not go in for what I had expected – ordinary sex. By three in the morning, the truth emerged. He was so terrified of AIDS that he had decided to give up sex altogether. 'Why take a risk,' he argued, 'when pleasure can be had in different ways?'

Using condoms makes sense – but even those were not considered safe enough by Demetrios. From what he had said, I believe that his intention was to give up sex altogether for life and not just in brief relationships like ours. His AIDS paranoia had also made him decide to give up the dentist, after reading about a certain American case.

I expect there are thousands of men and women in the world who think like Demetrios – though few so skilled with their hands. Apollinaire wrote prophetically in his *Les Onze Mille Verges* that masturbation was the coming thing. If he and the thousands like Demetrios are right, the world will end not with a bang but a whimper. There'll be no nuclear holocaust, no apocalypse. All the earth's billions will simply wank themselves, or each other, into old age and death without children or germs to be a nuisance to them.

Fortunately, this will not be the case – there are enough people left to let the side down by enjoying a good fuck from time to time. Yes, the unfortunate ones will keep the VD clinics in business. A small proportion – the severely unlucky – will die from AIDS until a cure is found. But that's life. The other choice implies the death of all mankind.

*

It was almost the end of my trip. Demetrios had to leave at six-thirty. He had determined to spend Easter on Mykonos. He liked to celebrate Easter on the islands, away from Athens. I told him about a friend's brother who had a T-shirt printed: 'I'll be buggered if I go back to Mykonos', after a much harassed holiday there. It was the sort of joke I was sorry I'd started – it required such a lot of explanation. We exchanged addresses. I wanted to see Demetrios again, but it would obviously not be until my next trip, if then. He gave me his parents' address to write to in Sparta.

Easter

The day of resurrection! Earth tell it out abroad.

John of Damascus, translated by Neale

N ext day, I caught the Skala Oropos bus and got off at a crossroads where one of the roads led to Kalamos. A couple of kilometres down that road I came to the Amphiareon. The guard on the door was so bored that he had stepped outside to solicit passers-by to come in and see his archaeological site.

The small excavations tucked away in the country are always happier experiences than the major ones in Athens. The few people who come to them are really interested. There's space to see them in your own time. You're not forced round in a swelling mass of tourists and there's not a camcorder in sight.

The Amphiareon is almost hidden beside a dried-up river in the midst of a wood of pine trees between hills. The situation is idyllic. There were so many unlabelled foundations that I wished I'd been able to find a map of the site before I went there. There'd been none in the English guides. I saw an elderly German examining a book, so I asked him if he had a plan. German books often seem to have more detail than ours. By good fortune, he even had a photocopy to spare with him, so I was able to find my way round the site.

Amphiaraos was one of the 'Seven Against Thebes'. As he fled after defeat, he was struck by one of Zeus's thunderbolts, after which the earth opened and swallowed him and his horses up. This meant that he was never caught by his pursuers. Personally, I believe that being swallowed by the earth has to be nearly as bad.

By the site of the hero's oracle there are the remains of a tiny theatre. The sacred spring was down by the river. It was at this precise point that Amphiaraos was supposed to have risen up again as a god. You can see the stagnant remains of the spring beside the masonry of an altar. It should be excavated further. The ancients, it is recorded, slung in gold and silver coins whenever they were cured by an oracular prescription from the god. Nearby, a colossal arm that lies in the grass within the precinct of the old temple of the hero gives an indication of former grandeur. The popularity of the cult is affirmed by a great many inscriptions on the stones near the entrance to the site.

It was the first time that I'd really attempted to look at Greek inscriptions. There's something rather moving and exhilarating about recognising the odd historic name from the past. Some, like that of the Spartan Lykourgos, are plainly visible on the bases where votive statues once rested. I began to understand the fascination of these sorts of remains for epigraphers.

Amphiaraos was recognised as a god for having instituted oracular dreaming. Everyone who came to consult him made sacrifices to the gods whose names were on the altar. The remains of the high altar are still visible. It's one of the biggest altars you'll see. It was divided into sections, although most of these divisions are no longer visible. The groupings within sections of this altar were curious. On the first part Herakles, Zeus and Apollo were lumped together; the second was for heroes and their wives; the third for Hestia, Hermes, Amphiaraos and his sons (except for the one who killed his mother – he's omitted, as are ex-cons from *Who's Who*); the fourth was for Aphrodite, Jason, Health and Athene. The fifth part – the part I came to look for – was dedicated to Pan, the nymphs and the rivers Acheloos and Kephisos.

It's interesting to speculate why some gods were left out of this collection. Poseidon is probably not appropriate a few kilometres inland – but Hera, Hephaistos, Demeter, Dionysos and Asklepios are all missing. Some of these, at any rate, might have been appropriate at the shrine of a hero who disappeared into the earth and who dealt in oracular dreams, a number of which were connected with healing.

After making his offering to the high altar's collection of gods, the suppliant then spent the night on the fleece of the sacrificed ram and waited for his dream. Those who wish to try it these days had better wait for a Monday when most sites are closed, then get over the fence. I doubt if the gatekeeper would allow it otherwise.

From the Amphiareon I walked on to Kalamos. It wasn't far. I had an hour to wait for the bus back to Athens, so I bought hazelnuts and sat in a little *kapheneion* and drank some of the best Greek coffee I've ever tasted.

It was Good Friday, but most of the shops were still open in Athens, contrary to what I'd been led to believe. I had been told by the insurance agent and the Greek Tourist Office that there would be a 'beautiful' procession that night from Syntagma Square to the Monastiraki area. I meandered through the streets to get myself a good place. Around the corners of Omonoia Square the traders were doing a roaring trade in Paschal lambs that had fallen off the back of a lorry. As men clocked off work they bought a carcass and staggered home with it (often unwrapped) across their shoulders. All the electrical shops were selling spits. Some had lurid models of plaster lambs covered in gore turning on them. It was enough to make me decide to turn vegetarian for a while.

I had a coffee in one of the cafés with a ringside seat, as it were, of where the procession would pass. A lot of other tourists were doing the same. When it came, I could hardly believe that it was the right one – a few crosses, a gaggle of ancient priests and a squad of soldiers. Hastings Carnival can do better. You'd have to be seriously religious to call that beautiful. One of my problems with religion is that I can't help noticing how it distorts logic and taste. I suspect anything that louses up the minds of its followers so much that they see bad music as good, poor art as something beautiful, and so on. Patriotism has much the same effect. A programme on Mrs Thatcher's favourite things showed her waxing lyrical about a perfectly ghastly bit of pottery that showed Falklands soldiers propping each other up. (Presumably they were wounded not merely drunk.) Only patriotism or religion could make a person who is supposed to be intelligent display such rotten taste before an audience.

The next day I took the bus to Paiania to see if it was the Pan cave that the curators of the monastery believed. (There's a line in one of Menander's plays, also, that refers to 'Pan in Paiania'.) Modern Paiania is a small town with expensive coffee shops where everyone lingers watching passers-by. I asked the way and was directed several kilometres further out of the town and up what I like to think of as the backside of Hymettos. I could recognise the aerials at the top. This was the other side from the part I'd climbed previously. Hymettos is known as a treeless mountain. There had been trees outside the monastery at Kaisariani, but they ran out higher up. Although that side was lush and covered with flowers, this was barren, apart from a few indeterminate clumps of prickles. The wind swept across this side. About three-quarters of the way to the top, I could see a strange, concrete, almost nuclear-looking installation disfiguring the mountain. When I reached it I found that it was the outside of the caves, with a cafeteria, gift shop, offices and car-park. There were hourly tours complete with a Greek lecture. I waited in the cafeteria for the next one to begin.

The amphorae here were even worse than those at Corinth and Delphi. You could buy them on key-rings or as miniatures filled with ouzo. These were alternated on the shelves with plastic temples and fluorescent bum-bags. There was no Greek coffee for sale, just expensive cappuccinos – or, rather, what the proprietor supposed to be cappuccino.

Once the next tour was called and I got inside the caves, I knew they had nothing to do with Pan. Glutinous stalagmite formations covered the walls like a series of castles designed by Disney, under coloured lights. It was the sort of cave that would make an archaeologist vomit. Most of my party were Greek families with kids. The kids didn't mind it – they're easily pleased. One of the women was nervous and clung to her husband's hand as we shuffled along dank, drippy passage-ways. Isn't it great to be feminine?

A great many stalagmites have been given names by the guides and the postcards in the shop – 'The Head of the Elephant', 'The Olympic Torch', 'The Columns of Olympian Zeus'. At one point in my tour the guide worked a cunningly concealed rheostat and brought the lighting down to complete blackness – everyone in his audience was meant to gasp. After that, he went through a series of switches to flood the area with blue, red or green light. For my money it looked equally boring in every shade.

I tried to analyse why I hated these caves but had liked the Korykian one which was also full of stalagmites. There's something repulsive about the organised, perfectly lit tourist attraction. The Korykian Cave had access to good mountain air and a most beautiful view of Parnassus from its mouth. This entrance was so concealed beneath concrete in the car-park that it felt like being forced through somebody's bowels while being asked to admire the sights along the way.

That evening, I was speculating on going out to eat something and sample a Greek church service. It was the last night of that trip. I'd been told by the Greek Tourist Office in London that the Saturday night service that led into Easter morning was something special. Demetrios was off on his Greek island and I didn't really feel like picking up anyone else. Just as I thought of Demetrios, the phone rang. He was in the hotel lobby. I put my new knickers on before I sallied down to meet him. There's a tradition that you should wear new clothes at Easter.

Demetrios had missed the Mykonos boat and gone to a nearer island instead. All the best society of Athens was there already. He hadn't been able to sleep, so he'd come back to see me. Whether it was the thought of me or the noise made by Athenian high society that had kept him awake, I wasn't too sure, but I was glad he'd come back. We went for a drink, and then listened at the back of the crowd outside the church in the Plaka. There was a camera crew on scaffolding filming the proceedings, but what was worth filming I couldn't see. Like the Good Friday procession, the whole thing looked remarkably feeble in terms of pageantry. Demetrios wasn't religious, so we both soon lost interest and walked back to the hotel. I managed to slip him back to my room. The proprietor had other things, like Easter, on his mind.

My white silk satin knickers were much appreciated. Demetrios was obviously almost as much a knickers man as a cunt man. I have always suspected that those who are over-fond of knickers or other forms of underwear are not into real sex – real sex by *my* definition that is, not Demetrios's.

After he'd brought me to orgasm, or sometimes while he was doing so, Demetrios liked to masturbate himself. He would accept no help in the operation and didn't like to be seen at it. He said 'Don't look!' several times, then said defensively, 'I'm only joking!' In the end I just lay back with closed eyes like a Victorian and let it all happen. I don't mind being passive, but I do like to see what's going on and I would have preferred *some* ordinary sex, at least. At times, especially as his fingers entered me from behind, what he was doing felt like ordinary sex, but looking broke the illusion. Perhaps that was one of the reasons he didn't want me to look.

It seemed a waste of a decent-sized cock not to let anyone else touch it. Perhaps he could have been persuaded to put it to use if I'd seen him more often. As it was, our relationship felt like a lesbian one. He might as well have been a woman for all I was getting.

After we were both tired by several orgasms, we spent the small hours learning to swear in each other's languages. We both laughed so much that the people in the rooms nearby must have cursed us. I had a pen and paper near the bed, so I wrote everything down and learned it for future use.

Being able to recognise how much people swear in another language changes your perception of it a lot. Now, when I listen, I realise that the Greeks swear at least as much as the English. The expressions you hear all the time are: '*Gamo to*' ('fuck it') and '*malakas*' ('wankers'). In fact, the Greeks call each other wankers all the time. I looked it up in my little dictionary. The respectable meaning of the word is 'softening of the brain', which seems to indicate that the Greeks have a similar opinion to Victorian doctors of what it does to you. In spite of his predilection for wanking, Demetrios was intelligent to talk to, which made a pleasant change. I'm more often fancied by the male equivalent of a bimbo.

We slept a little with the light out. I woke before Demetrios and was able to shower. In an hour or two, Demetrios was ready for more. My body seemed unable to have an orgasm any longer. I was suddenly too conscious of practical things like having to pack and get out of the hotel by a certain time. Demetrios had no such worries and so enjoyed himself more.

The proprietor glared as I settled my bill. I half expected he'd charge me for a double, but he preferred to glare instead.

His expression softened, though, as I wished him a happy Easter in Greek.

I spent the rest of the morning with Demetrios. He showed me the rather pathetic zoo off Syntagma Square with its tamed and shabby lions and wolves. I took a picture of him by the eagle's cage. We had some more furtive sex of his kind on benches in the less-frequented parts of the park. Then it was time for him to leave. He had promised to spend Easter day with his grandmother on the outskirts of Athens. Probably they would be having one of those whole roast lambs.

In the afternoon I bussed out to Koropi, not far from Paiania. According to my Baedeker it's next to the Paneion, a hill sacred to Pan. The only small hill I found there was covered in wrecked cars and rubbish. But perhaps the mountain ridges behind were the sacred bits. I'd prefer to think so.

The British School

This mean retreat did mighty Pan contain.

Dryden: 'The Hind and the Panther'

*B*y my third visit, I had joined the British School at Athens and was to stay there. I arrived sleepily at breakfast. As soon as the office was open I dropped in, hoping to pick up my museum pass. The Greek Museums should have processed it but hadn't. It was at that stage that I first became acquainted with the 'ephorate' system. The Greeks have an ephorate for everything. If you want to see some reserved exhibit or an excavation, you must apply to the right authorities in writing. Don't hope for a reply. The matter will only be expedited, weeks later, by one or more phone calls.

Helen, in the office of the British School, has a remarkable talent for dealing with ephorates in perfect, even-tempered Greek. Several phone calls later, my museum pass was delivered and she had also arranged for me to see the Cave of Pan on the Acropolis. I went bearing a letter to the Acropolis ephorate and was told to meet the head guard at a certain gate. I went there, still bearing my letter and the new museum pass, and was told to wait. Eventually the head guard materialised and led me to the closed area on the north side. There was another wait there while he called his underguards. 'Paulos, Dimitri, Vasili . . . !' he yelled several times with no results. They sounded like three familiar spirits. I was told to sit down and he went in search, still shouting out their names. Eventually, three young Greeks came running from various directions and I was escorted formally to the cave. The last part of the way up was a bit of a scramble across a double plank, one half of which was broken, and up a very old-fashioned wooden ladder, bleached grey with the sun. Quite why I needed an escort of four strong guards I couldn't imagine. There certainly wasn't anything to pinch in the cave, except two empty Loutraki bottles and a dead pigeon lying on polythene sheeting. I took some photos, trying to avoid the plastic water bottles and pigeon. The guards left all the offerings intact and went back to their business elsewhere after I'd been let out of the forbidden zone.

The cave was poky, but just about roomy enough for the couple in *Lysistrata* to consider making love there. It may not be the right cave, or the only cave dedicated to Pan, anyway. Archaeologists have worked on the assumption that because the larger cave nearby is dedicated to Apollo, it couldn't also be dedicated to Pan. This is not a very bright idea, when almost all his other caves are dedicated to other gods as well as Pan, or to nymphs at the very least. Most Greek archaeological records are so vague that you can't allocate the caves available by suitable finds or votive reliefs. If the National Museum has a record, it will probably just say 'The Acropolis' rather than designating which particular point or side of the area it came from.

I had the rest of the day to familiarise myself with the British School. In just a few hours, I realised that it was a place where a student could be almost too comfortable. In some subtle way, it undermines your courage. You could live there for years without speaking a word of Greek, hiding yourself away in the library, just emerging at meal times to fraternise with the other English, Japanese, Australians, Canadians, Italians – every nation that somehow comes under the umbrella-heading of British.

The library of the school is wonderful. You can slip in there at any time of day or night with your pass key and find new treasures on your chosen subject. All the archaeology-related periodicals in every language are there if you have the skill to read them. There's much that you couldn't find even in the British Library. The casual system of access to the shelves brings you in touch with many books that you've never heard of and would never have thought of asking for. The academic side of my nature could see the appeal, the temptation, of holing up in a library like that for years and forgetting about the outside world and things like sex. Some students do precisely that. After years in residence without learning a word of Greek, one threatened a nervous breakdown and burst into tears in front of a committee when it was hinted that he should get rooms outside as the places were limited. The other side of my nature sensed the danger of staying too long in the British School. When I travel, I speak more Greek and learn more about the people I meet along the way. My compromise was to stay there in short spells, while taking long field-trips to places outside Athens, breakfasting early and not returning till dinner.

Apart from the library, the other positive aspect of the school is the exchange of information. Archaeologists and classicists are free with this in a way that many other academics are not. Most are such genuine enthusiasts on their subject that they can be generous – it's part of their nature.

The British Schools are an odd institution. There are just a few left, scattered around the world – Athens, Rome, Ankara, Jerusalem, Mombasa. The school in Cairo closed forty years ago and those in Teheran and Baghdad more recently. They are almost like embassies – pockets of another country within a country. The closed ones stay closed on British-owned land. One day they may reopen, or not.

British Schools exist in part for the furthering of knowledge, in part for the keeping of the status quo. You don't have to mix with the locals. You can eat all your meals in, get your clothes laundered, buy beer from the fridge or make yourself a cup of English tea. If you need to go into the outside world – to direct a dig, for instance – you can hire an interpreter. The older generation of archaeologists, I'm told, don't stoop to learning any modern Greek, but valiantly bark the ancient variety at the natives in the most perfect of English accents.

For many, the school has an almost monastic atmosphere. Coincidentally, it is built on monastery-owned land. In the last war the Swedish used it as a hospital. There's no formal rule about not fucking Greeks on the premises, but it seldom happens. If you read the rules carefully, you might assume that bringing men (or women) back is okay as long as you accompany them everywhere, even in the shower . . .

I'd not slept, thanks to the night flight, so I had a brief siesta before dinner. Demetrios had written asking to see me again and I was to meet him later that evening. But the date had been arranged postally so I had slight doubts as to whether it would happen. Demetrios had left his parents permanently but was living with elderly relatives. They had the house and he had the granny flat without the phone. In theory, messages could be relayed through them, but he had not wanted to give me that number. He didn't like them knowing what he was up to.

Demetrios did turn up at nine. I went down to the lower gate and opened it at exactly the right moment so he didn't have to ring. We had always connected telepathically, which is a convenient but rare quality in any relationship. We went for a drink and then walked to Lykabettos and climbed to the top. Not being a smoker, he was fitter than most Greeks and so made it almost as quickly as me. He climbed it every two weeks or so, he said. I suppose he took a different girl up there every time – but that wasn't any of my business.

The way down was dangerous. It was lit so brilliantly that my eyes were dazzled and I nearly missed the steps several times and walked into a prickly pear. Demetrios sympathised over the prickly pear; he'd had bad experiences with them. This time, I was lucky though and came away without any spines embedded. We had Demetrios's kind of sex on a deserted bench up a side path. The only area in which we didn't communicate telepathically was my urge for real sex of my kind, not his.

We walked back to the British School. I would have liked to see Demetrios again as soon as possible, but I had to meet Nick and Kostas at the weekend for the tour of the red-light district. Nick had written, giving me Kostas's phone number, saying that they'd keep their promise.

I told Demetrios that I had to meet someone at the weekend who was to interpret for me while I did an interview for a magazine. It was work, I said – the truth, but not the whole truth. He looked a little sulky, but said he'd get in touch after that. I felt guilty. He'd been extra affectionate that evening, saying several times how glad he was to see me and admiring every garment I had on, from my dress to my knickers.

Mount Bedding

By many a haunt of Pan, and wood-nymphs' cave.

William Lisle Bowles: 'The Visionary Boy'

I spent the next morning at the Archaeological Museum. Some of the exhibits I wanted to see were in a closed section. One of the guards told me it was just for the weekend, because there was a staff shortage. Another said, with great satisfaction, that the room I wanted was closed for at least a year. I decided to make my next visit after the weekend.

About half the Pan reliefs were near the stairs to the upper floor. I concentrated on looking at these. I was gradually preparing a list of the items I wanted more information on. Some were not labelled at all. I'd been told at the British School that the museum curators were generally willing to supply background information as long as you applied to the right ephorate in writing. I might not get an answer on this visit – but I would eventually. Nine months later I was still waiting.

I got back to the school by lunchtime. I had promised to phone Kostas between twelve and one to arrange the tour for that evening. When I phoned, he was not there. His flatmate was vague. I said I'd go out for the afternoon then phone in the early evening.

I walked down to the Zappio and queued for a bus to Vari, where I hoped to find the grotto of Pan. I helped a woman with huge laundry bags full of shopping on to the bus. She turned out to be a Geordie working in an animal sanctuary. She didn't say so in so many words, but I got the impression she'd married a Greek, emigrated and been dumped. Her son had come out to Greece to join her some months ago. He looked in his late teens. He was tomato-picking now, but didn't speak a word of Greek.

The animal sanctuary was full of horrifically ill-treated animals, his mother told me. I suppose all sanctuaries are. Judging by the state of the cats around Greece, the animals in a sanctuary there would be in an even worse state than our waifs and strays. I wouldn't be quite so annoyed about the thinness of Greek cats if their owners were thin too and if they did not sell 'Beautiful Cats of Greece' calendars and rake in a vast profit by so doing. The cats on calendars are of normal size and sleekness, posed on whitewashed walls beside quaint houses on islands like Mykonos, beneath the bluest of skies. In theory, animal sanctuaries could raise money by producing the alternative 'Cats of Greece' calendars. But in practice nobody would want to buy pictures of two-dimensional mother cats too thin to feed their kittens against flaking walls beneath the pollution-clouded sky of Athens. Reality and calendars always have to be poles apart. Calendars are not there to make you think or cry.

The woman from the animal sanctuary got off at Varkiza, an attractive-looking fishing town with one or two beaches. Few people live in Athens now. The outward-bound buses are always packed to the brim in the afternoon with people going to their homes many miles away. The bus stopped short of its destination in the woman's village. It looked pleasant. If I'd had my bikini with me I'd have gone for a swim and forgotten the cave. As it was, I waited for the next bus.

It was only a few stops to the inland village of Vari. I got off in the centre of the place, such as it was. The grotto was supposed to be on a saddle of hill which is part of a mountain three miles north from there. About one and a half miles on I started asking my way. As usual I only found those who did not know – there were no handy Germans primed with archaeological information and spare maps.

I started my queries by asking for Mount Krevati – the name of the mountain I was going to. There were already several peaks to choose from on the horizon. You can always be sure that a Greek won't know the names of his local mountains. The first three men I asked at the local petrol-station-cum-mini-market had no idea. It seemed at first that I was going to be luckier with my fourth. He was local and on foot. He was speaking a mixture of Greek and English. Oh yes, he knew where Krevati was, he said. He kept referring to 'Krevati' rather than 'Vouno Krevati' (Mount Krevati) – but maybe that was its familiar name. He promised to take me there – it was quite near. Could I come back on Monday morning when his boss would have it open? I was getting a little puzzled by now – but then it was perfectly possible that the grotto had been turned into a vile tourist attraction with tickets – a little disappointing, but possible. I told him I'd like to see the outside anyway as I'd come this far and he took me a short cut across the fields.

By now we weren't much nearer the mountains and we had stopped at a sort of warehouse. I was about to opt out, suspecting foul play, but he said – in English this time: 'I have a magazine.' In I went, assuming I was going to get a brochure or map that would show me the way to the cave. But sonny boy had different ideas. I soon found myself locked in with him, his Alsatian and pile upon pile of mattresses and cheap beds. Obviously he had thought 'magazine' was the English for shop – it's not unlike the Greek *magazi*. I made friends with the dog while suggesting his owner let me out. 'But here is Krevati!' he said, trying to kiss me and pressing my tits. The Alsatian looked hopeful, too. I said no to all that in both languages, but he didn't seem to want to listen.

I kept wondering what 'Krevati' must be a synonym for. Usually men will take no for an answer when you've said it two or three times – but not this particular man. He was holding me in an iron grasp by now and there was nothing for it but to knee him in the balls. It was the first time I'd had to do it and I hope it'll be the last. He took it like a man and didn't scream. He got the keys from his pocket and let me out fast though. In fact, so eager was he to be rid of me that he escorted me to the nearest bus back to Athens. Mercifully, the Alsatian had made no attempt to defend his master. When I got back to the British School and looked up 'krevati' in my dictionary, all was explained. '*Krevvati*' – just one letter different but sounding the same – means bedding.

I remembered to phone Kostas, cursing him inwardly when his flatmate said he'd gone off for the evening. After dinner he phoned me. He couldn't bear to be alone on a Saturday night, he explained, so he'd driven an hour and a half out of Athens to spend the night with a friend. If I insisted he return, he would, of course. I left him where he was and we made an arrangement for the next day. The brothels would be quite as lively on a Sunday, he promised. Nick seemed to be left out of all this. Was Kostas doing the dirty on his cousin? It sounded as if he was no longer living with a woman, but was on his own. Most Greeks have a strange fear of being alone. If you marry an Englishman or an Italian, you are probably marrying their mother also. If you marry a Greek, you get the full package – mother, father, grandparents, aunts, uncles, brothers, sisters, cousins.

On the next day, I made another attempt to get to the grotto. This time I bussed on to Titsi, beyond Vari, and asked the locals there. I had coffee with a trader from Plaka who was having a second home built in the country. His Albanian worker had dug the drainage channel that morning and set a row of breeze blocks in place, but was now nowhere to be seen. 'I pay him five thousand drachmas [£15] a day, but Jesus

Christ I am disappointed in him!' the old man said. Titsi is a straggling new village encroaching on farmland and the hills behind. New houses are started there daily, I was told – usually without planning permission. The land is rich and full of laden pistachio trees, but it's being ruined fast. The old man told me proudly of all the pesticides with which the trees are sprayed, which made me vow to buy only pistachios from other countries in future.

A man in the local restaurant knew the correct mountain this time – he was definitely not a bedding salesman. It was thirteen kilometres away – he pointed to a white chapel on its top. I decided to walk across the land in between although I could have taken two buses part of the way. Eventually I arrived at the top, having trespassed accidentally on military land. I got off that fast, not wanting to be caught wearing a US army cap and carrying photocopies of Greek military maps, a good camera and a passport with a Turkish visa stamp.

All I could find at the top of the hill was a cemetery with several half-dug graves above a rather shabby cave with an attempt at a breeze-block house built within it. But I was not that far from the grotto, I discovered later.

The walk down the hill took me into Ano Voula, a town that's increasing daily with Albanian help. The houses look expensive and are adorned with sun terraces, frescoes, stone cladding, lions and everything else their owners can think of.

That evening I was supposed to meet Kostas at seven-thirty. I just ate the soup at dinner to ward off hunger. I wasn't sure whether eating would be involved or not on a tour of the red-light district. Unfortunately, I had told everyone in the British School of my planned adventure and they saw me sitting in the common room waiting. By then I had learned that Greek time-keeping is not British time, but I didn't realise Kostas wouldn't turn up until another hour had passed. At that stage, I rang Kostas' place and his flatmate claimed he'd left a short while before, so I waited and waited . . . Quite why Kostas stood me up I shall never know. Presumably, beneath all his male bravado, he was too cowardly to face taking me to talk to prostitutes. But then it was an offer he'd made, and he'd had every chance afterwards to opt out . . . I sat down and wrote a rude note to Nick – I only had his address, not Kostas'. He had told me that Greeks keep their promises. He had also said: 'You must say good things about the Greeks!' when I told him I was writing a travel book. Naturally, I mentioned both points. The letter was answered about a year later with a vague postcard blaming Kostas and encouraging me to try again.

Curiously, that episode seems symbolic of the whole of the Greek attitude shown in tourism and most other matters. Greeks demand our admiration and approbation without making any effort to deserve it. They should realise that what a travel-writer is interested in is telling the truth, not what a country and its inhabitants want to hear.

I didn't regret not seeing Kostas again, but I did regret having been led up the garden path. I would have to find some other way of doing my interviews on that visit to Athens, or my next. I also regretted having had to put Demetrios off. I could have had an evening of enjoyable foreplay with him, even if he didn't quite rise to sex.

In the next day or two, I wondered if I had alienated Demetrios permanently. Perhaps he'd seen through my 'interviewing' story. But three nights later he telephoned and I met him again. Once on the street, he asked me about the weekend. My trip round the brothels had been cancelled, I said. I hadn't met my friends since I was last in Greece. Had I slept with them? Demetrios asked. One of them, I said – but that was long before I met him. Men who withold sex can be very picky about who their girlfriends have it off with. I've come up against this problem before. Demetrios looked very pious and delivered an AIDS lecture. 'I was using a condom,' I said. 'It's not that big a risk with one of those. You're more likely to get killed trying to cross the road in Athens than by having sex using a condom.' My hint was not taken. Obviously Demetrios preferred crossing roads. We crossed a few on our way to his favourite spot on Lykabettos. I told him that I much preferred him to Nick, while we had a drink. That was perfectly true. I could have been very fond of Demetrios – he was tall, dark and handsome, intelligent as well – if only he hadn't been such a chronic coward about sex. He looked permanently erect when he was with me – it was such a goddam waste. I realised I was going to have to drop him sooner or later, if he couldn't be persuaded to behave like a normal man.

Of course, it was always possible that he might drop me first. The Nick episode had soured relations slightly. I hoped to see Demetrios when I came back from the Peloponnese. I told him as much. He was evasive and unsure about his plans. He'd been doing various odd jobs since getting his maths degree. His family also liked to use him to wait around for plumbers, plasterers, Albanian odd-job men *et al* at the house they were repairing to move to later in the year.

I was beginning to care less about whether I ever saw him again, though. There was a curious anomaly about our sexual relations. On the surface he was doing nothing but give. I was the one being given all the orgasms. Any he had were self-induced. At the same time, he was withholding the kind of sex that I wanted. Everything was done on his terms. Sexually, he reminded me of the kind of person who gets his own way with lavish but unwanted presents and flowers. The orgasms were my presents, but at heart Demetrios had a kind of meanness. He wasn't prepared to give me what I really wanted.

Personally, I'm inclined to subscribe to Freud's view of the different kinds of orgasm – clitoral and vaginal. Although I enjoy them at the time, as much as the next woman, I find clitoral orgasms deeply unsatisfying. Years ago, I couldn't really understand this, because I suspected that the vaginal ones were caused by the penis passing the clitoris and were therefore not really that far different. Masters and Johnson take that view, I believe. Recently, though, I talked to a woman who'd had a hysterectomy and had interviewed other women in the same position. She told me that there was a very distinct change in the type of orgasm they had after the operation. That would tend to prove old Freud right after all – right, that is, about there being two kinds of orgasm – not necessarily right though in the conclusions he draws about the women who prefer one to the other.

Although I've discussed preferences with several women, I've never, I don't know why, discussed the effect that several purely clitoral orgasms has on my body. I have no idea, therefore, whether my physiological reaction is the same as other people's. One clitoral orgasm I can get away with, but more, never. The next day, I feel quite a strong degree of pain located in the womb. It's a dragging sensation, a pull downward that is similar to severe hunger. It's certainly more severe than any food-orientated hunger I've felt. In the western world we only know the hunger induced by dieting or by missing a meal for a few hours.

I find it curious that I should suffer this effect. I have a high pain threshold in other respects. I've banged my head with impunity many times, my teeth are completely insensitive and I haven't had a headache for years. Maybe it's a psychosomatic reaction caused by my anger at the man's rejection of me. Probably not, though. In most cases there was no rejection – this was simply a method that we both chose because we were in a public place, or lacked condoms. Perhaps it's a sensation that all the women who prefer vaginal orgasms feel. I don't know. I shall have to start asking around. That will probably make me about as popular as when I tried to research women's opinions of blow jobs by asking friends and acquaintances.

Greek Gifts

Timeo Danaos et dona ferentes.
(I fear the Greeks even when they bring gifts.)

Virgil's *Aeneid*

*T*he following day, I headed for the Peloponnese. The minute I was off the bus in Tripolis I went to the museum. On the steps, I was given a handful of strawberries to eat. They were growing in amongst the roses. That's never happened to me at the British Museum. I had half hoped to get pictures of the Pan objects, but there was still a no-photography rule in operation.

Next morning I bussed to Alea. I had worked out that the museum of Tegea might be there. Tegea was an important ancient town. Its area is now made up of several modern villages and a large tract of farmland – all to the south-east of Tripolis. The remains I had seen before were part of ancient Tegea. In the village of Alea you find the remains of a large temple and the museum containing smaller finds from the area. While I waited for the museum to open, I walked around what's left of the temple of Athena Alea. Not being very well up in architectural terms, I tend to think of columns in terms of how many people it would take to reach around them, arms extended. Some columns can be easily encompassed by one person's arms. These stumps were three-man columns. The original temple must have been huge and impressive. It was built in the fourth century by Skopas of Paros in local marble on the site of an earlier, simpler shrine. The figures of heroes salvaged from the ruins are either in Athens or the museum nearby. There were statues of Athena, Asklepios and Health inside. The head of Health is now at Athens. Various nymphs were commemorated around the altar, including several who are connected with stories of the birth of Zeus and his being hidden as a baby, but there's nothing left now. The altar is only known through literature. I was to come on these particular nymphs' names again in association with Mount Lykaion, several days later.

I found the remains of the temple, discoloured a dark grey with age, strangely moving. When I was a child, only perfect, complete art moved me. As time passes, I am also attracted to ruins for the pathos of what once was – the inevitability of decline in everything. This temple carries a particularly sad atmosphere. Its figure of Athena was taken by Augustus, but I have not read who was responsible for the fall of the rest of the temple – perhaps it was Alaric who sacked the area at the end of the fourth century AD.

Games were held in honour of Athena in a stadium. There was also another temple – a small one – whose site is lost. It was entered only once a year by a priest. A portion of the hair of Medusa, given to king Aleos by Athena, was kept here. It was supposed to preserve the city from capture. Either the snaky hair was stolen first, or the talisman didn't do its job properly. The power of ancient Tegea is no more.

Most interesting to me in the museum nearby was a large relief of Pan. It is bigger than most of the reliefs in Athens, standing a metre high or more. The museum has labelled it as the 'Epiphany of the Arcadian God'. The surface of the stone is eroded – it has an acned look – but enough of the features are left to pick out details of the figure of the god under a fir tree. Pan's horns are high, shaped almost like a lyre, on top of his head. One arm is raised into the tree; his other, the left, holds the syrinx. Perhaps it's appropriate that Pan should be left-handed. A small goat stands looking reverentially up at him.

There were three sanctuaries to Pan near the outskirts of Tegea – one on the Sparta Road, one on the road to Thyrea, the other on Mount Parthenion on the Argos Road, where Pan showed himself to Pheidippides on his mammoth run to and from Athens at the time of the battle of Marathon. The latter shrine was pinpointed several decades ago by an inscription in bronze near the first arch of the railway viaduct below Palaiomouchli Castle. But the spot seems to have been lost since. In his notes to Pausanias, Peter Levi says that he could not find it. I didn't even try, feeling that my sense of direction and archaeological luck are probably worse than his.

Perhaps the relief comes from one of these three shrines, or perhaps Pan was worshipped as a sideline in one of the several temples to different gods that lay within Tegea itself.

The day was yet young, so I spent the afternoon going to Mount Mainalos, an area sacred to Pan where his music could be heard. The other main place for this phenomenon was Apollonia, but I drew the line at going to Albania on the off chance. My Greek is certainly bad, but my Albanian is non-existent.

I had a postcard which showed Mainalos in a romantic light. The shopkeeper had tried his damnedest to sell me every other postcard in the shop instead, because the one I wanted was grubby, but I stood my ground. I had bought a compass in a motor accessories shop in Tripolis. English letters were used for the four cardinal points, but, being a Greek compass at heart, it pointed south. Once I made the corresponding mental adjustment it was easy enough to use. I soon found roads to carry me out of Tripolis to the village of Silimna and on to Mainalos. The road winds through fir and pine woods where

Greek families picnic. It's pleasant country – not as wild as the remoter places I was to visit. It's just the sort of land for city-dwellers to pop out to for a little taste of nature. It was the weekend and a good few Greeks had driven out there. I had a lift for the last kilometre or two of winding road to Silimna. A little further on an old man on a motor-bike gave me another lift to the turning for Mainalos.

I didn't climb to the top of the mountain. Pan's music would be long gone, I felt. I just caught the view of the side of its craggy, tree-covered heights from the sleepy little town of Mainalos. I had read that the town was ruined but, when I walked into it, it seemed alive and well. I was not so lucky with lifts on the way back, but I made it before night. The south-pointing compass behaved itself impeccably. I was passed in a bright pink car whose tyres smoked. The man inside was all kitted up in racing leathers. Twenty minutes later he was tearing back from Tripolis again. When I had dinner in the park that night, a racing club was advertising for membership at a stand in the centre, complete with band and hot-air balloon. Trust the Greeks to enjoy tearing round on their terrible roads. Soon the pink car would end up with dowdier models halfway down a mountain, or in a dried-up river bed.

The next day I took the bus to Mantinea. I had expected it to be a depressing sight. Its original excavator, G. Fourgères, had considered it a melancholic, desolate spot, fever-ridden and subject to extremes of temperature. But that was back in 1887. These days it's just an unattended excavation site in the middle of farmland. It is much prized by archaeologists as an example of a Greek fortified city on a plain. Most Greek fortifications relied for their defensibility on being one hell of a climb up a steep hill – the Acropolis and Akrocorinth are obvious examples. A city on a plain needs much thicker walls to survive. Mantinea's circuit wall was elliptical and more than four metres thick. The perimeter was four kilometres. Along the wall, every twenty-five metres or so, there were square towers – one hundred and twenty of them in all. There were ten gates, each built in a different style. The river Ophis was diverted to flow round the city as an added protection.

A sizeable section, but not all of the city, has been excavated. Fourgères was led to finding the agora by the differences in plants in the area – particularly the appearance of hashish. It seems the Ancient Greeks had more of a drug problem than the modern ones.

In ancient times, there were many shrines in the city – even Poseidon was worshipped. On the surface this seems strange, as Mantinea is far from the coast. But it had a salty spring – the sea manifesting itself inland.

The theatre is the most obvious part of the remains to the casual visitor. Hera's temple was beside it. After a Delphic oracle, the bones of Arkas, Kallisto's son and perhaps Pan's half-brother, were brought here from Mainalos. His grave was called 'The Altars of the Sun'.

Across the road from the excavations are a chapel and war memorial – they are much more pleasing than most examples of modern Greek architecture. The church is covered in a curious patchwork of marble and small bricks – a folly standing out in the flat Mantinean plain. As I looked at the chapel I saw the one and only return bus go by. I walked a few miles along the way back to Tripolis before being offered a lift. The first part of the road was hedged with chicory and Lady's bedstraw. Away from the excavations there was a scattering of houses, which looked large and expensive. The Mantinean farmers are obviously well-off.

That afternoon I decided to walk out to the last of the old three cities before quitting Tripolis. Unlike Mantinea and Tegea, there is virtually nothing left of Pallantio, although the modern village is much larger than the others. All you can see that might possibly be ancient is the odd stone or two scattered in the fields.

Though so little remains of its ancient status, the name lives on in the Palatine hill at Rome. The Palatine hill was named by King Evander, a native of Pallantio. He was the son of Hermes and a nymph (the parentage most often ascribed to Pan). King Evander is probably responsible for the introduction of Pan worship to Rome. Pan became Faunus. Faunus may first have been an Etruscan god of similar form. The spot, now unknown, where the rites that started the festival of the Lupercal in honour of Faunus were celebrated was on the Palatine – the earliest area of Rome. Faunus was also known as Inuus, the Fertiliser, and Lupercus, he who keeps off wolves. The Lupercal was celebrated on 15 February. In Christian times it became merged with St Valentine's day. In ancient Rome, goats and young dogs were sacrificed in a grove at the altar marking the spot where Romulus and Remus were nurtured by the she-wolf. The priests were called the Luperci. Two youths of noble birth were led to them and touched on the forehead with a sword dipped in the sacrificial blood. The 'blooding' of the hunting fraternity in my country is probably a remnant of this custom. The blood was wiped from the youths' foreheads with wool dipped in milk. They were supposed to laugh out loud afterwards. Laughter seems to be connected with the worship of Faunus, as it is with that of Pan.

After the sacrifice, the Luperci ate a meal and drank wine. They then cut up the skins of the goats. They covered part of their bodies with these skins in imitation of their god. Strips of the goatskin were also cut into thongs. They ran through the city whipping passers-by with these – mostly women passers-by. It was considered lucky to be hit as it conferred fertility. The whip was also an attribute of Pan – the early Pan who was the son of Kronos and helped in the war against the Titans. There are paintings on many vases of Pan carrying a whip. In this context, it's usually an implement for controlling animals. A whip could be used on anything from goats and bulls to race-horses pulling a chariot. It was not appropriate for war-horses though – it made them too nervous.

The most famous member of the Luperci was Mark Antony. He even addressed the people in the Forum wearing only his goatskin. Julius Caesar was responsible for electing him high-priest to the Luperci. There were originally two classes in their college, but Caesar added a third – the Julii, or the Juliani.

The next morning, uncertain whether I would head for Sparta or Mount Lykaion first, I went to find out about bus times. It was Sunday, so there was no transport to Megalopolis until late morning. I walked down to another bus stop to see if there was anything going to Sparta. As I hesitated, wondering whom to ask, a car drew up – perhaps the driver was going to offer me a lift? But he got out.

'English? Deutsch?' he said.

'English.'

'I have a gift.' If I'd been German, I suppose it would have been '*Ich habe ein Geschenk*.' He was obviously another multi-lingual pest like Spiros. He fished in his car for his gift. When I got it I wished I'd said I was Welsh instead – he might, possibly, not have had a copy of *The Watchtower* in that language. The minute he'd driven off to find his next victim, I dropped the magazine in the back of an open van. Somebody else could benefit from this Greek gift.

Mount Lykaion

Of Pan the flowery pastures sing,
Caves echo and the fountains ring.
Sing then while he doth us inspire;
For all the world is our Pan's choir.

   Marvell: 'Clorinda and Damo'

I took the bus to Megalopolis in the end. From there, I
walked towards Lykosoura – a place that claims to be
the oldest town in Greece and which has some famous
remains. No one in Megalopolis now knows the old paths
which would have shortened my way considerably. I could
only get directions via the driving route, which covers thirty
kilometres instead of eighteen. I felt I was unlikely to get much
further than the site that night, but, near the tiny village of
Choremi, I got a lift the last part of the way to Lykosoura.

A path leads up to the museum and site from the main road.
The museum ought to have been open – it was still before three
– but everything was shut. I had the sensation that someone
had just left – all the tomato plants in the garden outside were
still dripping with water. Anyway, from what I'd read in
guides, the museum mostly contained only plaster-casts and
the real finds from the area were in Athens.

Below the museum you can scramble down slopes to the site.
The Sanctuary of the Mistress has been excavated, but not that
of Pan, who had an oracle there through a nymph called Erato.
She was the wife of Arkas. There is probably still much to be

excavated amongst the extensive foundations in the fields around. Pan's sanctuary is supposed to be below that of Despoina. The Despoina worshipped here is Demeter – 'the Mistress' is one of her regular titles, although she also had a nymph daughter, of the same name, by Poseidon.

I walked on, up through the village. The Blue Guide spoke of the key for the museum being obtainable there, but did not say from which of the few dozen houses. I couldn't face knocking on all those doors and being told, perhaps, that I should get permission from an ephorate back in Megalopolis, Tripolis or, worse still, Athens.

From Lykosoura the road climbs steadily upwards through the village of Lykaion to Ano Karyes. The scenery becomes very beautiful. Even the pollution of Megalopolis does not look so very bad from that distance. Mount Lykaion is one of the most beautiful and mysterious Greek mountains. Most tourists and many Greeks haven't even heard of it. From the top, you can see all the other mountain ranges of the Peloponnese. As you climb the long winding road that leads to Ano Karyes you are conscious of a positive symphony of birds and crickets. The area is particularly rich in butterflies of many different colours. A Brimstone and a Marbled White alighted fearlessly on my bright blue shirt as I walked. The area is also completely unspoiled by industrial pollution or Greek litter-bugs. These days, mountains without discarded tyres or Fanta tins in the streams are extremely rare in Greece.

There are several good springs on the way up. The road is shaded with oaks and the local nut trees after which Ano Karyes is named. The prickly holly oak which is ruining every other mountain top has not yet really got a hold here. There was just one piece of rubbish on the mountain – a raped and ravaged school textbook. The cover was long gone, Pythagoras had ballpoint spectacles and Thales of Milesios (one of the seven wise men) was adorned with a blue beard, red eyes and pimples.

Lykaion does not come within the realms of an obvious school history book like the one I had found. But the mountain, sacred to Zeus and Pan, is the subject of various odd legends. It carries the rival claim to Mount Ida for Zeus's birthplace. The infant Zeus was hidden here from his murderous father Kronos by three nymphs – Hagno, Theisoa and Neda. It also has the distinction of having been a place where human sacrifice was carried out. The top fifty feet of one of its twin peaks is entirely composed of the remains of sacrifices – ash and bone held together by dirt, grass and small plants. This area is a sacred precinct which carries a curse on men and beasts who enter it. They lose their shadows and die within the year. Death for intentional trespass was by stoning. The precinct used to be marked by two pillars topped with golden eagles, but you can imagine what happened to them.

One of the clearest legends about the place concerns King Lykaon. Like every Greek legend it has several versions. In the simplest (that of Pausanias), he is said to have killed a boy in honour of Zeus and mixed the child's remains with other meat as a test. Zeus kicked over the table and turned Lykaon into a wolf. In some versions he also struck his palace with lightning and annihilated all but one of his fifty sons. There are no remains of a palace visible now. The area hasn't been excavated thoroughly – even less so than Lykosoura – and there are probably still many buried foundations. Most of the information about the original sacrifices and rituals carried out in this area has been lost, although there's a curious story that has the unlucky eater of the bit of sacrificial meat that contained a snippet of human entrails having to go and live as a wolf for nine years. He only gets to resume his human shape if he avoids all human flesh in this time.

In the complex story of Lykaon, an interesting fact emerges. His kingdom passed not to one of his sons but through his daughter Kallisto to his grandson Arkas. In some versions

Kallisto, who was turned into a bear by Hera, was also the mother of Pan. Arkas is sometimes said to be the boy that Lykaon killed, inheriting the land as a sort of resurrected god, presumably.

I have taken a particular interest in the Kallisto myth since rehearsing the role of a fury in Cavalli's beautiful opera of her story. I was pipped from appearing by the clique-ridden nature of the group I had just joined. Most of the members I chatted to were unpleasantly right-wing; one even advocated shooting miners who went on strike. Being part Welsh with a second cousin twice removed who went down the mines, I objected feebly. Perhaps that's why some of the members of the group failed to tell the latest outsider where the final rehearsals were to be held. Consequently I had no costume fitting and could not appear.

When I got to Ano Karyes I had walked about forty kilometres of the way from Megalopolis. Buses only run that way occasionally. If you ask when they leave in Megalopolis, you will probably be told, 'Next week!' I had my eye on a solid wooden picnic table for passing the night. There were trees and a spring nearby – protection from the wind and a place to wash and drink.

I had already begun to notice a different kind of smell to this mountain – a heady cocktail of wild thyme and goat. Goat, contrary to popular belief, is not an unpleasant smell – it's just animal and earthy. I tried the local spring and found it good. There was an odd system of stone pipes and channels directing the water. When a goatherd came up to water his flock, I realised that I'd chosen the wrong point to drink from. The goats frolicked, paddled and swilled down water by the higher chutes. I climbed another kilometre or so up the mountain going anticlockwise – there was a choice of two paths. I turned back after reaching a marshy area near another spring. The first point was obviously a dryer one for spending the night. In the morning I would climb to the archaeological site and see the sacred peak. I told myself that the table was going to be terribly good for my back . . .

Then a car stopped and a woman asked me in Greek where I was going to spend the night. '*Edho!*' ('Here') I said. There followed one of those scenes of hospitality that I thought only happened in other people's travel books. I ended up spending the night with Mrs Tzevelekos and her family. I talked French to Mrs Tzevelekos – poor as it is, my French is definitely better than my Greek. After a coffee, I went as the guest of her family to one of the Village Association's get-togethers at the Folk Museum. I started to tell the Tzevelekos family that I was writing a book about the god Pan. Why was I interested in him? they asked. I started with the old Plutarch story where a sailor is given a message to take to an island, saying: 'Great Pan is dead!' I couldn't get to the end of the story or qualify it in any way, before one of my listeners interrupted in Greek as crossly as he could to a guest, saying that Pan could not possibly be dead, or all nature would be dead.

Since meeting them, I have often wished that the people of Ano Karyes were running the whole of Greece. They have a care for conservation that's largely absent elsewhere and they're prepared to set their aims extraordinarily high. It doesn't take an Olympic committee to arrange a major athletic event. Twenty years ago, unknown to most of the world, these villagers decided to restart the Lykaian Games. Ano Karyes is the nearest village to the old stadium where the games were staged in the honour of the gods Zeus and Pan. The games have a pedigree almost as honourable as that of the Olympics. They do not quite date back to the gods, but they do go back to the earliest dawnings of Greek history and the time of the first settlers in Lykosoura. Numismatic evidence proves their continued existence in the sixth century BC.

These days, there are only twenty-seven people left living in

Ano Karyes, but there's a strong Association, formed in Athens between the wars, that extends their numbers by giving membership to those who have some family connection with the place. There are frequent get-togethers in the folk museum, when the village's former inhabitants drive back from other towns, or all the way from Athens, to celebrate. It is this Association which got the Games going again in 1973. Every four years, the stadium is shaved bare, any trees that have appeared are uprooted, and lines are painted on for the races. The games are put on in August – a time when many Greeks are on holiday. There's a programme of twenty-four events – races of different lengths including some for children and one for old-age pensioners, discus-throwing and the long jump. Horse-racing has been left out of the modern version. No sensible horse is prepared to climb Mount Lykaion these days – you need a car with four-wheel drive or legs like mine to get you there. The events are advertised in local papers, but, surprisingly, Greek TV has not yet taken an interest.

The Folk Museum, where the Association's reunions are held, is the brainchild of Demetrios Karayannis. After the war, the village was emptying fast and becoming a ghost town. He collected together all the old tools that people had left behind – distaffs, looms, churns, cobblers' awls, etc. – everything that showed the old way of life. Once people knew what he was up to, the gifts came thick and fast, including a DIY raki press. Raki, for the uninitiated, is a delightful spirit made by pressing grape pips and distilling the liquor. It's similar to ouzo in flavour, but much better quality. These days it's easier to obtain in Turkey than in Greece. Some of the objects in the museum were barely recognisable until you looked at a picture beside the exhibit. It was once the custom, for instance, to bind sheaves of corn for carrying on your donkey with a sort of rope ladder. Most primitive-looking of all the exhibits was a blown-up goatskin without the head, sewn firmly across the bottom –

it was once used for carrying wine. It conjured up pictures of Dionysian orgies.

Propped casually amongst all the old everyday-life objects, there's a large inscribed stone. On it, some still readable, are the winners' names from one of the early BC Lykaian Games.

We ate in the next room – tomato salads with lavish quantities of barbecue-roasted pork. Fortunately, there were no human entrails in my portion. It was all washed down with red retsina – locally trodden and fermented, of course. Demetrios Karayannis's son, Elias, was the only English-speaker around. He told me of the dilemma that was emptying Greek villages. He would have loved to live in this peaceful spot, but could only get work and get educated elsewhere. He was a lawyer now, in Athens. He was spending time in France, also, where he was completing his legal education.

Although there are other universities in Greece, Athens carries a great emotional pull for almost all Greeks. It's looked on as the centre of civilisation and the only place to get an education, so much so that it has become an ever-growing Mecca. Anyone who wants anything more than being a goatherd has to go there. The city grows visibly, day by day, as new cheap tatty housing is built on its outskirts – and the pollution gets worse and worse.

After the meal, some of the couples began to dance. I noticed then that there were no children in the place and few young people. I still felt full of energy, so I wouldn't have minded joining in, but the family I was with wanted to get to bed. I am firmly convinced that driving and being driven are more tiring than walking.

I said goodnight to Elias. He was not sure about what remained of the Pan sanctuary, but he promised to show me the way to the top on the following morning. We made a date for nine o'clock.

As I walked back to the Tsevelekos house, I noticed that the

sky was full of stars; but I wasn't astronomically knowledge-
able enough to pick out Kallisto the Bear.

Wolves

*T*he next morning I woke with a cricket on my cheek and a lizard chuckling on the wall – evidence of the life of the place. I heard the cry of wolves in my sleep – but that was only to be expected. I had asked the villagers, the night before, if there were any local ghost stories. Perhaps there had been, I heard, but all the really old people who knew the best stories were dead.

Lykaon was the first werewolf in literature. He is mentioned briefly by a variety of authors from Hesiod on. But presumably there were even earlier traditions – he lived back in the mists of time. Sometimes it's useful to compare mythologies. Lykaon has some similarities to Abraham, offering God a wrong sacrifice and also founding a dynasty. There's the same chumminess with the Almighty, that only seemed to happen in ancient times. Zeus kicks over the table with the human sacrifice. The story implies a shared meal between him and Lykaon. But Lykaon is pre-Flood, so he can perhaps be more aptly compared to Cain – the first murderer. His transformation is the equivalent of the 'mark of Cain'. Lykaon's father, Pelasgos, was the first mortal of any prominence and the founder of the most ancient Greek race, the Pelasgians. He therefore can be compared with Adam.

It's usually accepted that Lykaon and Lykaion are connected etymologically with *lukos*, the Greek for wolf. Our word lycanthropy also comes from that root. There are a few other etymological suggestions that connect Lykaon with the Etruscan word for king and various ancient words for light.

Our 'werewolf', like the Greek *lucanthropos*, most likely means 'man-wolf'. The belief in human transmogrification is a curiously persistent one. People were even tried as werewolves up until the last century in France. Although the tradition spread almost worldwide, France probably has the richest material on the subject, due to the many well-documented, rather than legendary, cases. Once an aberration becomes a court case, real names and life details are recorded. The French were fairly lenient to their *loups garoux*. Most cases ended up in an asylum rather than executed. Symptoms of being a werewolf almost always included the eating of human flesh. Hannibal Lector is our modern werewolf.

The transformation scenes quoted in court did not always imply magic. A man might dress up in a rough skin, then go out for a little armed robbery rounded off by a cannibal feast. While the human didn't necessarily have to grow hair as the moon came up, he usually became possessed – his usual nature changed. The transformation is similar to that of a *berserkir*. The most psychopathic Vikings fought by giving up the conscious mind and allowing a sort of possession, or perhaps their lower nature, to take over. In this state of frenzy, the warrior became so strong and ruthless that nothing could stand in his way.

Some men suffered transformations by accident or enchantment, others for wrongdoing, others by deliberate choice – a pact with the devil. Some werewolves had pitiful stories to relate. Some were mentally retarded, poverty-stricken people who grew up amongst animals, hardly able to speak, let alone write. They were rounded up when they became a menace to society by robbing graves. A werewolf could behave like a hyena or, more sinisterly, he could abduct living prey, often in the shape of children. Red Riding Hood's wolf is clearly one of these. Like that particular wolf, the *were* kind can seem respectable on the surface. One of the ways you tell them from the next man, or your granny, is by looking for hairs on the palm of the hands. That legend still persists. One of the jokes in my snobbish school was to get people to look for hairs on their hands. 'People with hair on their palms are mad!' Every sucker scrutinised their hands, only to be told, 'If you look for hairs on the palms of your hand where no human has any, that *really* proves you're mad!' Werewolves were never mentioned, but it's obvious which particular form of insanity was implied.

It is remarkably hard to find books on werewolves. You could spend several years reading about their near relation, the vampire, but werewolves have caught the imagination of far fewer writers. Many histories of witchcraft contain a mere page on the subject, tucked away and often not indexed. Libraries are similarly lacking. The London Library contained nothing when I looked. The only book I could find elsewhere on the subject was Baring-Gould's *The Book of Werewolves*. Baring-Gould has had to pad his work with an account of Gilles de Retz's trial. Sinister as he is, Gilles de Retz hardly rates inclusion. While the mass abduction, torture, rape, murder and dismemberment of dozens of children on behalf of Joan of Arc's right-hand man – one of France's military heroes – is interesting to speculate on, I can't go along with any definition of this nobleman as a werewolf. He is more akin to Dracula – suave, super-sophisticated. Apart from Lykaon, later werewolves are very working-class, compared to vampires.

One of the things that interested me about Lykaion, once I had heard the legend, was the fact that the mountain and its games were dedicated to Lykaian Zeus – the wolf-aspect of the god – together with Pan. It's an uneasy pairing – werewolf and weregoat. Goats and wolves, as every shepherd knows, are traditionally not the best of friends. Only in one story can I find any links between them. Baring-Gould relates a legend from Périgord:

> It is always at night that the fit comes on. The lycanthropist dashes out of a window, springs into a well, and, after having struggled in the water for a few moments, rises from it dripping, and invested with a goatskin which the devil has given him. In this condition, the louléerous run upon four legs, pass the night in ranging over the country, and in biting and devouring all the dogs they meet.

The goatskin could, therefore, provide a disreputable but cosy form of clothing for the lunatic to go berserk in, out in the cold night air. This disguise also echoes the costume of the Luperci in ancient Rome.

The story of Pan's successful affair with Selene, the moon, is also located on Lykaion. He seduced her by a trickery similar to that of the Périgord werewolves, donning a silvery white ram's fleece to lure her down to a cave, behaving like a wolf (or, rather, a goat) in sheep's clothing. The tale reminds me of a wonderful illustration to a religious tract. I treasured it for years until it dropped to bits. Three wolves were on the front, in sheep's clothing that looked remarkably like Victorian-style woollen combinations. They were leering wolfishly as they fastened their fly buttons.

Perhaps the ram's fleece used by Pan had a magical power. Euripides quotes the tale of Pan bringing the lamb with a golden fleece to Atreus (he of the House of Atreus – the head of one of the world's most unlucky families, which managed to clock up more murder, madness and mayhem than all the episodes of *Dallas* combined.) In the Euripidean version, in *Electra*, the quarrels that ensued over the lamb are connected to a change in direction of the sun and a drought. Mount Lykaion's sacred secrets are also concerned with the position of the sun and the bringing of rain. The sacred enclosure was a place where the sun threw no shadows. Rain was produced on the mountain by the priest of Zeus Lykaios putting an oak branch in the spring Hagno. After this, vapour would rise and become mist, then a cloud. Then other clouds would form. The Arcadians of this area were considered specialists in terms of curing drought. Pan, I think, must also have been involved in their rain-magic, judging by his inclusion in the invocation elsewhere, at the beginning of the Sacred Way that leads to Eleusis.

Mount Lykaion has a further animal myth, in the shape of the Kallisto story – bears as well as wolves. To add to this menagerie, persons who strayed into the sacred precinct were sentenced to death. They became *elaphoi* – stags. Anyone could hunt and kill them, thus aiding the sacred curse of death within a year.

The only work of literature I can think of that connects these particular animals is the interesting medieval poem *William and the Werewolf*. The French original of our version was composed in the twelfth century. The early parts of the poem are tender and beautiful, but the plot is over-complex and reads, as do many texts of the Middle Ages, like a garbled version of some earlier truer story.

To sum it up as briefly as I can – Embrons, King of Apulia, Sicily, Palermo and Calabria, had a son named William by his wife Felice, the daughter of the Emperor of Greece. Embrons' brother bribed two ladies to murder the child. While the child was at play at Palermo, a wolf ran off with him, swam the Straits of Messina and carried him to a forest near Rome. The wolf looked after him well and managed to keep his gold clothes in one piece. While the wolf went off to find food, a cowherd took the child and adopted it. The wolf was a werewolf – Alphouns, eldest son of the King of Spain, enchanted by his wicked stepmother so that her sons could inherit. The cowherd lost the child when the Emperor of Rome took a fancy to him while he was hunting. William became the page of the Emperor's daughter Melior and she fell in love with him. She was in two minds about degrading herself by the match, but went ahead. Her friend, Alisaundrine, caused William to fall in love with Melior by a spell. There was a secret betrothal. William went on to prove himself as a knight. The Emperor of Greece sent an embassy seeking Melior's hand for his son. The lovers fled, sewn into white bearskins as a disguise. People noticed the couple of bears walking on their hind legs and they were followed. They met the werewolf in a den and he helped them on their journey. The lovers went on to Benevento – a place renowned for witchcraft. Here, the wolf killed and flayed two deer for them and they went on disguised in the skins as a hart and a hind. They crossed the Straits of Messina and Queen Felice welcomed them also dressed as a hind. William promised her help against the Spaniards. He captured their king and prince, thereby forcing Queen Braunde to change the werewolf back to his human shape. There were marriages all round and William was elected to become Emperor of Rome when his father died.

On the everyday level, the tale does not work. Travelling sewn into skins would probably finish you off in the first few kilometres. Crossing the Straits of Messina without a boat would be another non-starter. In the old days it had Scylla and Charybdis. Now it has strong currents and sharks. Though the distance is small, I've never heard of a swimmer attempting it.

The tale therefore belongs to the myth genre. The use of animal skins implies a ritual. The use of bearskins immediately makes me think of Artemis of Brauron and of Kallisto. Artemis's bears all seem to have been female children from the Athenian nobility. I dismiss that idea therefore. That takes me back to Kallisto. The couple's next disguise as fleeing stags puts me in mind of the trespassers in the sacred precinct of Lykaion who became *elaphoi*. This is further reinforced by the werewolf connection. The couple had stayed in the wolf's den – a kind of trespass. Alphouns, the werewolf, is like one of the Arcadians who spent part of their lives as a wolf but eventually returned to their own form. He is obviously not a cannibal wolf. He steals a child, but for good reasons. And so, he is allowed to regain his shape. The territory covered in the story is also relevant – the foot of Italy and parts of Sicily, particularly about the Straits of Messina, are areas where Pan was worshipped. Rome too worshipped him in his Latin form, Faunus. His sanctuary was in much the same spot on the Palatine as the hut of Romulus and Remus, who, as we all know, were brought up by a she-wolf. William parallels their origins by his relations with the wolf and the fact that he becomes Emperor of Rome. If the original legend had made William be adopted by a goatherd rather than a cowherd, there would be even more of a connection with Pan and the myths surrounding Mount Lykaion. I'd hazard a guess that the original legend did. Goat- and sheep-herding was more prevalent in ancient times. The fact that the cowherd was in a forest sounds unlikely also. Cows are less adaptable than goats to difficult territory. The twelfth-century poet who first put the tale into verse probably just used whatever type of herd fitted his local knowledge of farming.

It's reassuring to see that William and Melior survive their trespass and animal guises. Plutarch puts on record the case of an Arcadian, Cantharion, who had violated the sanctuary and sought refuge in Sparta. He was returned as an *elaphos* to be stoned to death by the Arcadians. Kallisto and her son Arkas were turned into bears to join the stars at the same spot. Perhaps the *elaphoi* became immortal too.

Ovid connects the story of Syrinx to this area – yet another transformation, although not an animal one. Considering that Pan is supposed to have dedicated the pipes that he made from the reeds she became at a cave near Ephesus, one or other version of the story is probably radically misplaced. If Syrinx's story really does originate in Arcadia, rather than elsewhere, it's interesting to speculate whether her fate resulted from setting foot in the sanctuary rather than a maidenly escape from rape, known as 'Panic Marriage'.

As far as humans went, there was a different sentence for involuntary trespass. The rules said that these men were to be sent 'to Eleutherai'. No one quite knows the meaning of this word. *Eleutheros* means free, so some commentators assume freedom was what they got. Another possibility is that the involuntary trespassers had to make a pilgrimage to Eleutherai in Boeotia. Eleutherai is a small town that was founded by one of Lykaon's sons after lightning struck them in the palace. Places struck by lightning and people who survived were generally considered sacred. Slaves could also become free if struck by lightning.

The human sacrifice made on top of Mount Lykaion is still a bit of a mystery. To date, archaeologists have not found human bones on Zeus's altar. Some like to think that this proves that the sacrifice was merely symbolic. To my mind, it seems more likely that they didn't dig deeply enough or in the right spot. The Greek Archaeological Society excavations at the beginning of this century recorded a lot of fragments of plates and two iron knives found in the area, but in those days technology was not good enough for much analysis of tiny burnt bone fragments.

The most thorough account of the religious ritual is in Plato – he gives us the tale of the portion of human entrail in the feast.

Other authors skirt around the subject. It was at this ritual that one of the Arcadians became a wolf. Pliny attaches this cult to the family of Anthos. Lots were cast among his family (by entrail?) and the chosen man hung his clothes on an oak-tree and swam across the marsh to become a wolf and associate with his kind for nine years.

Interestingly, a boxer, Damarchos, is credited with having attended one of these sacrifices, where he was turned into, or elected, a wolf, going on from there to Olympia, where he became a champion. It's not recorded whether he spent nine years as a wolf getting there. In the tradition of Odysseus' needlessly long voyage (perhaps due to the lousiness of Greek maps), it's a distinct possibility.

The Neda Gorge

O'er the chasm's fearful brink
Hangs she, on the topmost height,
Where the crags abruptly sink,
And the path is lost to sight.

Schiller: 'The Hunter of the Alps'
(Victorian translation)

*A*fter breakfast I went round to the Folk Museum and was unable to resist more coffee and Greek cookies while I waited for Elias. We climbed, via a short cut full of thistles, on to a higher reach of the road. The road was always bulldozed smooth for the cars and coaches before the Games, he explained. The hippodrome was grass-covered when I saw it, but its amphitheatre shape was obvious. A few scattered blocks to the north showed evidence of classical remains. These were probably the remains of the sanctuary of Pan, I discovered later from old archaeological reports. Bronze statuettes of athletes – portraits of ancient champions – were found in the area. One of them was pictured on the back of a small colour brochure produced by the village as a sort of programme for the Games three years before. I had been given a copy the previous evening.

Elias pointed out areas of the mountain where pines and firs – trees sacred to Pan – were being replanted. His grandparents had donated the first piece of land for this, then others followed. The money raised by the Association was also used to preserve the local springs by building masonry and channels round the spots where they bubble up. We passed the spring Hagno on our way – it's named after one of the nymphs who hid Zeus. Neda is remembered in the name of the gorge. Only Theisoa goes without a spring or anything to her name. When I talked to them the night before, the villagers called these three 'good spirits' not nymphs – a kind of Christianisation, presumably.

The shepherds and goatherds are guardians of the land, Elias told me. Not a person or a stone moves on the mountain without them knowing. As he said this, I could see one seated on an opposite slope, a transistor held to one ear. As I climbed alone, later, I was always conscious of being watched.

Lykaion is full of the sound of springs, and its vegetation is bright green even in the height of summer. Wild thyme, Lady's bedstraw and thistles grow everywhere amongst the grass. Even on the higher reaches, I was still conscious of the smell of goats I'd noticed the night before, although there were no animals in sight on that part of the mountain.

Elias left me a little higher up the road to continue my walk to the top. It was not that he was afraid of the curse of Zeus, he explained, but he had to do some odd jobs for his father before returning to Athens.

There's a chapel of Elijah near the highest peak. A great many mountain summits are dedicated to Elijah – his name in Greek is only one letter different from the word for the sun. Inside the chapel there are sinister, murky icons of the prophet being fed by ravens and carried off to heaven in a chariot of fire.

I decided to risk the curse on the last fifty feet to the top – after all, it was only on 'men and beasts'. I'm told that the local women climb the peak to light the sacred flame when the Games are on – and none of them has died in the last three years.

There were no trees on that last fifty feet – just the odd thistle and other tiny scrubby prickly plants like the butcher's broom with which Victorian prostitutes used to beat their clients. I could see no obvious fragments of bone or potsherds, but some of the grey grit amongst the flakes of stone I was walking on might have been ash.

It was comforting to find that my shadow was still intact at the top. But was it my fancy that it looked a little paler than usual? There's a tiny concrete post – perhaps an observation point – right at the summit. I sat and drank some water while I looked around. The view is spectacular. Virtually every other mountain in the Peloponnese is visible. Even the two power stations of Megalopolis, known locally as Megalopollution, didn't look quite so bad from that distance. I went up the other small peak also. The path up is marked by a pile of stones. I had decided to strike out in the direction of Bassae. Apollo's Temple was unmistakable there under its four-gabled tarpaulin.

Elias had said that Bassae was about twenty kilometres away and that I'd find a road leading off the main one, the beginning of which hardly even looked like a path. I took a turning of that sort, but it soon led me into trouble. By the time I reached the trough at the bottom, I realised it was the remains of a stream instead. Still, I was heading in the right direction. Once over the next peak, I'd see Bassae again, or so I thought. The trouble was, the next peak was so covered in Kermes oak that it looked impassable. I deviated down the river bed, climbing down various falls and going far off course. By the time I could find my way up again, Bassae was out of sight. I walked back along a ridge but found getting down it on the other side would be more difficult still. I came to dead end after dead end at sheer limestone drops. A large carrion crow and a bluebottle were hovering hopefully. For a while I wondered if the curse of Zeus had struck. What else can you expect of a mountain with twin peaks?

Eventually, I found a limestone face that had a couple of reasonable ledges I could use as steps and so I clambered down to a lower level. From there I walked and scrambled on loose stones and dirt amongst trees. Several times I slipped and landed on my bottom. I saw a female goatherd passing below me whooping to her goats, but could not get down in time to ask the way.

Further down, I came to a dirt road leading away from Ano Karyes. Several kilometres later it came to houses, but there was no sign of any human beings. Perhaps everyone was having a siesta. The village had a Marie-Celeste-like quality.

There was a signpost pointing back to Ano Karyes and Megalopolis after the last house in the village. My way must be one of the other two roads – but which to take? Eventually, I worked out that one was only going to the tiny stone village of Petra and that the other must be my road on to Bassae and Andritsaina. I was worn out by the scrambling up and down ridges, which is much more tiring than ordinary walking, and my water was running low. I had intended to refill both one-and-a-half-litre bottles in Ano Karyes, but that had been forgotten as I talked to Elias. The side of the mountain I'd come down from had only had one tiny spring, so slow-flowing and muddy that I could not get much water from it.

Fortunately, a couple of kilometres up the road I was offered a lift with a family to Andritsaina. In the morning I could return that way and try to find Phigaleia. I booked into Hotel Pan again. Was it my fancy, or was it the same dead moth lying in the bath?

I remembered from my last visit to Andritsaina that it was about fourteen kilometres away from Bassae and that the signpost there showed a further thirteen to Phigaleia. If the worst came to the worst I could walk the whole distance there and back in a day if I set out early enough. I went and equipped myself with two bottles of water and a kilo of cherries to keep me going. I reckoned I was likely to get short lifts on the way to and from Bassae. There were cars passing every ten minutes or so. But the dirt track to Phigaleia was another matter.

In the morning, the tourists all passed me by on their way to Bassae but a local man gave me a lift for a few kilometres in the middle of my walk, before he turned off. I saw the temple differently this time round. The story that you'll find in most guide books is that the local Greeks demolished parts of it in the last century so that they could sell the tiny bits of scrap metal that connected sections of columns. But this process was arrested and the temple saved. Recently though, the tarpaulin had been erected to avert further deterioration. Everyone who sees it wonders why anything that has stood so long needs protection from rain or frost. An archaeologist at the British School suggested the reason. He believed that the temple had been undermined by members of his own profession – the sort of scientists who like to cut a ball in half to see why it bounced so well. He claimed that they had dug away sections of the foundations to study ancient building methods. The stone and rubble had not been replaced quite correctly afterwards. To him, though, the tarpaulin was not a monstrosity. He considered it a modern work of art, like those curtains across valleys in the USA. When I'd seen it from distant Lykaion, I could almost see what he meant.

I stopped at the temple – I found the back of my heel was beginning to rub. I'd got grit in my shoe. I remembered I'd left my packet of Elastoplast at the hotel, but I decided to carry on walking anyway, leaving a hail of cherry-stones in my wake.

A few kilometres down the dirt road to Phigaleia I was offered a lift by a good-looking biker. He asked me to guess his age. For once I did it accurately – he was twenty-five. He was called Georgios, but wanted to be called George for short. It wasn't long before he was suggesting we had sex. 'Sex' is a word that seems to have transferred into Greek and a great many other languages, although all of these languages have perfectly good words of their own.

I decided that sex might not be such a bad thing. There were parts of me that Demetrios had left unsatisfied. There's something about a bumpy ride on a bike while you're clutching someone so as not to fall off that works instead of foreplay. I'd never had a biker before, either – I was curious. A little further down the road we stopped and climbed up the bank and went behind some trees. There were odd Arcadian prickles among the grass so he spread his jacket. I shoved my culottes in my bag. I didn't want to get sperm anywhere near them. It's awfully hard to get out – especially when you don't quite like to tell the dry cleaners what that stain really consists of. If you catch it while still wet with soap and water, it goes like magic – but leave it to dry and it'll probably adorn your clothes for the rest of their life.

I kept my blue silk jersey T-shirt on. It's long enough to work as a mini dress. It would save my tender skin from any prickles the jacket didn't cover. He flung his trousers and bike keys into the bushes with reckless abandon. I made a mental note of where the keys had fallen.

We started kissing and he lay on top of me. I realised pretty soon that he was going to be one of those men who can't support his own weight. He started to touch my cunt – but oh, what a difference from Demetrios. He was all fingers and thumbs. Perhaps actual sex would be better. He was very erect by now so I reached for condoms from my bag and started to put one on him. But he preferred his own technique and wrenched it on – breaking it of course. He was luckier with the second condom and we managed a very brief fuck.

Sometimes when you've had poorish sex once, trying again is the answer. But sometimes the second time is twice as bad . . . George's main problem was that he liked to thrust before he'd got his cock well-positioned. Often it would hit the perineum hard. Men who won't wait that split second that it takes to get the thing in place properly just end up frustrating and hurting both parties. Disdaining all help, he hauled another condom on inside out. The third one ruptured and he chucked it into the bushes after his keys. He tried again with the fourth one – my last. It popped off the end of his cock and landed in the grass. It wasn't punctured, so he put it back on again hopefully. He hadn't quite got it pulled well up, so off it went again.

At this stage, I told him I wasn't going to have sex without a condom. That was my last one and he didn't have any. He decided to have one more try with the acrobatic but still unpunctured condom. Just as he was about to enter me I saw him pull it off and chuck it away. I should have figured that a biker who carried his helmet rather than wearing it while riding wouldn't be into condoms. I twisted my body quickly, so that he didn't enter me but came on my hip. At that moment, like some character out of de Sade, he bit my upper arm violently and I let out a yell so loud that he thought he'd excelled himself. Fortunately he'd bitten me through the silk jersey so he didn't puncture the skin. I had two crescents of bruising that lasted for a week.

I dressed in angry silence. I was seriously tempted not to tell him where he'd thrown his keys to serve him right. He had forgotten already and was searching his pockets. On the other hand, if I didn't, I might be stuck with a fellow walker liable to decide he wanted a condomless fuck round the next corner. I passed him his keys and he gave me a lift down to the point where he was turning off for his village.

The only good thing to be said for that fuck was that the bite on my arm was so painful that it acted like acupuncture and made my rubbed heel feel perfectly all right again. This was fortunate, as I still had several kilometres of winding track to follow to the village of Phigaleia.

By the time I got to Perivolia, three kilometres from Phigaleia, I was round on the other side of the Neda gorge and near the bottom of it. There was a small village with a fountain of good water. Somebody had dumped an old black crimplene skirt in the corner of the square trough at the bottom. A frog was sitting on it. I thought about kissing him to see if he would turn into something better than the biting biker.

The last three kilometres led me down to Phigaleia, but there were no antiquities to be seen other than a few ancient blocks used to rebuild the fountains at the bottom of the town. And there wasn't a cave in sight. Past the village, I saw a signpost leading onwards across the gorge to Dragogi, which was almost certainly the village the biker had been heading for. If I went straight across it would save several kilometres of the way back. A few hundred yards on, the road got more and more overgrown and then branched without further signposts. I went back to the long way round – it was safer. I couldn't afford to get lost with no hope of a lift and a very long walk back.

When I was almost at Bassae, some German tourists offered me a lift. They stopped at the temple. I waited outside and gave directions to some lost Brits who wondered if the Phigaleia road was drivable and whether it would get them to the sea. The Germans returned – a little disappointed by the tented temple – and I had a lift back to Andritsaina.

It was six o'clock, so I had time to look at the Folk Museum, which was supposed to be open for an hour or two in the evening. It was a block away from the main square. A thin middle-aged widow holds the key. The Archaeological Society's excavation reports from the turn of the century said that objects from the Pan temple behind Andritsaina were kept there. Unfortunately, the objects are no longer on show. No one, least of all the Archaeological Society in Athens, now knows where the whole collection is. One of these objects, though, is in America. I've seen a picture of it. It's a small bronze figure of a shepherd holding a lamb, dedicated by someone called Aineas. It's now in the Metropolitan Museum of Art. If anything remains of the temple, again no one seems to know. Baedeker had placed it on the hill behind Andritsaina – that had caused my last fruitless search. The Society's report from the original excavation placed it some hours south-west of Ano Karyes. In other words, what remains of it may still be out there somewhere in the vast, scarcely inhabited mountainscape that lies between Lykaion and Andritsaina – unless it too has ended up in America.

The tragic-looking widow showed me round the museum. I remembered her – I had eaten dinner in her restaurant, the other side of the square, the night before. The museum is a perfectly preserved example of a Greek nineteenth-century home – very cosy, with a lot of red in the weaving and embroidery. The walls are covered with tapestry pictures, cross-framed texts and sepia photographs. There are several dummies in costumes of the day – large-bosomed and seriously short.

I praised the museum and bought postcards out of politeness. But I was disappointed that there were no antiquities left. The woman insisted I come for a coffee with her to the restaurant. She showed me a photo of her handsome husband, now dead. It was on the wall behind the stove and counter, amongst pictures of the museum, and various prints and reproductions. Some of these looked left over from the 1930s – a winter scene with bare trees, a rumpled, soot-smeared Bassae, a man out shooting birds with his dogs, a fruit bowl, and a fairy appearing to children. The combination was strangely depressing. The woman who ran the restaurant looked broken and tearful. She insisted I have a slice of cake with a coffee while she lifted the heavy pans full of the evening meal on to the stove. My Greek was too poor for much sympathy. I tried to make up for what I could not say by the expression on my face.

I thanked her and left. Perhaps she expected me to eat there again later – I don't know. I wasn't hungry enough after getting through the larger part of the cherries.

That night when I showered, the moth had gone from the bath – was it a good or a bad omen? Part of me had wanted the moth to stay there for ever as a *memento mori* of Greek hotel-keeping. I wanted Andritsaina to stay the same in every detail, from its strange spring to the tinkling sheep-bells and cicadas. Staying in Andritsaina, in the very same room as before, I had been filled with a feeling of *déjà vu*, although there was no Stephanos around now. I did not fall through the bed this time round, but I did switch off the hotel's illuminated sign – an unexplained switch near the bed. When the proprietor came up to complain, I remembered, too late, that the same thing had happened the year before. Andritsaina is beginning to change. Some of the dusty old shops with their pans and brushes are being replaced by smarter establishments full of toys and magazines. But at least 'Greek Art' has not found its way there yet, and there are no cat calendars.

Prophetē Elias

And now, while happy peasants sleep,
Here I sit lonely and forlorn;
No one to soothe me as I weep
Save Philomel on yonder thorn.

William Julius Mickle

*T*he next morning, I caught the early Tripolis bus out. It
was crowded with old women in black, laden with bags
of fruit and suitcases. I decided to get off at Asea, from
where I could walk the eight kilometres or so to Arachmites
Asea. It is hilly farming country, not unlike parts of England.
Peter Levi's notes to Pausanias hinted at remains of a Pan
shrine on the hill dedicated to Hagios Elias. The villagers
mostly didn't know which hill was which, but one of a couple of
little boys with a donkey collecting brushwood directed me to
a slope covered with prickly oak. For once, the oak was so bad
that it beat me. A good many of these specimens, intermingled
with fir trees, had grown to above my height. Added to that, a
water course, dry in some parts, wet in others, was mixed up
with all the vegetation. I got to the top, more or less, but could
only see out of the thicket in places. If there's anything there,
it's lost until all the oaks are felled. Of course, maybe Peter Levi
and the little boy were just joking . . .

After spending that night in Tripolis I took the bus to Sparta
in the morning. Sparta is a pleasant town with a small museum
full of interesting mosaics. There's a strangely lifelike one of

Alcibiades that remains in your mind, even at times when you can't quite remember who he was. A few kilometres away, the most popular excursion is to the Byzantine ghost town of Mistras. What is less well-known is that Sparta is the nearest town for climbing the highest point of the Mount Taÿgetos range, Hagios Elias.

Pheidippides encountered Pan on his round trip between Athens and Sparta. It seems significant to me that there were many shrines of Pan along the route he must have taken. While the worship of Pan picked up in Athens after Pheidippides' meeting, Sparta did not really take to him in a big way. It was not strictly Pan territory – but while I was there, I thought I might climb one of Greece's better-known mountains. After the Hagios Elias dedications on Lykaion and at Asea, it was also possible there might be a tenuous connection between the prophet Elijah and Pan.

Patrick Leigh Fermor, in his book *The Mani*, mentions local legends that connect the whole range with a Pan-like figure. The other name of Taÿgetos is Makrynas. Makrynas, in folk tales of the area, is a devil who appears to travellers in deserted places at noon. Women who meet him usually run away shrieking at the sight. There is also another tale of this mountain which relates to Pan. In one area, near a watershed, there was a spring and a wild fig tree. Three goat-footed nymphs lived there. Their speciality was luring travellers into dancing with them until they fell down some ravine. Perhaps these nymphs were the offspring of Pan. I had certainly seen no goats' feet on the representations of the nymphs that were worshipped with him on the marble tablets in the Athens museum. They sound more like the Christianised view of the pagan world voiced in Ronsard's *Hymne des Daimons*. His spirits are transformed into nymphs, fauns, satyrs and Pans. They are all lumped together in appearance as having hairy, speckled bodies, hoofs, long ears and horns and reddened faces. They dance through the night at crossroads, or by a murmuring brook. Trust later Christian writers and legend-makers to take away the beauty of the nymphs. The word that used to mean 'beautiful' in ancient Greek is now used to mean good. I bet Christians are responsible for that. A new word for beautiful has been invented. It gets applied liberally to thousands of things that don't deserve it. Tourists are forced to agree that every town and every vista in Greece is *oraia*.

I had determined to dare Taÿgetos alone, goat-footed nymphs and all. Away from the town, I might be lucky enough to find something that was genuinely *oraia*.

You're unlikely to get much help from the office of the 'Tourist Police' of Sparta if you're into climbing. They don't own a detailed map of the area and have no idea how far away anything is. Quite which way to take out of the town, they'll also be unable to tell you. What they will give you is a ground plan of Sparta drawn from a diagonal aerial view. There are no street names marked on it. The roads are just drawn as broad straight bands of black. If you go on making a pest of yourself asking questions about Mount Taÿgetos you will be directed to a photo shop one block up the Mistras road from the town hall and on the opposite side. You may have difficulty finding it, because they will also have given you the shop's old owner's name. The shop is now called Georgiadis. Inside, you can purchase an Alpine Club map of Taÿgetos which gives detailed instructions for ascending its highest peak. This is marked as Hagios Elias on maps but is known as Prophetē Elias locally. What you will not be told is that the shop holds the all-important key to the mountain refuge which could provide your only protection from hypothermia.

There's a local custom whereby Spartans climb this mountain peak on a particular day in August, stopping off for the night in the refuge. It's something they do perhaps once or twice in their lives. Some even spin out the trip, sleeping on the

159

top of the mountain as well. They take little food, and all the space in their back-packs is filled with warm winter clothing. If you climb the mountain either earlier or later than August, the weather can be dodgy. There are sudden rainstorms. The top of the mountain can be snowbound until June, the month when I was climbing it.

Once you're armed with your map, the next stage is to get the local bus service to Paleopanayia – the last proper village on the way up. The road sign there gives you distances – eleven kilometres to Boliana (accessible by car), then a walking distance of two hours to the refuge at 1,650 metres. It's a sandy dirt road. With good four-wheel drive or a jeep you could probably make it most of the way to the refuge before your real walk begins. After my first few kilometres, I was lucky enough to get a lift from an Austrian botanist who prided herself on having the same name as one of the Valkyries. Taÿgetos is famed for its plants. These include a variety of orchids and a small, lilac-coloured cyclamen which can only be found there.

When I walked the last bit of the road to the refuge I found it was thoroughly padlocked and covered with heavy cast-iron shutters which offered not the faintest hope of breaking in. The over-optimistic signs beside the shelter say that the ascent takes two and three-quarter hours – but it has been timed by commandoes who never stop for snacks or water.

At that moment a couple of shepherds came and offered to show me a short cut up 'Prophetē' as the peak is known for short. Their four dogs went with us. The head dog, a bit like a foxhound, went in front with a bell, and another kept his nose to my backside, pushing me up the boulders like a recalcitrant sheep. The dog had definitely got my scent. If I got lost, perhaps it would come, armed with a keg of brandy, to find me. After that first slope, I was on my own. The path is well signposted and easy enough walking. The view of distant mountains is spectacular. At the time I should have reached the summit I came to the gap in the ridge, marked by a pile of stones, that is known as Portes. This is almost at the top of the mountain and is the first point at which you see the other side. Because the Taÿgetos range runs from north to south, passing from east to west involves a dramatic light change. I found myself standing on the edge of the greenest of valleys, bathed in sunlight, amongst a herd of bulls and cows. It was a strange and unexpected sight – a bit like dying and going to heaven. The bulls and cows fled across the valley at my approach, their lowing and bellowing bounced off a series of peaks like the call of the yeti.

I continued along the path to the left. After a couple of signposts more, I decided to give up, perhaps a hundred feet from the top. The going was beginning to look dangerous with lots of loose flints and an area higher up roped off about a hole. This peak, I learned later, is known as 'The Pyramid' from its shape. It could almost be an artificial addition, like the fifty-foot altar of Zeus on the top of Mount Lykaion. Apparently there is a tiny path up it, but it's hard to find. Eventually it leads to a small ruin, tucked away – perhaps the remains of a church. This is the focal point of the annual Spartan pilgrimages. Perhaps it was once a centre of Baal worship by the Phoenicians. There may be some older stonework to be found under the chapel's remains. It has been suggested that all the peaks dedicated to Elijah were formerly sacred to Baal. Personally I doubt if the Phoenicians, traders rather than agriculturists, would have ventured so far inland.

When I passed back through the Portes gap the light already looked dimmer. I could see clouds settling on the mountain below me. Probably I should have stayed up in the valley where there was some shelter from the wind, but I decided to attempt a fast descent. Maybe I would get back as far as the refuge, where I could curl up on the concrete bench outside. When I came to the cloud I was surprised at the visibility within it – everything looked a little greyer, as in mist, but it was not dangerous. I was conscious more of a change of smells than a change of visibility. The cloud smelt like the essence of damp earth, not unpleasant exactly, but faintly depressing. Soon, I was out of it and descending as fast as I could. By nine-thirty, I was past the spot the dogs had pushed me up to.

At that stage the last of the visibility went as completely as if someone had put the light out. I thought about going on with my torch but decided that particular stretch would be too dangerous. I only knew the way I'd come up and it had certainly been more precipitous than the rest of the route. It was the sort of path that would be infinitely worse going down than up. There was nothing for it but to try and sleep where I was. I was already on the edge of that descent, so I wedged myself firmly between a limestone boulder and a pine tree.

I could see odd lights and one fire glimmering on distant hills. There were a few stars and an almost full moon, but the night seemed short on light. I resolved to try not to look at my watch until morning. I had other clothes in my pack, but it would be hard to open it in the dark without spilling them down the rocks. I would try and manage in what I was wearing. I put the military cap I use against the sun back on my head – they say you lose warmth from that area quickest. I wrapped a headscarf round my bare legs. The rest of my body was fairly fully clothed. I had on a silk T-shirt under a man's shirt, and culottes to the knees. Already, I was beginning to feel the difference in warmth between the silk on my upper body and the silk and cotton mix of the culottes. As time passed I put my face down the neck of my T-shirt and breathed heavy warm breaths on to my body. I shivered violently for most of the night. I told myself that was healthy – shivering keeps you from hypothermia. Occasionally I slept, but I think only for a few minutes at a time. I managed not to look at my watch until half past one. By then, an owl had joined my solitary vigil in the tree above – you'd think at least it would have been a nightingale. He was to keep me awake for most of the rest of the night.

Soon after that the wind came up – sudden icy blasts from the north. I shifted myself further round behind the pine tree, but it was no better. A pine tree is about as much protection as an umbrella with no material between the spokes. Never go under a pine tree when it rains. The weather seemed set to break. I'd heard one or two distant thunderclaps on the way up the mountain and seen a tiny pocket of snow left in a crater. I could just about stand the cold, but I couldn't face rain or snow as well. The wind kept up, but it was still fine by dawn which came at five-thirty. Considering it was almost midsummer, Greek nights seem to be at least an hour and a half longer than ours.

I got up, drank some water, finished my cherries and brushed the goat pellets, pine needles and dust off my clothes. Then I started to walk down in the grey early-morning light. My legs had gone dead under me and felt like jelly. I couldn't go fast. In about an hour I reached the shepherd's hut below the mountain refuge. I had thought of leaving his invitation – six-thirty seemed a bit early to call – but his wife beckoned me across. Her husband and sons were busy with the sheep. The younger son was little more than a child. I didn't take to him. He kept giving the animals the odd smack for no good reason.

His mother had two fires on the go. The family did all their cooking outside as their small house had no chimney. Her fires were made of pine branches surrounded by a little wall of stones, open at the front. She had a huge cauldron of sheep's milk simmering on the larger fire. She gave me two tiny brass coffee pots to set in the little fire. When the water boiled, she mixed it in with the coffee and sugar we'd measured into our cups, then set the mixture back in the fire. I've used her method since on an ordinary stove and found that it makes better Greek coffee than simply putting water and coffee on together.

163

I sat on a log watching the coffee. Soon it was raining copiously and I was loaned the family umbrella – a sturdy British gentleman's type of the best quality. The wife carried on stirring her milk and adding wood to the fire, pushing it in close to the flames with her bare hands. Occasionally she came across to ask me a stream of questions. Her husband brought a pan of milk to add to the cauldron. It was strained through a sieve made of a rough wooden frame and chicken wire with a piece of canvas spread loosely across it. The canvas was rinsed out afterwards. It was a necessary precaution – sheep have been known to shit in their milk. Several large plastic carriers contained the water for washing and drinking. Probably these had to be filled daily somewhere lower down the mountain and brought up on the tractor trailer.

I was offered some hot sheep's milk and accepted it gratefully. A smaller saucepan was put on a little tripod set on the fire that had been used for the coffee and some of the milk was transferred into it. When it had boiled I was given a mugful and a toasted roll to dip. I was interested to taste sheep's milk and was surprised at its similarity to cow's rather than goat's. It's pretty much like a creamy Jersey full-fat milk. The rain had stopped and soon I was on my way again. The legs were back on form. A kilometre or two downhill it started to rain copiously. I was reminded of the scene in *The Lord of the Rings* where the Hobbits and their party are assaulted with every kind of malice by the mountain Caradras. Tolkien chose the name of that mountain carefully – it's almost the same as the Greek word for a ravine. It's a word I came across time and time again when I read Greek accounts of the position of various Pan caves, which were mostly in ravines, or by streams named after them.

I looked back at the peak I'd just come from and found it was totally obscured with clouds. If I had waited at the shelter, I'd never have made it up at all. I began to feel glad of my cold night. At least I'd reached that mystical green valley and come very close to the top. Soon, though, I was totally soaked. I comforted myself by thinking that at least I must smell better now the rain had washed from my clothes all the sweat from yesterday's climb and the flavour of the goat-droppings on which I'd spent the night. A few kilometres above Palaeopanayia I got a lift on the open back of a van full of shifting milk churns. It was not the most comfortable ride of my life, clutching the wet rope that held them. The cold metal churns slid up against me every time we turned a corner or hit a bump in the road – and that road had plenty of bumps. In Palaeopanayia I managed to flag down the bus just as it was leaving. I left a very damp patch on its seats.

I was still thoroughly wet on the Sparta bus that took me, fast asleep, all the way to Tripolis. I told myself I was bound to get pneumonia from sleeping in wet clothes, but I was wrong. I didn't even catch a cold.

Caves

The murmurous haunt of flies on summer eves.

Keats: 'Ode to a Nightingale'

*T*he next morning I left for Athens. Before returning to the British School I intended to visit the Pan cave at Daphne. I had not found any ancient writing about this cave, but I had met others there who'd seen it.

The pine wood to the left of Daphne monastery smells more like incense than any other pine wood I've come across. To get to the cave you have to pass through it. There are several paths. The cave is visible, eventually, about two-thirds of the way up a hill. There's also a point at which you can see it from the main road. Locally it's known as 'Panon'. I'd have expected it to be called 'Paneion' in the way that most shrines are derived from the gods' names, but no, the men at the monastery and a stranger in the wood on a motorbike quite clearly referred to it as 'Panon'. It's a small cave like that at the Acropolis. There was no dead bird, nor any Loutraki bottles, but there were more flies than I'd ever seen in my life. I hate to think what lurked at the back of the cave. I didn't dare to penetrate far into that small space, for fear of swallowing or inhaling a cloud of Beelzebub's servants.

The cave at Daphne is quite simply the easiest Pan cave to visit. The bus passes near. People actually know where it is and it's visible from the road. Interestingly, from the flat terrace outside you can see the grounds of the psychiatric hospital, across the main road.

Helen of the British School had fixed me an appointment next day at the Zappio. I was to be allowed into the area by the Olympic stadium to look for the remains of a shrine to Pan, the nymphs and Acheloos. A map in John Travlos's *Pictorial Dictionary to Athens* had marked this spot. I waited in the office of the Zappio for one of the officials to accompany me with a key. It was soon after the Olympic ceremony, and so security was tight in the area. I always enjoy seeing what pictures people have in offices. Predictably, there were several of nineteenth-century Greek politicians, and some large marble busts. Beside them was one of St Veronica and her hanky – the statutory bit of religion. Next to these there was a surrealistic one of Athena with the Acropolis on her head, and, less understandably, a shipwreck scene and a brace of lesbian maids.

The man with the keys puffed and complained all the way across the road. There was nothing there, he said, and it turned out he was right. The Travlos map is misleading. Somewhere, near that stadium area, there was once a shrine, but the site is lost now – it might lie smashed to smithereens beneath the road.

A rather unusual dialogue by Plato is set in this area. In it, Socrates discusses love with Phaedrus, a young pupil. The text is very interesting, but it never ends up on the school syllabus or in selections from Plato's works. There are definite under-currents to the rhetoric. Phaedrus seems to be attempting to seduce Socrates by arguing in the words of another philosopher that having a relationship with someone when you're not in love works better than when you are. Seductions by logic are always doomed to failure. Phaedrus should have made a quick grope if that was what he wanted. Of course, then there'd have been no dialogue. Literature owes a great deal to unrequited lust and the failures of lovers.

At first, Socrates gives similar arguments to those of Phaedrus and produces a speech that logically proves his pupil's point. After a while though, inspired by the spot – a grotto dedicated to the nymphs and Pan on the banks of the Ilissos – Socrates begins to undo his former reasonings. His arguments, he considers, have been a kind of blasphemy against Eros, the god of love. Christian moralists have continually seized on Socrates as a sort of hero. They translate his *theos* as 'God' rather than 'a god' and choose to gloss over all his religious reverence to a multiplicity of other deities. It is patent from all his works that he was a thoroughly religious pagan, with all that that implied. His dialogue with Phaedrus ends in a beautiful prayer to Pan and the other gods. The *Phaedrus* is one of Plato's most interesting works. By Socrates doing an about-turn and arguing both ways on the same question, it becomes a study of true and false rhetoric as well as a logical examination of the nature of love.

The Travlos map had not pinpointed the lost grotto, but ancient Athens was a small area. The Hill of the Nymphs, Socrates' prison and the strange relief by St Photini's are all a short walk away. I'd hazard a guess that the relief was all that was left of the real grotto. The Ilissos is long gone. The Athenians turned it into a sewer – they would.

The only other Pan site in the area is the Asklepeion on, or rather below, the Acropolis. I had seen it from below, several times, but this time I climbed to its locked gates and looked between the iron bars. It's now a tiny chapel. Its copious spring has dried up or been diverted. The path up to it is badly neglected. The old stone steps are grown over with spiky butcher's broom. It's hard to manoeuvre your way up without getting thoroughly scratched. I was joined by a helpful stray dog – a lean, yellowish mongrel – who wove between the plants, looking back over his shoulder and showing me the easiest way to climb. I had taken to saving my breakfast egg when I stayed at the British School – to have something to give to the starving Greek cats – so I was able to reward him for his help. I poured some water for him too in the hollow in the middle of a stone near the gates. Of course, he followed me down and tried to follow me up the road. In the end I had to pick him up and point him back towards the archaeological site, which appeared to be his only home.

I spent the next two days chasing the Vari cave. My third and fourth attempts took me via Voula by the Blue Guide's instructions and a rather confused page of advice from an American archaeologist who was working on the Agora. Unfortunately, he had described the cave as 'past the cemetery' and 'past the aircraft installations' – this led me back down into the town of Ano Voula again. The 'aircraft installations' are a set of empty offices that were once used for radar, I'm told. There's still a barrier across their entrance and notices about security. From near the entrance you can see a smashed plane on an opposite hillside lying crushed like a fly against the grassy slope.

The cave is, in fact, roughly halfway between, not past, the two landmarks mentioned. It's well-concealed, off the main road. Another archaeologist, an Australian, had told me to watch out for a hill with three trees – but all the trees had bred wildly since he'd been there. To complicate matters further, Tiffany's Discotheque, mentioned as a landmark by the Blue Guide, had long since been demolished. Time and again I ended up at the cemetery. I was becoming very familiar also with Voula – an unlovely new town that's split into three areas. There's the Voula on the seafront. Then there's Ano Voula, a bus ride away inland. 'Ano' in a name means upper. To confuse the issue, there's a third Voula which is higher up the mountain and still being built. It is this Voula that is nearest the cemetery and the grotto. On my last solo attempt I asked a workman in Greek for the cave of Pan. He only caught the Pan word and asked if I meant the Panorama Mini Market – the main local shop. Probably every Greek in town could direct you there, though few these days bother to visit the grotto.

Back in the British School that night, I heard that the American School was going on the very next day to the grotto at Vari. It had been an excavation of theirs decades before and was always included on their summer-school field trips. I decided to give up trying to find it alone. Getting in touch with those who ran the trip meant I would have to gatecrash a party that night.

The American School and the British School are next to each other without the formal separation of a wall. You can meander from garden to garden and the tennis courts are shared. Often the British are invited to the American parties. I had been to two already, although I was told that there had been a cut-down of socialising of late because the British scoffed too many canapés. I hung around, going up to every man who came in, asking if he was Bob or Clayton, the men in charge. I just took a glass of lemonade and kept well away from the canapés, trying to be the honourable sort of gatecrasher.

I was soon introduced to Jere Wickens, the author of a book on Attic caves, who was able to give me some useful advice on others to visit. Slightly to my surprise, the Americans welcomed me on to the field trip. It was to be an early start, at seven-thirty.

It was a strange feeling for me to be one of a party being taken to sites. Most of the students were of university age, with the odd older classics teacher thrown in. The student next door to me had the job of giving a paper on the site at Brauron, our first stop. I had not thought that any of the sites along the way would connect with my Pan theme, but I was wrong. Brauron was the area where Artemis's bear cult once held sway. Was whatever went on there so far from the other animal cult of Lykaion? Kallisto, of course, had been turned into a bear and she had been connected to Artemis.

Iphigeneia and Orestes were supposed to have brought the original statue of Artemis from the Taurians' land to Brauron, accompanied by Pan. From the little that's known, the cult in its new form involved the training and dedication of young girls as 'bears' to the goddess. Quite what this training consisted of is not known – it could, I suppose, have been anything from domestic-science lessons to child abuse. The chosen initiates were from the best families in Athens. A great many statues of rather chubby little girls and boys were dedicated – some of the older girls might have been Artemis's bears, others were perhaps given in thankfulness (or hope) for the birth of a healthy child. Dozens of these statues survive in the museum by the cult site.

Looking through the museum, I became conscious that all cult offerings tend to look rather like each other. Small terracotta vessels and toys turn up everywhere, as do fairly anonymous-looking female heads and figures. Only the Pan figures amongst such collections in other museums could define them as belonging to one of his caves.

Outside, on the temple site, our guides pointed out the sort of details our eyes would certainly have missed unaided – metal linings in the indentations in the marble that once held the pivots of doors, other slots where couches had been fitted in.

From Brauron we went on to some *tholos* tombs at Thorikos. I lost a lace on the way up a small hill and spent the rest of the day gripping my left shoe tightly with the arch to keep it on. Inside the curved structure of a *tholos* tomb, you become conscious most of all of how many similar graves might be lurking in every curved hill, ready to be fallen into if you're singularly unlucky. Probably, though, most of them have already been opened up by hopeful tomb-robbers after gold or antiquities. Perhaps others have been protected by making the area sacred, or cursed. I had a romantic fantasy of there being something similar, complete with treasures, under the area I trespassed on at the top of Mount Lykaion. That fantasy probably has no truth in it. I haven't heard of other *tholos* tombs being found in that area. Besides, part of the sacred mound had been excavated without that kind of find.

From the tombs, we went towards Laurion and the old lead and silver mines. Much of the old system was intact, complete with its original air ventilation shafts, but there's little ore left now. You can look through barred gates into the opening of the mine with its neat pit props before the tunnel vanishes into darkness. It reminds me of a human mouth – a rather unsavoury one. The air that comes out is unpleasantly organic, like a very bad case of halitosis.

Several decades ago, a French company worked its way through the Ancient Greek slag heaps nearby which still contained a high enough percentage of silver to keep them in business for thirty years.

From Laurion we reached Sounion, where the cafeteria did good business assuaging American thirsts. Attention was flagging as students longed for lunch or a dip in the sea – or both. Poseidon's temple, out on the headland, is one of the most complete and obviously beautiful you'll find. We all ducked under the ropes around the temple to view the spot where that vandal Byron had carved his name in curly writing. Where other authors do book-signing tours, Byron seems to have preferred using any architecture he passed in his travels.

I ate a Greek salad with the tutors in a restaurant above the beach. The students had brought packed lunches. I had brought fruit, but was now hungry enough for more. There was little time left, so I plunged into the sea full of lunch. I chose the wrong patch and hardly dared put a foot down because of sea urchins, not to mention the baby jellyfish that were floating purposefully towards me. I thought one of the urchins had got me on my way out, but mercifully it turned out to be broken glass. I paddled my way along the rest of the beach, half dressed, and found that every other bay was sandy and pleasanter than the one I'd chosen. Sounion is the first point at which many Athenians will consider bathing. Most of the sea nearer Athens is supposed to be too polluted.

Last stop of the evening was the grotto of Vari – I kept fearing that this part of the trip would be cancelled as it was getting late. It turned out to be not too far from Voula cemetery, but more or less impossible to find without good directions, as the whole area is riddled with caves. We left the coach on the main road and walked across to a saddle of hill. At the junction of paths, someone had dumped several old mattresses. They were half burnt and covered in shit. Mount Bedding's name was explained.

There is a large metal grid across the entrance. Beneath that, a worn and dangerous set of steps leads down into the cave. There were candles left in the old niches sacred to Pan, but none of the Americans were smokers, it turned out. Nobody had a single match. The cave was very dark in parts, so we needed our flashlights and torches. The cave is sacred to Apollo and to Pan as well. Near the entrance, an inscription proclaims that Archedemos, a nympholept, decorated the cave for the nymphs. The word 'nympholept' means 'one seized by the nymphs'. It's usually taken to mean a form of madness, perhaps including the prophetic gift. I wondered if modern Greek doctors recognise such a state. Were there any nympholepts in the hospital near Daphne?

There are two possibilities. Either Archedemos made all the carvings, or else he was only responsible for one or two. Others then would have been added later by worshippers who considered him a cult hero and joined his name to the list of deities already worshipped there. If Archedemos was responsible for all the reliefs – against the odds, I'd like to think he was – he must have been an extraordinary character. His form of madness was a kind of genius that drove him to adorn an ordinary cave with carvings that are still a source of marvel and mystery to archaeologists twenty-five centuries later. Perhaps his nympholepsy was something like the experience of those who were taken by the fairies into a hill for a night of dancing in old legends. Fairy 'nights' often lasted seven years, or even a lifetime, of course. Personally, I would like to believe that Archedemos enjoyed being dominated sexually and that three beautiful women (the nymphs) collared him, locked him up and forced him to do their decorating.

Archedemos has left us several interesting carvings including his self-portrait in a full-skirted costume wielding a mallet. There's also the figure of a seated goddess, which now has no head. Most seated goddesses are reckoned to be Cybele. Figurines of the same shape as this statue turn up in many caves. But it seems to me that other goddesses can be seated too – when worshipped in one aspect. We had seen a seated goddess earlier that day – an image of Artemis of Brauron.

There were also several inscriptions whose words are ambiguous. There are boasts of building a dancing floor for the nymphs down there, and a garden – presumably outside. At one time a lion's head and an omphalos sign were also visible. More recently, I have wondered if what was taken for a lion's head was in fact not a goat's. That thought struck me as I watched a programme on the restoration of the Portland vase. The script talked at large about the two scenes on either side of the vase, but failed to mention the goat's head, presumably representing Pan, that separated the pictures. As the camera dropped down, the goat's horns were cut off. At that point the head became a lion's. Although I would never have thought of the two animals resembling each other, it struck me then. When a goat's face is given more width and fleshier cheeks by an artist, it is nothing more than a lion with horns.

The carvings are not great art but they are the work of a competent craftsman. Stone is not easy to work. I can only begin to imagine the years of chiselling in every figure and inscription. The Vari grotto reminds me of an ancient version of Charleston House in Sussex, where Duncan Grant and others of the Bloomsbury Set personalised their surroundings. Although it is not high art like the Acropolis or the temple at Bassae, it has a quality which leaves room for endless speculation. I am fascinated by enthusiasm – a person fired by that, more than genius, has the 'infinite capacity for taking pains'. It's a quality you come across in quite ordinary people – gardeners, retired men who spend their lives carving a schooner out of a piece of ivory, and so on. It's a celebration of manic devotion to a cause. I will always wonder about Archedemos's life.

Just outside the grotto, one of the archaeologists stooped and picked up a tiny bronze coin. It was so damaged that you could not see anything on it. He let it fall again after he'd showed it to us. It was not worth collecting anything you found now with the trouble involved in recording and 'publishing' collections.

Like many unprotected sites, the grotto has been damaged greatly across the years. The steps down were already dangerous. The grill is left unlocked. There are no guards to save the place from harm. The carvings that have lasted so long are in poor condition – eroded by time and chipped away by vandals. Mercifully, though, it's one site Byron never visited.

When I got back, the annual party of the British School was in full swing in the Director's garden. A man had sidled up to Helen and was asking her, *sotto voce*, if she could see about getting a pot of Marmite brought over in the British Embassy's diplomatic bag. 'It's not for me, you understand,' he said. 'My wife and daughter can't live without the stuff.' Helen said that she thought she could arrange it.

The day had been one of those seriously hot ones – about forty degrees centigrade, so I was told – and I thought mistakenly that a gin and tonic or two would cool me down nicely. It was the same mistake that has taken all the planters and embassy officials down the road to ruin in Graham Greene books. The trouble is that natives (i.e. any non Anglo-Saxon) can't be trusted to mix a safe drink. Gin and tonic, for instance, tastes pretty much the same whether it has a millimetre of gin and a few measures of tonic, or vice versa.

I had three gin and tonics in a tall glass while I was talking. I had turned away while the Greek waiter poured them. I was told afterwards that the only single measure in them was the tonic, the rest came in what was probably a quadruple measure, not that measuring had come into it. I was perfectly all right until I went to a nearby bar with some of the other students and took one sip of beer. Then, the creeping paralysis struck. Fortunately for those around me I was not sick, but it took two archaeologists to steer me back – one on either side. They were obviously both past masters at that kind of thing.

Instead of the bad head I expected, I woke up hyperactive at six-thirty and went into the library to work. I never had a hangover from that gin, but I was slightly drunk for several days afterwards.

It was the last day of that trip in Athens and I had little to do – there were only a few more photos to be taken of the Pan reliefs in the museum and one other in the Agora. My flight was in the small hours. That evening, Demetrios telephoned. He had tried to call me the night before when I was off getting myself drunk. He had not got my postcard. He told me that what is posted in village post boxes is virtually never sent on. Knowing locals would give their mail straight to the bus drivers to post in the main cities only. Then, it might have a slight chance of getting to its destination . . .

Obviously, Demetrios had forgiven my attempt at unfaithfulness. I decided not to tell him about the biker – it wasn't as if I'd enjoyed it. We spent that last evening together. He was more affectionate than usual, telling me he'd miss me and seeing me to the airport bus, helping with my things. It was then that I realised what, precisely, I'd got from this particular relationship.

Many of us do things in our lives either too late, or out of order. This was the teenage relationship I'd missed out on. Being in a single-sex school is quite damaging to your ability to relate to the other sex as human beings. Fortunately, mine was only a day school, so I met some boys in the evenings or at weekends. I had some dates as a teenager and snogging sessions at parties – but the two things never interrelated. The boys I kissed at parties were not the ones I went out with. The people I had crushes on were totally unsuitable and unattainable. I had no relationship at that time that included talking and foreplay. The dates I had were usually one-offs with rather frightened boys who did no more than the most social of goodbye kisses.

In TV soap operas, every teenager has a romance, but in real life many schools dish out too much homework. Besides, the boys you go out with or talk to may be homosexual. At sixteen or so, I was going for coffees after art classes with a boy who was not only thoroughly homosexual but into very little boys only. It was a great deal easier to hold an intelligent conversation with him than with the heterosexual boys I knew at that time.

I could talk to Demetrios. He was very intelligent. In fact, I was more able to hold a decent conversation with him than with men my own age. Most of them are so bitter and jealous of my career that they spend all their time bitching and finding fault with me. That, rather than physical reasons, is the main reason why I prefer younger men. They have their hopes intact and don't feel they have to try to destroy mine.

Demetrios's wanting to stop before full sex made him seem like a teenager, rather than someone of twenty-two or so.

Maybe doing military service will change him radically. The Greek government hasn't caught up with him yet. I would hope that military service, in forcing him to 'be a man', won't turn him into someone useless sexually, like the other Greeks I'd had, whose technique only ran to the quickest of fucks.

If Demetrios was like a teenager in his undeveloped sexuality, then what was I in this 'teenage relationship'? While Demetrios wasn't young enough to be my son, he must have realised that I was a good deal older. Without make-up, I can pass for ten years younger – so perhaps he saw me as just slightly older than himself. Greek women age worse than their British equivalents. I never lie about my age, so I was pleased Demetrios never asked it.

But there were other ways in which the relationship felt like going back in time for me. By ceasing to express my need for full sex and going along with what Demetrios wanted, I regressed to a typically passive teenager. Snogging or mutual masturbation in parks, walking hand in hand – all that was the stuff of teenage romances. Perhaps I would have hated an older man for holding back from me. I would also, I'm sure, have felt less comfortable hand in hand with one. I walk faster than most older men and we would not have fallen in step so easily, or always met each others' eyes when we looked across.

The fact that this relationship was a kind of late substitute for the teenage romance I never had made it easy to let go. It was complete in itself. It needed no future.

The charter section of the airport was swarming with Britain's vilest export. I kept my pack on my back. Those that had light luggage or tiny children also held them up out of the flood. There wasn't an inch of floor that was dry. We were all paddling in Heineken and Amstel, laced with the odd puddle of vomit. Those that had trolleys left brown mud tracks through it all. Since I first visited it, Athens has been one of my least favourite airports – but that was a black day even by Greek standards.

The plane home was icy – I'd have thought it was the fact that there was now gin running in my veins instead of blood, if the woman next door hadn't noticed it too.

Penteli

I can say that I have seen Michelangelo at the age of sixty, and with a body announcing weakness, make more chips of marble fly about in a quarter of an hour than would three of the strongest young sculptors in an hour – a thing almost incredible to him who has not beheld it. He went to work with such impetuosity and fury of manner, that I feared almost every moment to see the block split into pieces. It would seem as if, inflamed by the idea of greatness which inspired him, this great man attacked with a species of fury the marble which concealed the statue.

An eyewitness account by Blaise de Vigenère, quoted in Mrs Jameson's 'Memoirs of Italian Painters'

*M*y next trip was in August, the hottest time of the year in Greece. Athens was half empty, which meant that the air was clearer and the roads safer to cross. There's something to be said for going when most of the Greeks are away on holiday. Unfortunately, all the city buses were also on strike – a fact that was to make for even more difficulty in getting to the sites connected with Pan.

The orange buses to some of the surrounding towns were still running, which was why I opted for another visit to Marathon. I looked again at the area of the Pan cave. This time I had a compass and could pinpoint exactly how the mess of stones fitted with modern descriptions. I still had time also to look for another cave – Pigi Drakonera sounded interesting. At one time it was thought to be the Pan cave, till the real one was found. Sometimes it was spoken of as a dragon's cave – a title which survives in the name of the village. To get to Drakonera you must first go to Kato Souli. You leave the main road there where it heads towards Rhamnous and take a tiny road out into marshy fields. On the left, there's a series of hills.

I took a long time to find out which road was which – the locals had long ago forgotten the existence of Pigi Drakonera – the Drakonera Spring. Why didn't I ask the Englishman? they asked. The problem with the Englishman at the local bar was that he hadn't been there long enough to know where anything was and was far too pissed to articulate Marathon, let alone Drakonera. I showed him my maps. He held one upside down, muttered 'Here's the sea!' gesturing vaguely inland and tripped over his own feet. He was so far gone that his eyes were rolled in. The staggering reminded me of early Chaplin films. The surrounding Greeks assured me again and again that he'd be able to help in English, in my own tongue. I left him to his staggers in the end, retrieving my maps before he vomited all over them. I headed down the unmarked road opposite.

One of the Greeks came after me and asked if I wanted to go to Drakonera. I don't think he, or the others, had been able to believe I wanted to go there. From the tourist point of view, they believed that there was nothing there. He gave me a lift. He knew where Drakonera was, he said, because he'd once owned a house there. There was a scattering of houses along the road. The marshy land on the right was fenced off into some sort of huge complex with humming power lines. He dropped me by three hills. The cave, he assured me, was near the top of the second one. I climbed and found nothing. If only I'd trusted my map I'd have gone on to the furthest hill and looked low down. Never trust the word of a Greek where directions are concerned.

At that stage, I had to turn back to catch the last bus which was due to stop at Kato Souli at six. Perhaps it was just as well I didn't find the cave. It's supposed to have a drop of a few feet at the entrance, bridged by a ladder down to the spring. If the Greeks have forgotten where it is, then the ladder would not have been maintained. The Greeks never care if ladders have bits missing, anyway. The ones by the Pan cave at the Acropolis were pretty defective, even though they're supposed to be in regular use by the excavation team.

I got back to Kato Souli before six, but there was no bus. I waited and waited. Eventually I had to start hitching a lift. Two men stopped and drove me back to near the centre of Athens. They were both carpenters. One spoke only Greek. The other talked a mixture of Greek and English to me. When he learned where I was staying, he said: 'We don't like archaeology. We have the new technology now, in Greece.' His view is shared, I believe, by ninety-nine per cent of the Greek population.

In the evenings, I found myself running down the new Greek technology to a Scottish student who'd just arrived on his first visit to Greece. He had been horrified by the lack of interest shown even by museum staff. I compared the filthy chemical plants at Eleusis to those at Grangemouth in Scotland. John was horrified and pointed out that at least the Scottish refineries were brand-new. He was right, of course. Part of the trouble with Greece's 'new technology' is that it's several decades out of date. It's a very short-sighted policy to ignore and despise your archaeological heritage for that.

The underground was still working, so I decided on a trip to Penteli next day. If the buses had been running I could have arrived at the village of Nea Penteli before starting a walk to the quarries. As it was, I could only take the Metro to Marousi and follow the road from there. It was a long climb, but there was a fresh breeze on the mountain top. I had been warned that it was an unpleasant walk, but I couldn't agree. There's something fascinating about seeing the bones and substance of a mountain laid bare. You won't find marble more beautiful than the white one from the Penteli quarries. Several kilometres of the mountain consist of quarry after quarry – some old and no longer worked, others freshly cut. I'm told that the staff of the British Embassy hike up there on New Year's Day to clear their hangovers – but it's probably just a wonderful story.

When I was near my goal, a man on an ancient motorbike stopped and asked if I needed help. I showed him my map and was offered a lift to the Daveli cave, which is just below the one I wanted. It was a circuitous, bumpy ride on the broken marble paths between the quarries.

The Daveli cave is an infinitely more pleasant site than the Paiania tourist trap. Not many tourists go there. Those pot-holed, broken marble roads wouldn't do much for the average car. It's a huge cave with the sound of dripping everywhere and a muddy floor at the back, but no apparent signs of a spring. The huge hall that makes up the main cave echoes wonder-fully. It's far bigger and higher than the other caves I'd visited – a reason perhaps why it's not dedicated to Pan. On the right of the entrance there's a church of St Nicholas, long since fallen into decay.

My self-elected guide turned out to be an Albanian goatherd, pasturing his animals on a grassy section of the mountain, away from the quarries. He was tanned like old leather and had an impressive array of gold teeth in his expansive smile. He was enthusiastic about the cave – as proud as if he owned it personally.

The little church is Byzantine. I went inside it after I'd inspected the main cave. The frescoes of saints by the altar were worn away to almost nothing, but there were some tiny reliefs on the wall. I might have missed them if the goatherd hadn't pointed them out. They appeared to be three incised drawings – one or two of these might be the risen Christ, or a winged archangel holding an orb and cross. There were also several Christian symbols and some centuries-old graffiti.

There was a grid in the floor that appeared to lead somewhere. I wondered if it covered a well or a way down into the cave. I couldn't resist going down inside with my torch. There was nothing there. The space was big enough for a body or so.

The Pan cave was supposed to be located about a hundred metres directly above the Daveli cave, about eight hundred metres by the road. The Albanian denied its existence, but I went up to look for myself. I had a hard job explaining in Greek and gestures that once archaeologists had finished with a cave it might not look like a cave at all. What I was looking for was in fact a pit. The roof had fallen when the cave and all its antiquities were excavated in 1975.

The Penteli cave contributed an impressive array of objects to the museum at Athens. Two of the best Pan reliefs come from there. In one, with a surrounding like a small Greek temple, three figures of women with their heads covered follow Hermes and Pan. Pan's face has blurred with time, but there's bags of character in his sturdy posture, two perky horns on top of his head, a club over his left shoulder, pipes in the right hand by his side. Above his powerful goats' thighs, there's a small, discreet erection. His stomach and chest are slightly thrust out. In front, appealing to Pan, are three tiny mortals – bearded men, stereotypes, all similar to each other. Mortals always come in a smaller size than gods. Their right hands are raised. Their left hands conceal something in a fold of their garments – a tiny offering perhaps. This relief was dedicated to the nymphs by Telephanes, Nikeratos and Demophilos. Their names run across the bottom of the stone.

The other relief has a more roughly shaped cave surrounding. Everyone is more casual, less formal here. Pan is again the central figure. This time he's seated on a rock, cross-legged, about to play his pipes. His horns are spread in a wide V. His face is better preserved than that of the other Pan. This is a benign Pan with eyes that slant down at the outside corners, a luxuriant beard and drooping moustache. Hermes stands behind him. The three nymphs are at their ease. One leans against the cave wall talking to another. The third is seated. The reason for the casualness of all the immortals' poses can be seen on the right. A boy is pouring a libation from a jug into a bowl held by an older man. It looks as if Pan will be the first to receive the wine, if wine it is. This relief was dedicated by Agathemeros – the inscription is preserved separately. Perhaps he is the older man holding the bowl. Both of these reliefs date from the fourth century BC.

Apart from the large reliefs, an array of terracotta lamps was found, as well as small figures of Pan and tiny herms – boundary gods with a head of Hermes on a small marble upright, punctuated halfway down with a discreetly erect phallus. Unusually, there was also a broken-winged figure of a woman. I have only seen a rather unclear photo of this, so I can't really guess what other religion or cult it might have come from.

The cave area had been so well stripped by the archaeologists that it was hard to find. I think I did in the end, but I wouldn't like to swear to it. All I could look out for was a section of marble lintel and a bit of dry-stone walling in marble also – what else could you use on Penteli? There were several pits on the way up, at roughly the right distance. I hope I found the right one . . .

Soon the Albanian joined me and pointed up to the top of the quarry above. His Greek, being acquired recently, was naïve. Three girls, he explained to me, larger than myself and made of marble, had been taken down from the mountain in that place and carried off to Athens. His words gave the sense that sculptures were found within the marble and not created by the skill of the artist. There are a few anecdotes by classical and renaissance authors that would suggest this also. Michelangelo is supposed to have seen marble in this way.

Seeing the artist as a medium or a diviner, who merely finds the blocks that carry a spirit within them, was an idea wholly alien to me. The sorts of sculpture I'd tried only involved modelling – building up clay, a formless substance, into solid form. All the credit for what was done was mine. The only time I had any sense of the form within a block was when I did a plaster cast from a head I'd modelled in clay. That involved chipping out the head from the mould. But then I knew quite logically that the head I'd made was there, concealed in the mould around it. I knew exactly what it was going to look like. I just had to be careful not to chip off any vital bits like the end of the nose and to clear areas like the hollow bits in the eye, around the pupil, where it's customary to have a deeper relief to give a sensation of colour.

Up on the mountain, though, amongst several kilometres of pure Pentelic marble, I could almost feel convinced that there were a host of gods, goddesses, pillars, reliefs and mythical creatures waiting to be released. I couldn't resist putting a few odd lumps of the marble from the quarries in my back-pack for future use as paper weights. They were just stonemasons' scrap – small stones with odd chisel-markings where they'd been chipped off the larger blocks.

Fortunately, considering the stones in my bag, I had a lift on the motorbike back to Kephisia, where I was able to get the train to Athens. On the way we stopped and climbed up to a tiny modern chapel near a copious stream of good water. I filled my water bottle. It had begun to leak, though, and was quietly wetting the side of my culottes. Still, it was a hot day. The goatherd also stopped halfway down to look up the mountain for his goats. Being goats, they hadn't stayed put where they should have done. He'd find them on the way back, he hoped.

Pharsala

And we are here as on a darkling plain
Swept with confused alarms of struggle and flight,
Where ignorant armies clash by night.

Matthew Arnold: 'Dover Beach'

*B*y using Pausanias as the mainstay of my researches, I had limited myself to central and southern Greece – the areas he covered. I believed that there might be caves further north, or even out of Greece.

I had begun reading Philippe Borgeaud's book, *Recherches sur le Dieu Pan*. In it there was the briefest of mentions of a cave of the nymphs and Pan not far from Pharsala, the scene of the ancient battle between Caesar and Pompey. Yet again, there was a connection between Pan and war. The victories of Marathon and Salamis were directly attributable to the intervention of Pan causing panic terror amongst the enemy. Could something similar have happened at Pharsala?

The most famous account of the battle is in Lucan's *Pharsalia*. A supernaturally caused panic is certainly recorded. But why should Pan side with Caesar, not Pompey? His allegiance to Greeks rather than Persians in former wars was easier to understand. Caesar of course claimed divine descent. He was also epileptic. Epilepsy could be a state created by Pan. It was sometimes called *Panolepsy*, although *Panolepsy* could be a form of mania too. The faces of some epileptics have a curious, faun-like quality.

I would hazard a guess that Pan sided with the inspired, the one who claimed divine origins. Caesar was, of course, a much more charismatic figure than Pompey. Although Pompey was described as the 'Great' in his time, his greatness fails to span the centuries. Certainly he is still known as a name, but by far fewer people than know Julius Caesar. Though Caesar did many bad things, he had film-star style. He went into world legends, even rude rhymes. My father had one that started: 'Julius Caesar let a breezer...' Pompey never became a subject for schoolboy verse. Perhaps his face was too ordinary. I had a female Latin teacher who looked awfully like him – if you can imagine him with a perm. We christened her 'Pompey' behind her back.

But where was the cave of Pharsala exactly? To get some inkling I looked in the library until I found the excavation reports in an Italian magazine. Every tiny object was catalogued – the usual sort of collection of female heads, Pan figures and so on. The finds were not kept at Pharsala. Although it's a big town by Greek standards, it has no museum. They had been taken further north, to Volos – a resort and port with ferries to various Greek islands and even to Syria.

You get a bad impression of Volos as you walk out of the bus station. Its town centre is tatty. But once you make your way to the waterfront, all that changes. The air coming across the sea is warm and clean. Everyone stays up late in Volos, for the café life. There is good food at the tiny ouzo shops along the waterfront before you reach the central area of town, but the cafés further along are more impressive places to sit, with their comfortable cane armchairs covered in deep cushions. A lot of Greeks seem to spend their holidays here or use it as a take-off point to the surrounding islands. I had no time to go up into the mountains but the pictures of their traditional, partly wooden houses in the local tourist office's brochure looked a distinct improvement on most village houses I'd seen.

Sitting in a café I could feel the tension that was driving me fast from place to place unwind. Unlike empty Athens, Volos was full of people – perhaps I should pick someone up? There was a slight problem there, though. All the picking-up along the waterfront seemed to be exclusively gay. I settled for a large plate of calamari instead.

My hotel had a most beautiful view across the sea from the balcony. You needed to get out on that balcony though, because the en-suite lavatory smelt of drains.

I left my hotel early the next morning and walked along the waterfront to the museum, which was right next to the public beach. I was reminded of a film called *Cocoon*, where the octagenarians from an old folk's home in Florida find a kind of latterday fountain of life in a neighbour's swimming-pool, which is being used by extra-terrestrials to bring round friends they left behind a few million light-years ago. The sea was full of joyous, bobbing pensioners – men with flappy dugs and brown leather paunches, women with breasts down to their hips and vast crepe thighs. As they came out of the water they took up positions on the rocks – more like gargoyles than mermaids – to dry and sun themselves. It's sights like that that remind me just what the sun does to skin and reinforce my determination never to sunbathe.

The museum opened promptly and I started looking for the collection from the Pharsala cave. Most of the objects would be similar to those I'd seen in Tripolis, Marathon and Eleusis, I thought, but at least I'd be allowed to photograph these as they'd already been published. Eleusis had allowed photographs, but no flash – not a lot of use as the museum is not well-lit. The Italian magazine had shown photographs of every single object except for one erect statue of Pan. That I would have to see for myself.

I walked round the museum. Everything was well displayed and labelled. It seemed in fact a model museum. Most beautiful and unusual of all was the huge collection of painted grave steles from the nearby ruins of Dimitri. Though carved steles turn up in every museum and its garden, painted steles are rare.

It's not a large museum, so I exhausted its contents quickly. Where, oh where, were the Pan cave objects? I brought out my pile of photocopied pictures from the Italian magazine as proof that the objects were (or should be) in that particular museum. Eventually I was shown next door to the curator's office. At first, she told me that I should have sent a letter to the Larissa ephorate – Larissa being nearer Pharsala than Volos is – if I wanted to study these things. I told her I didn't want to study them, just take a quick look. She agreed to that and gave me lemonade while she scoured the museum's catalogue.

The catalogue was a rather indecipherable-looking file with rows of numbers, mostly in faint pencil. The only entry she could find near the date of the relevant excavation and under Pharsala showed that the museum owned four boxes of mixed terracottas and one of bronze. Perhaps this was the collection. A couple of strong guards were sent to fetch them into the office and I was allowed to examine them on the floor.

I decided not to try to identify the bronzes. Those in my list were so insignificant – damaged tiny coins or plain rings – that they would look like those from any excavation. The terracotta figurines were the only things that could be identifiable. I was also able to discard another box quickly. It was full of half life-sized terracotta masks of goddesses or women's faces – all far larger than the objects I was looking for.

It was at this stage that I began to notice the condition of the boxes. All four were riddled with woodworm. The wood was orange-box thin and the sides of one box were bowed, either with the wood's rottenness, or with the weight of the objects within. The boxes were leaving a trail of sawdust on the carpet. There was also a lot of sand in them. Perhaps it had come from the excavations, or, more probably, filtered down from some derelict Greek ceiling in the storehouse. Inside the two boxes that were left, everything was in plastic bags – broken bags full of holes. Every object had its museum number marked in pen, but that was all. Two or three bags had an area of Pharsala mentioned on labels, but most of the stuff was without record of where exactly it had come from.

I sorted through it all carefully. At first I was nervous of touching ancient objects. Soon, though, I came to the conclusion that I couldn't do anything worse to them than had been done already. Some of the bags were so full of objects that unlabelled fragments had broken off. Every bag had a sort of terracotta grit in its bottom made by the objects rubbing against each other. The bags were made up according to contents rather than source. There'd be thirty female heads in one, ten statues of Cybele in another. I spread my photos out on the ground and eventually found a female head and a Cybele that more or less matched and might be from the collection. I could not be sure, though. Such objects are usually made from a mould – early mass-production. There were no figures of Pan in the boxes – not even flaccid ones.

I was beginning to feel profoundly depressed by my first experience of a behind-the-scenes look at Greek museum-keeping. What point had there been in that original Italian excavation if the Greeks into whose safe-keeping the objects had been delivered had managed to lose or mislay a whole collection? What point was there in any foreign country pouring in money to help Greek archaeology if this was a typical result? What point was there in the exorbitant museum charges throughout Greece if the money was spent on ephorates and bureaucracy and not on the preservation and accurate cataloguing of collections?

The Greeks, of course, are blessed or cursed with more objects to preserve than a poor country can afford. Perhaps a radical solution might be to sell some of the real stuff to tourists once it has been recorded. There are so many duplicate statues, vases, etc. that it would surely not be missed. Israel takes this way out. You can buy antiquities quite legally in Jerusalem. Wouldn't the mass-produced ancient Cybeles be better on ten tourists' mantelpieces than left to break up in a box in the museum storehouse?

Most of the terracottas I'd seen would have been no great loss to Greek art. There are thousands like them all over Greece. On the other hand, there was one rather different figurine in one of the boxes. It seemed to be of marble or stone. It was such a filthy dark grey that it was hard to tell. A few inches high, it showed a child seated on the ground with his legs sprawled out. Artistically, it was superior to the other pieces in the boxes, yet it was being given the same rough treatment. At that stage, I hadn't seen anything quite like it elsewhere. The nearest things were the life-sized statues of children – the gifts to Artemis at Brauron. It was only after a visit to Turkey that I realised what that tiny figure was. The main archaeological museum in Istanbul has a case full of larger statues of children in a similar pose – sitting with one knee up, the other on the ground, to expose the genitals. Fortunately whoever did the labelling in Istanbul does not share the usual prudery of museum curators and has labelled the case 'Temple Boys'.

I was left alone in the curator's office and it would have been awfully easy to pocket the uncatalogued temple boy and save it for posterity. The Greeks trust strangers too much. But, of course, I just put the little figure back in the crate to crunch together with all the Cybeles, female heads, spare arms and pottery fragments.

After lunch, I took the train to Palaiopharsala under the

delusion that this is where the ruins would be. (*Palaio* means 'old'.) I asked several people on the station but no one seemed to know. The ticket-office man told me quite rudely that if there was an archaeological site nearby he couldn't be expected to know – he only knew about the trains. Outside the station I could only see flat, empty farmland without a vestige of caves, hills or the town's acropolis. I decided to go back to Pharsala itself on the next train. I went up to buy a ticket, but the staff in the office were too busy having a loud argument to sell me one until after the train was gone. I had to wait another three hours or so until the next one. I had two coffees from the station buffet and fed crumbs to the hens and a cockerel that were strutting up and down the platform. There was definitely nothing else to do. By then I had begun to hate Thessalians and filled in several postcards to friends saying so.

The town of Pharsala is about three kilometres from the station. I had just enough time to walk there before the daylight went. Fortunately I didn't need to ask the way. I could see it across the plain. As I was nearing the town, a man stopped and offered me a lift into the centre, directing me to one of the hotels. Although there are about fifteen thousand people in Pharsala, I ran into him several times during the day I spent there.

The atmosphere in Pharsala seems quite different from that in most small Greek towns. The girls are very pretty and there's much more mixing of the sexes. There's a lot of English spoken and people were eager to practise on the only English person they'd met. Pharsala's off the tourist beat. I was probably the only English person to visit it for years. It's a pity because although the town itself is very small and ordinary, the acropolis behind is well worth seeing.

As soon as I'd popped out of the hotel after cleaning myself up, I ran into the man who'd given me a lift in the square. I sat and drank lemonade with him and his bright eleven-year-old daughter. She spoke excellent English, having started it at five. It's the only way. By the time most English schools get round to teaching us languages, the memory part of our brains has become inflexible and deeply flawed. That's my excuse. If I ever get round to having a child I should be tempted to start it on Latin, Greek and an Oriental language at five. After that, any other languages would be easy.

Later I went on to the local bar with Chrysa's older sister Nansi and her cousin Demetra. Demetra offered to set me on the right road for the acropolis early the next morning. The bar was seething with men and women, mostly in their teens and twenties. There was a free mixing of the sexes – none of that furtive herding of boys with boys, girls with girls, while each lot eyed up possible partners for life. Men and women were talking to each other as human beings. It was totally different to anything else I'd seen in the towns away from Athens. The music was mostly Greek pop. Tonight was a quiet night, I was told, as it was Tuesday. If this was a quiet night, Saturday must look like one of those occasions when they try to cram fifty people into one telephone box for the Guinness Book of Records.

It's hard to find an explanation for the freer atmosphere of Pharsala. According to my Baedeker (although the Greeks might well not agree) there's a lot of Turkish blood in the town. This could well explain the markedly better-looking women, but it would hardly explain the freer atmosphere. While I've seen a reasonably free mixing of men and women in Istanbul, smaller towns in Turkey are as bad as those in Greece. Strict Muslim women also keep to their own sex, even in Istanbul. You can see them picnicking in the parks and shopping in groups without a man in sight.

Thessaly has a long witch tradition, dating back to Medea. Lucan, in his *Pharsalia*, maintains that the area is particularly rich in poisonous plants. But since Lucan's day they've all been used up. I couldn't even find a mandrake (something common enough in Turkey), henbane or thorn apple. Yet I'd seen these plants in profusion in other parts of mainland Greece. I'd like to think that the magical traditions are what have made for the different atmosphere. Perhaps women from witch stock believe in themselves enough to talk freely to men as their equals.

Thessaly has a number of important firsts in the mythological history of Greece. The first warhorse sprang out of rocks that were hit by Neptune. The first ship, the *Argo*, was launched here. Coinage was started by King Ionus. Thessaly was also the home of the Python before the serpent went to live at Delphi.

Demetra kept her promise to show me the start of the road to the acropolis. Her home backed on to the bottom of the hill. Her next-door neighbour was building on to his house, but had discovered ancient remains in his garden, she told me. The town was full of them.

A dirt track winds steadily up the hill. You could drive most of the way to the beginning of the old walls. The hill is triple-peaked these days. Older guide books call it twin-peaked. There are pine woods on the lower slopes. A man grazes his goats there, surrounded by noisy dogs. The hill is probably only a hundred metres high at most. About two thirds of the way up you come upon layers of thick wall of various periods from the Mycenaean epoch on. The fortress was repaired in the Middle Ages. It's far from complete now, of course, but there's enough to give a feeling of the city's former importance. One writer suggests that it might have been Phthia, the home of Achilles. There are two gates between the main peaks.

From the top, looking south, away from Pharsala, you can see mile upon mile of farmland, empty of people and buildings alike. It's pleasant, undulating landscape, bordered by mountains. What's curious about it is that it looks well-tended, but absolutely empty. I couldn't see as much as a goat in that vast expanse.

The battle of Pharsala was fought on the flatter plain to the north of the town. Caesar was positioned not far from the railway station. Most events in Roman history seem to have been attended by a record number of portents. The Battle at Pharsala was no exception. A sacrificial bull did what all sacrificial animals should do – ran like hell and escaped. There were fireballs and waterspouts when Pompey entered Thessaly. Swarms of bees covered the standards, making them almost too heavy to carry. Bees were connected with the worship of Pan. They were sometimes dedicated to him in a hive as an offering. They also went to the lips of the baby Plato when he was brought by his parents to Pan's cave on Hymettos, the world's most famous honey-producing mountain. They are very much part of small-time farming, together with goats and sheep. They provide one of the other basic necessities of life – something to sweeten food. Yoghurt with honey is the average Greek breakfast – so we hear. Most Greeks I met would prefer to settle for coffee and a fag.

Pompey's army was afflicted also by midday darkness. Midday is the time associated with panic fear if you accidentally come into contact with Pan or hear his music. Most interestingly of all, the armies of Pompey suffered a kind of mass hysterical hallucination – they saw Pindus collide with Olympus and the Haemus range subside into a chasm. They also heard the plain of Pharsalus ringing with battle through the night and saw blood pouring from Mount Ossa. This general demoralisation springing from some unseen source resembles that which caused the defeats in several other areas connected with the worship of Pan. Marathon and Salamis are the best known, but you can add to these similar incidents in Phyle, on Parnassus, near Acharnai, at the siege of Megara and by Apollonia.

In terms of numbers, Pompey certainly should have won. His total army was fifty-four thousand, Caesar's only twenty-three thousand. Caesar only lost two hundred men, Pompey lost fifteen thousand. These facts may in part be explainable by good military strategy, but that is probably not the whole story. Even if you do not believe in supernatural happenings, you would do well to believe that the witch followers of a god could create certain effects by trickery.

The article on the cave, copied from an old Italian magazine, opened with a long, rambling sentence that gave the location of the cave – in theory anyway. It said that it was about an hour out of Pharsala, in the area called Kukuvaia. But no one in the town had heard of Kukuvaia. But then, most district names and the names of mountains, rivers and ravines are not known to local people. They exist only in the minds of map-makers. There's an Israeli joke about a Bedouin leading a pedantic Englishman and his interpreter through a desert somewhere in the Middle East. Every time they came to a mountain or other geographical feature, the Englishman would ask through his interpreter what it was called. He would then write down an English transliteration of the name for his map. The Bedouin didn't actually know what most of the mountains were called – besides, he was hungry, tired and generally pissed off. The first few features got polite names like 'Mountain One' or 'Mountain Two'. By the end of a few hours' camel ride they were all named after Arabic swearwords. Anyone who understands Arabic might be slightly surprised that the last mountain on the map has a name that sounds remarkably like a phrase for 'Go and fuck a monkey – I want my dinner!' It's supposed to be a true story.

My Italian article went on to say the cave was on the summit of a hill which stretched in a range to the west. The next clause was damnably ambiguous. It could have meant that the cave was on the first of those on which the acropolis stood, or it could have meant that this was part of the same range. It seemed that my best bet was to search the whole side of the acropolis hill. It couldn't be on the further side, because the cave was also supposed to be visible as a flash of white from the Thermopylae road. There seemed to be no roads in that empty, undulating country on the other side.

I worked my way through the thickets to no avail. I can personally guarantee that the acropolis hill of Pharsala is completely caveless. Perhaps the cave lies instead in the next range over to the west. Another article places it an hour and a half west of Pharsala. The entrance is a narrow slit. Only the parts of the cave nearest to the surface have been fully excavated. All that remained then – they may perhaps be obliterated now – were a damaged inscription commemorating a dedication of the wreaths of Pantalkes and Phanippos to the gods, and a twenty-line hexameter poem headed '*Theos*' – god. The shorter inscription, which dates back to the fifth century BC, has been filled out and reconstructed – in this form it seems to record Phanippos dedicating the laurels he won in the Games and hanging them on the tree consecrated by Pantalkes to the goddesses.

Judging by the objects found, the gods worshipped here were the nymphs, Pan, Dionysos and Aphrodite. The fourth-century inscription in the form of a poem adds other gods to the dedication – Apollo, Hermes, Herakles, Cheiron the Centaur, Asklepios and Hygeia. There's such a medical feel to the last three that the shrine must have been used for cures. The poem goes on to mention Pantalkes and his role in improving the cave and planting the area. Presumably the tree of a former inscription had seeded itself and there was now a positive plantation.

Pantalkes's role in the poem is remarkably like that of Archedemos in the Vari cave. If the bowels of the Pharsala cave were fully excavated perhaps further carvings would be found. An article by Domenico Comparetti, written shortly after the excavation early this century, makes further leaps of imagination to connect the two caves. He would have it that Archedemos was a Thessalian. He believes that there's a mistake in the Vari inscription. Archedemos is described as a Theraian. He believes that the 'th' should be a 'ph', which would make him from Thessalian territory. It's not exactly probable, but neither is it impossible. Even in modern Greek those two letters get mixed up. I've seen it in roughly scrawled notices in shops. Turn the Greek capital *Theta* (Θ) on its side and the horizontal bar across the circle becomes the vertical division of the letter *Phi* (Φ).

Personally, I believe that Pantalkes and Archedemos were separate but similar men. Probably every cave had the names of its founders or early priests inscribed originally. Such names would not have survived in moister caves like the Korykian one. I had seen the lime deposits on even the most recent graffiti there. Later, I was to read of, though not to see, an inscription including a priest's name on a Pan cave in the north of Israel.

The Parnes Cave

Such my cry as rapid, I ran over Parnes' ridge;
Gully and gap I clambered and cleared till, sudden, a
bar
Jutted, a stoppage of stone against me, blocking the
way.

Browning: 'Pheidippides'

And they stood there on the meadow
With their weapons and their war-gear,
Painted like the leaves of autumn,
Painted like the sky at morning,
Wildly glaring at each other . . .

Longfellow: 'Song of Hiawatha'

I now had just one important Greek Pan cave left to see. I had only met two people who'd found it, and they were Jere Wickens and our lecturer at Sounion. Both were American. Perhaps only Americans can find it. They'd both talked as if the cave might still be in use – it had that sort of feel to it. I knew that there were several possible ways of getting there and that they were all difficult, near impossible, without a guide.

It's known as 'the cavern of the lamps' because dozens have been unearthed there. These can be seen displayed in Athens's main archaeological museum. Most are ordinary, but one has a couple copulating in an unusual position on its upper surface. Various tablets and inscriptions have also been found there.

I made my first approach through Phyle, a site still visited by archaeologists. It's on the border between Attica and Boeotia, commanding several passes and ravines. A few kilometres above the modern town there's a section of wall and tower preserved. I'm told that a kinky Greek scoutmaster likes to bring his cubs and scouts up here dressed as Indians, complete with feathers and war-paint, before he chases them along the wall's precipitous edge.

On my first visit I opted for the road to the monastery instead of the one that leads to the old walls. From the outskirts of Acharnai I took a taxi to Moni Kleiston – 'The Monastery of Our Lady of the Defile' as Baedeker calls it. The driver pointed out on the way the place where Procrustes had lived. From the monastery itself I could see a cave, or rather a grotto, across the deep ravine. Two hikers were meandering precariously among the stones, on the opposite side. The grotto was filled with icons.

I got some advice from the monastery about the way to the Parnes cave. The taxi driver had said it was near the ruins of old Phyle and the monastery gardener told me it was up and over the mountain behind, but that it was easiest to go back to the fork in the road and then walk via the village of Hagia Paraskevi. I compromised by taking mountain paths and trying to go up and over the mountain that way. I found my way to another road at one point but returned to the mountain and climbed to that particular peak's marked top. On the way down I found a cave – perhaps the one the man in the monastery was directing me to. But it wasn't deep enough, there were no niches that had once held votive offerings and the floor was wall-to-wall sheep shit. Not only did the place look different from that I was looking for, but judging by my map, it was also on the wrong side of the ravine.

That particular spur of Parnes was scratchy even by Greek mountain standards. Not only were there well-developed specimens of Kermes oak, but the paths were often barred by fallen charred pine trees from past forest fires. Burnt trees are hard to climb over. If you use a branch for support, it often breaks off like a stick of charcoal. I didn't get to see the Pan cave that day. I walked back down to Phyle afterwards. It was a pleasant walk – the road reaches the level of the stream-bed before it enters the town. Once in Phyle, I found the fastest taxi I've ever been in. He whisked me back to Athens for a minuscule fare by going through most of the red lights along the way. He was the last pleasant taxi-driver I was to encounter in Greece.

On my next trip, I opted to go via the famous fortifications of Phyle. It was the Feast of the Assumption of the Virgin – a general Greek holiday – and I had great difficulty getting a taxi. In theory taxis ought to be safer than hitching a lift, but it's not always the case. The man who eventually picked me up told me how lucky I was I'd found him. That sort of remark is always a bad sign from men – in relationships as well as with taxi-drivers.

It wasn't long before he was driving the wrong way, turning back towards Ano Liossion. I pulled out my map and corrected him. Perhaps he simply didn't know the way. Once we were in the town of Phyle, he started diverting up side roads. I saw the mounting fare on the meter and suggested he fix a price if he was going to take the long way round. I told him what I'd paid the last taxi driver and he agreed to take me up to the fortifications for about twice that.

The reason for the side roads soon became apparent. At first he offered to take me sightseeing next day for an exorbitant sum. I told him I'd seen everything in Athens that I wanted to see already. Then he offered to wait for me while I saw the Pan cave, for a price. I argued that the cave was a very long and difficult walk from the road. I couldn't be certain when I'd get back. He told me he knew exactly where it was and could take me there quickly. I had serious doubts about that – it didn't fit any description I'd read. But, on the other hand, just in case he was telling the truth, I thought I'd try not to fall out with him.

From then on, he started making passes. He wasn't bad-looking and was about twenty-five – if he'd had a more sensitive, kinder nature, I might have been tempted. But no woman wants a man who's trying to cheat her. He was also obviously educated by porn magazines. He told me he wanted a kiss and hung out a flickering tongue, hopefully, like La Cicciolina. When he didn't get that, he told me how women loved giving blow jobs and started to unzip. I told him most women found them boring, but he obviously didn't believe me. He had a look on his face as if he thought he was about to do me a great favour.

Fortunately the road was fairly empty as he swerved along it trying to get his way by collaring me round the neck. Eventually he got the message and stopped. The fact that the road had run out into a track of chalky lumps that might damage his car had more to do with his giving up than any sense of mercy. I paid him off at the rate agreed. I had to argue about getting a receipt and he also tried to get more money. At that stage, he did admit that he'd never been to the Pan cave. He had tried to take an archaeologist there years before, but they were unable to find it.

When I started walking I realised that he had taken me miles higher than I'd wanted to go. It was a long way back to the fortifications. Lower down, at a restaurant, I asked the way and the ruinous wall was pointed out to me through the window. There were no paedophile scoutmasters around that day.

It was at these fortifications that Thrasyboulos and his men held out against an army sent by the Thirty Tyrants. Pan is generally credited with the snow and the noon-day darkness and other things that scattered the assailants.

From the fortifications I was able to find my way to Krya Pigi, a plentiful spring near another restaurant. There was a long queue of men and women filling up water carriers. It's one of the best springs in Greece. I kept a little in the bottom of a bottle and it still tasted as good weeks later. I had a Greek salad at the restaurant before going on. There were young Albanian boys serving – they were probably still of school age. They spoke a very broken kind of Greek. There were a great many families having lunch together. Huge heaps of lamb bones lay on every table.

I had a set of typed instructions of another route to the cave. The path should have been over the next hill above the restaurant, but soon I found a multiplicity of paths from which to choose. The instructions depended on knowing the names of the ravines ahead, but ravines are never labelled.

I walked back to Phyle. This time I was lucky – there was a bus waiting. The army had laid on a skeleton service to some destinations outside Athens while the strike was on. When I got back to the British School, everyone knew I hadn't found what I was looking for. There's a running joke amongst archaeologists that you haven't found that particular cave unless you've been lost for three days and the helicopters have been sent out.

The evening of the Assumption of the Virgin I had dedicated to the purpose of visiting an Athenian brothel. I had come back early from Phyle for this. There were few heterosexual men left in Athens in August. A cursory walk around Omonoia Square had told me that, as had the fact that I'd had few offers and none worth taking. Omonoia Square seems to be solely a homosexual pick-up point in August – hopeful soldiers, the odd Albanian (that is, apart from the man with the slipped toupée and the barrel belly who couldn't afford to stay away just in case that was the one night in the year he was destined to get lucky).

With any luck, I thought, the trade in the Athenian brothels would be so slim that the prostitutes wouldn't mind wasting their time being interviewed. My obscene Greek is okay, but the rest is so shaky that I decided to take an interpreter. I had met Philip from the British School at the end of my previous visit. This time we had become friends. He had been seen with a Greek girl leaving his room in the morning and was fined £30 – a bit of a blow when you're operating on a meagre grant. It was not a fine officially, just the rather exorbitant price of having a non-member to stay as a visitor. 'I could have had Professor So-and-so in my room for anal sex and they wouldn't have cared,' he fulminated, 'but I bring in a Greek girl . . .'

He was so down about it that, for a joke, I put up a notice that said: 'Members of the British School of Athens are requested only to sleep with each other. Bringing in Greeks is subject to a surcharge of £30, per night, per Greek.' The notice had vanished by breakfast and I heard that certain people in charge were not amused. Questions were asked, but I was the one person they did not suspect.

Philip was the only person at the British School who spoke good Greek. In fact he speaks it like a native after years at Thessaloniki University, not to mention a policy of constant fraternisation. He also had a certain sympathy with my project, having done a spell as an exotic dancer in Blackpool.

The results of my interview are recorded elsewhere. It was illuminating to find that Greeks take an average of two and a half minutes for sex, and that includes bargaining time and undoing their flies. In some cases, it also included the most popular Greek fantasy – pretending the prostitute was their wife and quarrelling before having sex. Obviously I had been singularly lucky in that some of my partners had taken three or four minutes. Demetrios had taken hours – but I don't really count what he did as sex. It was just pleasant foreplay that never got any further.

The other thing that surprised me was the standard of looks of this prostitute's clients. Out of the four clients she had in between questions, two were young and handsome, the other two quite passable. In a world where I had imagined only seedy old men as customers, it shook me. It seemed sad that men who had everything going for them in looks had decided to pay for sex purely as relief, rather than find it, together with affection, from a non-professional.

It's in a prostitute's interests for the man to come as quickly as possible. These men would go on through life believing that little or no foreplay was okay. That spells tragedy in their own lives. While many married Greeks have mistresses, it's also true that their wives – in the larger towns, at any rate – have the tourists. Presumably the mistresses also have the tourists. What woman could be satisfied by a man who takes two and a half minutes?

I had just enough time left in my August trip to make one more attempt at finding the Pan cave on Parnes. There was supposed to be another approach by road. When there are buses in Athens, they can take you up to Hagia Triadha, near the top of Parnes, but the strike was still on. Next day, I walked to the foot of the mountain from Acharnai and hitched up the road that zigzags across the face of the mountain.

It takes a long time even to drive up that road. I was with a large family in a sort of mini-bus. They were all laughing and joking. It was obviously a picnic party. They dropped me before Hagia Triadha. The first of the landmarks on my map, a sort of sanitorium hotel, had closed down and there was no road through. A little higher up though, a turning was marked leading to the cave of Pan. A Greek road sign for a cave – that made a pleasant change. I could hardly believe my luck – that is, until after I'd long passed the seven-kilometre distance the sign mentioned, and found no cave.

Although Greek maps are a joke, the distances on signs are usually pretty accurate to within a kilometre. I had with me also a military map and some information from the Blue

Guide. I soon abandoned the map when I found that my road had twice as many wiggles in reality. The Blue Guide made mention of 'a conspicuous pine tree' near the cave. In a walk of ten kilometres or so, down from the top, I had found round about twelve pine trees scattered amongst the firs. None of them could have been described as 'conspicuous'. I determined to be pedantic and write to the author of The Blue Guide before my next visit.

Nonetheless it was a pleasant walk. The road is extremely rough – you can feel the soles of your shoes wearing down on it. I saw no cars on it that day – it wouldn't be the best place for a breakdown. There are a few camping sites near the top, but as you wind down to the bottom of the ravine there's not a person or an animal in sight. At the same time, you have a curious feeling of being watched. The trees in the ravine are a mixture of deciduous ones and the omnipresent firs. The stream-bed contains a series of young plane trees, stretching their roots down to the water's underground sources. When the stream is alive in the winter, these trees must be bedded in the centre of it.

Browning has made a most curious mistake in his poem, 'Pheidippides'. He writes of the runner's vision of Pan on the route between Marathon and Sparta. The ancient historical placing of the vision is on Mount Parthenion at a spot that hasn't been pinned down in modern geographical terms. Partheni – the modern name for the range – is on the Peloponnese. Yet Browning has transferred this vision to Parnes. He describes the rough, rugged quality of that range accurately enough. It's an extremely curious mistake, because the fact of there being a site sacred to Pan on Parnes was not well known in Browning's day. Locals, presumably, still used the cave, but it is not mentioned in Pausanias or other historical authors. The main literary source for the cave was only discovered just over thirty years ago. Menander's play

Dyskolos, *The Misanthrope*, had been languishing in a manuscript tucked away in an Egyptian monastery. Almost everything we now have of Menander's work comes from Egypt. Interestingly, sections of other Menander plays are still coming to light as part of the papier-mâché lids of mummy cases. But in Browning's day, only the quoted fragments of these plays were known.

Throughout Menander's play, Pan's shrine is on stage with a statue in front of it. On either side of his shrine there are two farmhouses, which belong to two of the main characters. The prologue is spoken by Pan. Pan gives us something near to a synopsis of the play and sets all its characters in context. The daughter of the Misanthrope is shown to be under his special protection because she worships Pan and the nymphs. Here, Pan is shown to have a role like Oberon in *A Midsummer Night's Dream* as he declares that he's made a rich man's son fall in love with the girl.

Pan does not appear again in the play. Knemon, a very bad-tempered old man, is made softer and allows the marriage of his daughter by the end, without divine intervention. The catalyst to this change in his behaviour is his unlucky fall into the well by his house. One of the characters suggests that this is a revenge of the nymphs. Perhaps Knemon turns into a nympholept.

The rich young man's mother – as with Knemon's daughter, her real name is not given – is an interesting character. She only has a handful of lines in the play and yet we feel we know her by what other people say of her. She makes regular sacrifices to different gods, involving her family and servants in day trips to the shrines around the area, carrying all the paraphernalia needed. It is from this outer frame of the story that we learn most about the sacrifices made to Pan – more, probably, than can be learned from any other source.

Every character who passes the statue salutes Pan. Even

Knemon greets it regularly. Sostratos' mother is in the habit of having dreams. This is why she spends her time sacrificing to the gods. This time she has had one that proves to be prophetic in a metaphysical sense. She has seen her son having chains put on him by Pan and then digging his neighbour's land. She comes to sacrifice in order to avert the omen. She is very precise in her orders. She tells Parthenis, a hired double-flute-player, to play Pan's hymn, whatever that was. They must not approach the god in silence. Perhaps my mistake in my attempts to find his caves was arriving in silence. When the party of revellers have got to the cave, Sostratos' mother instructs them to prepare baskets, water and cake. The water was needed for sprinkling. The baskets were to hold barley which would be scattered on the victim. Cakes could be either edible ones made with honey and sopped in wine, or little blocks of incense.

The cook employed by Sostratos' mother gives the most vivid details. He has had to carry a sheep – when he picks it up it makes passing munches at the shoots of fig trees. When he puts it down it won't walk. And who could blame it? Another servant brings a collection of cooking pots and pans, rugs, cushions and mattresses.

Knemon is about as happy as a man living next door to a house used for raves. He thinks about demolishing his place. The nymphs and their worshippers make noisy neighbours. He complains that sacrificers bring hampers and wine-jars for themselves, not the god. All he will get is incense and a barley cake plus the tail-bone and the gall bladder of the lamb. (These are left only because they're inedible.)

It's a comic, earthy, messy play with its pots and pans and the live sheep on stage. It seems suited to the countryside I walked through. Phyle is renowned as a place for buying lamb. Many Greeks drive out there – for a carcass for the freezer rather than sacrificial meat. The land is not rich. The play describes it as rocky and growing savory and sage. Yet the stage set has farmhouses on either side of Pan's shrine. I would suppose that they were very makeshift houses though, in that Knemon talks of pulling his down. Commentators have speculated on the impossibility of there being houses in this position. Photographs of the cave show that it's set in the ravine at the top of an irregular flight of stone steps cut into the cliff. Menander has probably used a bit of poetic licence, unless they were tree-houses. I wish though that there had been some kind of habitation in the area – it would have made my task a lot easier if there'd been a Misanthrope from whom I could ask the way.

What I had to look for, but did not find, was a cave cut into the rock with rough steps leading to it and a plane tree in front. Inside, all that's left, now that the archaeologists have moved on, is bare rock with niches that once held tablets or statues, and a floor full of hollows like basins where water might collect. The niches sometimes contain recent offerings from those who still worship Pan, or candles to give light in the darkness.

On a later visit, I tried scrambling my way along the sides of the ravine – it's mostly loose rocks. It's easy to fall if you walk down among them. Some are covered with a treacherous layer of leaf-mould. But you can't fall far, there are always more tree roots to stop you.

There's a stage at which the ravine and its trees look quite unlike any other landscape I've seen. Somewhere near the seven-kilometre distance mentioned on the signpost at Hagia Triadha, everything began to look very old. I recognised a similar landscape on television in a programme on some naturalists searching for a creature – half-ape, half-man – in the primeval forests in China's mountains. The trees in the bottom of the ravine on Parnes have grown tall and sparsely leaved in their efforts to reach the light, like roses in a

213

backyard. The Chinese forests in the television programme had something of that same quality. It is in this 'primeval' stretch that you get the strongest sense of being watched. There's the odd rustle among the trees as if something has moved, but I didn't see as much as a goat that day.

I looked up at the opposite side for some vestige of a chariot-shape on the rocks opposite – another landmark mentioned in The Blue Guide. There were at least two white rock-formations that could have more or less fitted that description, but there seemed to be no cave on my side.

On the rock beside the road, someone had painted an arrow and the name of the cave in Greek – this time the adjective meaning sacred had been included. I was on the right road, but where was the cave?

Near the bottom of the ravine, you can hear the buzzing of bees before you come upon a vast array of hives on a stretch of grass where the road loops round. I reached the bottom of the ravine that day, but I knew I was now too low down for the cave which lies thirty metres higher in the side. I had failed again. I would try once more on my next visit to Greece. If the strike was over, things would be a lot easier. I could get there early at any rate, and spend the whole day looking.

Back in the British School that night, I met an artist, Mary Louise Colouris, the daughter of the actor George Colouris. She was currently exhibiting in a gallery in Kephisia, Menander's birthplace. The gallery-owner, an old friend, had told her of a cave of Pan near there. Could that be the one on Parnes? It's not near if you're travelling on foot, but it might be considered so by car. The gallery-owner was in the habit of taking day-trips like Sosostros' mother out to the hidden shrine. Unfortunately, she was abroad and so I was never able to find out the truth about the place she visited.

Ephesus

Or snorted we in the seven sleepers' den?
John Donne: 'The Good Morrow'

*T*here's just one image of Pan in Istanbul's main archaeological museum. It's from Tirnovo, a place I can't even find on the map. It's intrinsically different from the other Pan images around. It has the same shaggy legs, small erect cock and bare torso as other statues and reliefs, but the proportion is on the grotesque side. It has the look and feel of a Gothic saint. The head and hands are large, the body, though more muscular than anyone from the Middle Ages, seems twisted. Pan looks as if he has a hump from the posture of the front part of his body, but there isn't one at the back. He could almost be a medieval beggar playing the pipes to earn a little money before limping home. Nobody with this body would walk well, let alone cope with rugged mountain tops. The face and hands are as coarse and stupid-looking as those of a Brueghel peasant. If the statue were badly executed, it would be easy to dismiss it as a piece of poor workmanship, but it's not. It must therefore be taken as another view of Pan – one essentially different from the ones that appear in Greece.

The first thing you see on entering the museum is a gigantic statue of the Egyptian god Bes. It's a Roman copy, as, for all I know, the statue of Pan may also be. The god Bes is holding a lamb or a kid upside down by its legs. He's using the body as a

215

sort of gigantic fig leaf. Other statues of Bes usually sport an erect cock. Bes, in the mythology of card manufacturers, is usually compounded with the god Priapus. Priapic cards prove a great seller to tourists at most of the major sites in Turkey. They are always mislabelled as pictures of the god Bes. In his usual representations Bes is shown as a pot-bellied dwarf with a small erect cock and a large head. True Priapic figures have the sort of cock you could hang your hat on, even if the rest of the body's only a foot high.

The form of Pan in the Istanbul statue seems to have been influenced by the shape of Bes. Bes came late into Egyptian mythology; he may have been imported from Somaliland. He had long arms and crooked legs, cat-like ears, thick hair and a beard and coarse lips. He is usually depicted wearing an animal skin and always shown front on. His statues have a symmetrical feel. He was a god who had connections with war, music and love – functions that overlap with those of Pan. If Bes had been made to play the pipes, a statue like that of Pan might have resulted. Raising a set of pipes and blowing into it throws the body into an asymmetric position, unlike those assumed by Egyptian gods in their cult statues.

Although Turkey now covers a huge proportion of what was once Greece, I could find a mention in classical literature of only one place associated with Pan. Achilles Tatius wrote that Pan consecrated his syrinx in a temple in a sacred wood by Ephesus. The Oracle of Syrinx was founded there for testing virginity. It's natural that virginity should be considered important in an area largely dedicated to Artemis and most famous for her multi-breasted cult statues. If a virgin passed the test, the syrinx was heard. If she failed, a groan. The doors of the cave would then fail to reopen and, presumably, Pan had his wicked way with her. She did not reappear.

The original etymology of the word 'syrinx' is interesting. It comes from the Sanskrit *surunga*, meaning 'an underground passage'. Such passages are a feature of many rituals – either in the form of natural caves or man-made grottoes. It would also be a fair description of the cervical channel in a woman. The doors of the cave, which either open or remain shut, are an emblem of the hymen.

I would like to think that remedies for failed virgins were available. Goddesses like Hera and Venus had bathing spots where they could renew their virginity. Curiously, it is still possible to do this in modern-day Istanbul. A few of the quack chemists in the Sultan Ahmet area (definitely downtown) stock DIY virginity repair kits. They used to be a lot more common. I have asked a friend of mine who lives there to buy me one and translate the instructions. I have also told him to ask if it's any good for one long gone. But, understandably, he keeps forgetting.

The Turks I've met in Istanbul seem to have a far more relaxed attitude to virginity than other Muslims. In Egypt, the situation is horrific by comparison – a non-virgin is often forced to become a prostitute, or, worse still, shot by one of her brothers in an 'accident'. I think of Turkey as being 'soft-core Islamic' – downing a few rakis during Ramadan carries no penalties, nor does sex. Turkish men, I'm told, are a little too respectful of Turkish maidenheads, though. A Turkish woman who wants to screw around generally arranges to lose it with a foreign visitor first to smooth her path.

I had decided to take a bus to Ephesus – an all-day journey. The Topkapi bus terminal has a seedily romantic aura. The huge ruins of the old city walls provide a backdrop. It's not a conventional indoor terminal like those in other countries. You get your ticket by going to one of the small agencies, talking to a tout or stopping one of the coaches that's setting out. Conductors stand on the step of their buses crying out their destinations as they start out on their appointed route. It's an amphitheatre-like space – bustling even in the small hours with sellers of all kinds of food from kebabs to croissants. Any traveller would enjoy reading the lists of names on the agencies' windows – Trabzon, Damascus, Budapest. Anything seems possible in the Topkapi bus terminal.

I opted for a bus to Izmir. The direct bus to Selçuk, the nearest town to the Ephesus site, didn't leave till late morning. Every long-distance bus stops for refreshments. Passengers' hands are also liberally doused with cologne by the conductor from time to time. On this particular bus, every passenger was given a large chocolate-cream biscuit and a bottle of lemonade – sickly sweet – against travel sickness.

The bus took about an hour and a half to clear the outermost suburbs of Istanbul. After that the whole coach was driven aboard the ferry. Most people got off the coach to stretch their legs. All the ferries out of Istanbul have people selling teas off large trays which they suspend on chains from one shoulder. Tea-sellers are always either boys or old men. I've never seen women selling tea, or for that matter junk food, in Turkey. There are plenty of women in the top jobs, but none at the bottom.

From the other side, the coach went on to the big modern town of Bursa. A guide I'd read had enthused about the kebabs in that town. They seemed much like any others to me – the only difference being that they had tomatoes on the side, not mixed salad. I was sitting next to a young German hiker on the bus. He'd changed his place to be next to me as he knew no Turkish. I was glad of the company.

By the early evening the bus reached Izmir, after one more food stop. Izmir looks beautiful by sunset, but not so good by day. It's full of modern buildings, but as the sun goes down you're only conscious of the red sky and the water-line. Turkey has cleaner air than Greece, and so does a much better line in sunsets.

My second bus got me so late to Selçuk that I took the first hotel offered by a tout. I bargained over the room price, which went up once I'd climbed the stairs but went down rapidly again once the owners saw I was about to leave. The tout, a relative of the proprietor, had spent time in Australia and had the accent to prove it. He was sufficiently Turkish, though, to give me apple tea and hint that he could sell me a carpet.

I set out for Ephesus in the morning. It's a pleasant walk of a few kilometres. I don't know why so many tourists drive there, either by car or in locally hired traps. I have a deep instinctive dislike of people who choose to be pulled around by tired horses in carriages. I don't feel at all the same about riders, so I don't suppose my concern is entirely for the horses. Perhaps I have too many plebs in my ancestry to feel comfortable with the sight of lazy people being pulled around fancying themselves.

You can take a road parallel to the main one to avoid most of the traffic. A turning leads to the Grotto of the Seven Sleepers. A French book on the excavations of the area, *Ephèse et Claros* by C. H. Picard, suggests that this was the site of the Pan cave where the oracle of Syrinx operated.

The hill where the cave is sited is the right spot, but I very much doubt if the Christian site is the correct one. Before I reached it, I saw the remains of several other caves and went over to explore them. The hill is gradually breaking up on the side facing the town. Old caves fall in and become clefts full of wild fig trees. The other side of the hill seems to be part of farm land. Perhaps the real Pan cave will be found when a sheep, a goat, or a shepherd falls into it one day.

The French book puts forward the theory that ancient sacred spots usually went on to be used as Christian sacred spots – and that therefore the new grotto must be the old grotto. The only Pan cave I'd seen taken over was the one at Kephalári. All the others had continued their existence as pagan sites only – perhaps their inaccessibility helped keep them inviolate. While Roman Catholicism in Italy seems happy to absorb pagan divinities and parallel them with its saints, I'm not so sure that the same is true on Greek or Turkish land.

The Grotto of the Seven Sleepers is oddly named. I'd expected something more cave-like. What I found instead was the ruins of a complex of buildings, including an early Christian basilica, built of narrow bricks in the style you see all over Rome. If the area was once a cave, it certainly ceased to look like one after the Christian property-developers had moved in.

The 'Seven Sleepers' – Maximianus, Martianus, Joannes, Malchus, Dionysius, Constantinus and Serapion – were martyrs in the reign of Decius in the middle of the third century. They were sealed into the cave by the emperor after they had hidden in it to escape having to worship idols. This is precisely where the French theory falls down. If you're too Christian to worship idols, why on earth would you go and hide in a Pan cave with a working oracle, not to mention all the votive offerings – marble tablets and terracotta images of the goat god, erection and all? It's like Mrs Whitehouse and Lord Longford seeking a bit of peace and quiet in Raymond's Revuebar.

The sensible version of the story is that the Seven Sleepers died once the air, or their food, ran out. The miraculous version has them hiding in the cave, then falling asleep for one hundred and ninety-six years. When they wake up one goes into the town, full of fear and trembling, to buy food for their breakfast. He is surprised to find that everyone is Christian now. He behaves so oddly that he is brought before the bishop. At that time there is a heresy going the rounds regarding the resurrection of the dead. The bishop, the emperor Theodosius and quite a few of the townspeople go to see the Sleepers and their faith in resurrection is renewed. The Sleepers can then go back to sleep and die a natural death. Quite why a sleep of one hundred and ninety-six years is thought to prove the resurrection of the dead, I can't fathom.

What interests me about the story of the Seven Sleepers is its relation to all the other long-sleep tales. All the other stories concern fairies, or the 'Little People'. The catalyst that kicks off a supernaturally long period of slumber is some meeting or dealings with them. Rip Van Winkle plays bowls with dwarfs in the Catskill Mountains. Innumerable children are snatched by fairies. Young men are taken by female fairies who have fallen in love with them – these particular fairies are surely descendants of the nymphs. In most of these stories the Little People live in a hill, and caves or subterranean worlds are involved. Mount Coelian, near Ephesus, is a hill where Pan worship went on in a specific cave – like the one near Vari. In each case, nymphs are involved. In Ephesus, it's Syrinx. Those who like to believe in the supernatural might care to think that the Seven Sleepers were nympholepts like Archedemos. If so, a splendidly decorated cave is still waiting to be found. Perhaps it lies hidden in the hill behind the current ruins.

The number seven is, of course, a magical number much used in amulets and spells. If a longer version of the Seven Sleepers story existed, perhaps there would be a more concise explanation of what put them to sleep. In many fairy stories the mortal touches fairy food or drink. Even in the late story of Rip Van Winkle, the hero makes the mistake of swallowing the dwarfs' grog. All these tales have a touch of the Persephone myth – eating or drinking underworld food binds you to that world for a while.

The Seven Sleepers could, of course, have been lulled to sleep by music – the pipes of Pan or Syrinx. These pipes have vanished from Greek music. They are not even recorded in the museum devoted to it in the Plaka. Probably the only countries that play them now are in South America. The British

Museum owns a set from Peru, made of fourteen reeds. It's perhaps not a coincidence that South America has become a symbol, the Mecca of conservationists. Any programme on saving the rainforest will contain the music of these pipes in its theme tune. There are sections of rainforest elsewhere in the world, but it's the South American ones that have caught the world's imagination. Brazilian substances like guarana have also taken off and surpassed the sales of any home-grown herbal stimulants. At one time, the pipes of Pan were only heard in a changed flute-like form in early French films. In these, the sound symbolised nature in the form of raw sex lurking in the great outdoors. Now, the sound of the pipes has left Europe and become a symbol of Indian tribes and Nature itself under threat.

How good a sleeping place would a cave make? While prehistoric peoples knew nothing better, by the middle of the third century cave-dwelling was very much a thing of the past. The Roman catacombs – an artificially created labyrinth, similar to caves only in material and temperature – were not used for living in, only as temporary hide-outs and places of worship. But shrines of the cave type could be slept in temporarily, perhaps for the procuring of oracular dreams. Psychologically, sleeping in a rough, cave-like place must symbolise a return to prehistoric times (or the womb) – a drawing on ancestral strength.

Aristophanes' play, *Lysistrata*, includes a Pan cave as a place for sexual experience. I had not, at this stage, found positive evidence of them as sleeping places. The images I had seen in the Reggio museum were like nymphs in beds, but I was only to find bed-like depressions in caves when I went to Italy.

Above the church of the Seven Sleepers, there's a 'Healing House'. Probably it was once a place of pilgrimage and miraculous cures. Now, the tourists who come to the Grotto of the Seven Sleepers often don't bother to look higher. Most of the floor in front of the Healing House has caved in. If you stand back from what's left of the building, you can see what remains of its curved ceiling holding up the hill above. There's probably a great deal to be found in the whole hill, when, in the course of time, other ceilings fall in and inner rooms, or other caves, are revealed.

I went on to the main Ephesus site. I had seen it before on a less crowded day in spring. Ephesus, when it's uncrowded, is one of the most beautiful places on earth. On my way, I passed some ruins which were labelled 'The So-called East Gymnasium'. Turks are in the habit of translating archaeological comments absolutely literally.

The main site was seething with visitors. The soft-drinks traders were making a fortune. It's one of the finest classical sites purely on appearances – far better, I think, than the Acropolis – but it's one that must be caught near empty in early spring or late autumn. A great deal of what has survived is Roman rather than Greek building, so I don't suppose it would appeal to purists. I particularly like the remains of the library of Celsus – a vast, well-preserved, two-storey façade opposite a broken-down brick brothel. It is interesting to speculate what books it once contained. Ephesus has a very long tradition of magic, dating back to the earliest times. Most of the early practitioners were Jewish Kabbalists working in the tradition started by King Solomon. 'Ephesian Letters' were a widely used magical formula written on parchment. They made their owner invincible. An Ephesian once used these in the Olympics in the way our athletes might use steroids. Once the parchment bound to his heel was removed, his wrestling opponent threw him thirty times.

I walked back to Selçuk and stopped off at a sort of nomad's refreshment tent. As I drank some *Vishne Suyu* (sour cherry juice), I noticed the flies circling the tiny wooden stool next to mine. A second look explained all: the Bedouin blankets on the floor were peppered with sheep shit. I reminded myself to stick to ordinary-looking cafés in future. Shit shows up plainly on lino.

It was a seriously hot day and the fruit in my bag had been fermenting. Just outside Selçuk, I decided to feed my grapes to the sort of goat who looked as if she'd eat anything.

I intended to look at the museum in case there were any exhibits with Pan connections. I got waylaid by a Kurd with a shop nearby. He pointed out that a coach party had just gone in and that I would have the museum more or less to myself if I waited twenty minutes or so. I made it very plain, from the outset, that I was not in the market for a carpet. The Kurd explained that he merely wanted to practise his English and show me the differences between Kurdish and Turkish goods. I still don't know precisely what those differences are. Very soon carpets were being rolled out. You have to be a man or woman of steel to escape Selçuk without buying one. I explained that I was about to work my way down into Greece and would have to walk in some areas with a pack on my back. The last thing I wanted was to have to carry a carpet as well. Yes, I did like Turkish carpets. One day I would return to Turkey and buy one, or several, when I was not on my way to Greece, carrying all that I had with me on my back and hoping that pack would get lighter not heavier. Of course, he offered to send one separately. I countered that by telling him the true tale of someone I'd met who had his beautiful cheap carpet sent to England. The customs didn't tell him it had arrived and he was charged several months' storage. He could have bought a similar carpet more cheaply at home.

He was the only Kurd I've ever met. I'm told they figure in Turkish jokes in much the same way as the Irish do in British ones. I was interested in finding out what Saddam Hussein hated so much about these people. When one nation seeks to get rid of another there is usually some reason, albeit not a logical one. The Jews have been frequent victims throughout history. Sometimes the oppressors claim it's because Jews are bleeding them dry through the usury trade, or that they are running all the country's business. A Russian from the BBC told me that Jews were hated in Russia because they had all the best jobs in education and medicine. These kinds of hatred are usually based on the envy of success. Similarly, Indians are hated in some parts of London for running newsagents' or grocery businesses that are open all hours. All these people make money because they work terribly hard – that's a fact missed by those that oppress them. Did the Kurds have some similar sort of success story? I wondered, but did not ask. Perhaps the explanation lies in what I was told of the business methods of the man before me. After the season was over, he shut up shop and went in search of new stock. He travelled through all the villages of Eastern Turkey with a van full of new machine-made carpets which he would swap for antique ones. Money seldom changed hands. It reminded me of the lamp-seller in Aladdin.

When the Kurd saw that there was no hope of getting my money, he asked me out to hear traditional music in a nearby village. We were much the same age, he said – he was a widower with a small girl – perhaps we might hit it off. What he didn't realise is how far down in the attraction stakes the ownership of metal teeth places a man from a western woman's point of view. I would consider sex with a man with metal teeth only if he was the last man on earth and we were the sole hope of perpetuating the species. In those circumstances, I would insist on a prenuptial agreement that specified that there would be no kissing and, above all, no cunnilingus.

Eventually I got to the museum. It was fairly empty. One of the curious features of the place is the assortment of ornamental birds kept like a harem in an inaccessible inner courtyard. Occasionally, one of them comes up and peers through glass at the tourists.

The archaeological collection is small. Pride of place is given to two impressive statues of Artemis standing in semi-darkness. There are several small cases of tiny objects and a figure of Priapus that's much photographed. Strangely, the picture I took of him displayed a curious effect. A spiritualist would perhaps make much of it. On the print, there's a blazing rectangle of light in his face, where the eyes should have been. A faint shaft of light descends from this rectangle, irradiating the tip of his vast cock.

There are a few other minor sites in Ephesus. I had seen the so-called 'Mary's House' last time I was there. Jesus' mother is supposed to have spent her last days in it, looked after by St John. The faithful visit it with appropriate awe, but the shrine commanded very little from me. It was something about the smell – someone, or something, had urinated in it and there was an old leaky gas heater that had gone out. I think the gas, on the whole, smelt worse. The only point in the place's favour is that there's a spring of good drinking water nearby. Presumably it has some curative properties, but I wasn't ill enough to feel them.

Nearer central Selçuk there were a few things I hadn't seen – the Artemision, the ruins of an old basilica, a mosque and a castle up on top of a hill. I took the Kurd's advice and saved these for the early evening when the air was a little cooler. I spent the hours between in the local Turkish bath – a particularly pleasant one. The slab where you lie is a vast octagon of warm marble. In the dome above there are three circles of tiny glassed holes like stars. The dome has a powerful echo. When the man massaged me with the sort of strength that only Turkish masseurs have, he pushed my head to one side and my neck gave a crack that echoed in the dome like a pistol shot. It had been stiff and out of place thanks to all the time spent sitting on buses.

In the early evening I went to the other ruins with a renewed spring in my step. There's little left of the once-famous Temple of Artemis. Her city was built by Amazons – it's an area of woman power. Turks have told me that this Artemis was more of a fertility goddess than a virgin huntress.

The greedy goat nearby was being taken home by a little boy. I wondered, guiltily, if her milk would taste of fermented grapes. I climbed the hill to the basilica of St John. The favourite disciple was supposedly buried here and the dust known as 'Manna' from his grave used to be exported widely. Perhaps it was used in medicines or amulets. On the way up I passed an ancient Turkish bath of the fourteenth century. In some towns, such old buildings are still in use.

In the castle grounds at the top, a man offered to be my guide in Spanish, his second language. Without speaking it, I more or less understand Spanish from its resemblance to Italian. He gave me the guided tour round the battlements and down into an underground cistern. Then I was persuaded to climb up the minaret of the disused mosque. I put my water and notebook into a tiny pack on my back to decrease my width and leave my hands free, and climbed. Soon the stairs became narrower and narrower. My helper was climbing eagerly behind, so I had no chance to stop. I had visions of getting stuck in the top of the minaret. The local emergency services would probably need a shoehorn to prise me out.

The actual top of the minaret was broken off. You could sit there and view the town from above. I never actually stuck. My hips are not as narrow as a *muezzin*'s, but there was just about enough room.

That evening I had dinner with a lonely young German who joined me at my table outside a little café. 'This beer is shit!' he said convivially, before ordering another pint.

The Former Haunts
of Priapus

*N*ext morning, I took the little local bus to Izmir. Local buses are like grubby, well-worn vans. There are no tickets – you just give the right money to the driver, who drops it into an open box. The fares are incredibly cheap. Sometimes the buses halt between stops to pick up travellers. I get the feeling the driver only does this if he likes the look of them. Nomads with huge bundles never get lucky.

Getting into the Izmir terminal is like shoving toothpaste back into a tube. Several bus lanes converge and everyone wants to be first in. Miraculously, we eventually made it without an accident. From Izmir terminal I picked up a coach to Çanakkale. I planned to take a quick look at the Hellespont. I hope to swim it some day. There are also a couple of sites where Priapus was once worshipped on that side of the Dardanelles. There are some parallels between Pan and Priapus. Priapus became the guardian god of Roman gardens. His images were also reddened. He was capable of creating panic in thieves who were after your fruit, even if he couldn't do

so in the battle context. He is also the god of a kind of poetry –
satire, in his case. I've always liked him for that and other
reasons. I once lowered the tone of a radio programme by
stating that he was my muse.

The bus wound through hilly country much like Greece,
before arriving in the late afternoon in Çanakkale. The minute
I got off the bus I was handed a hotel card which I kept for
later. I'd noticed a museum, three kilometres or so outside the
town. I planned to see it next day. In the meantime, I reckoned
there was just about enough time to visit Troy. I got on a tiny
local bus. It was stuffed full with villagers. Most of the women
wore veils and carried heavy loads of shopping. One near me
was pregnant and was also carrying a tiny baby. She had a
bruised face. Her husband sat down leaving her to stand, but
an old woman moved up and there was just about enough room
for everybody. The battered wife had palms hennaed rusty red
as dried blood. At first glance the henna used by a tiny
percentage of Turkish women looks like stigmata. The baby
cried continually in a fretful, feverish way. Its mother glared at
me as balefully as an ancient Thessalian witch – or so I thought
at the time.

The next man to me turned out to be a professional guide to
Troy. He told me smugly that I was on the last bus and
wouldn't be able to get one back. When I got to the site, there
was an hour or so left – enough time to stroll around. I'd missed
all the crowds of the day.

There's a wooden horse standing about fifteen feet high near
the ticket office. It has something like a Wendy house or garden
shed on its back with open windows. The Trojans would have
been complete mugs if they'd let something like that in. A
coffee shop nearby sells small wooden horse replicas and
hand-made chariots large enough for a Shetland pony and
child.

Almost everyone I've met has told me not to bother with

Troy. Although it doesn't have the impressive façades of a site like Ephesus, I found it interesting. The foundations of the city from nine periods of settlement have been revealed – parts of city walls, a temple and a theatre. The excavations are in flat fields. The area is inland and higher than Çanakkale. A quiet breeze blows across it. The air is healthy and clean. The sight that is most moving amongst all the other fragments is a near perfect ancient stone ramp. Rightly or wrongly, I could envisage the wooden horse that proved the city's destruction being wheeled up it and through the city gates.

Perhaps Geoffrey of Monmouth and other medieval historians are right about the British being descended from the Trojans. When I first read Homer I felt more on the side of the Trojans. I feel more empathy too with the Roman civilisation. According to the traditions cited by Virgil, the Roman people were also of Trojan descent.

I started to walk back towards Çanakkale. When I got on to the main road I would probably be able to hitch a lift – it was thirty kilometres or so – far too much to walk in the late afternoon and evening. I was offered a room in the village. Turks are very enterprising at letting one or two rooms in ordinary houses in out-of-the-way villages. I was half tempted to stay there, but realised it would delay my journey too much the next day. I met the battered woman I'd seen earlier. She greeted me like a long-lost friend. She was wreathed in smiles as she mentioned meeting me on the bus. Obviously I'd misjudged her expression before. Now, she looked happy. Presumably the baby was at home and asleep.

A lorry stopped on the main road and offered me a lift. The driver gave me a parting gift of three peacock's feathers. Just in case there's something in all those bad-luck stories, I decided to part with them next day.

Back in Çanakkale, I attempted to book in at the hotel I had a card for. It was up a maze of back streets. The façade was

231

weather-boarded and pure American Gothic. It could have been built for the Addams family. The last room had gone and I was rather glad. I ended up in a more conventional place near the front.

Çanakkale is a boring town. It's only worth stopping there as a jumping-off point for Troy, a tour of the Gallipoli battle site or a ferry to Istanbul. The only bad Turkish meal I've had was in one of the fish restaurants on the front. The fish had run out so I was stuck with kebabs. They came half an hour late, neither hot nor quite cold.

Just as it's hard to leave Selçuk without a carpet, it's difficult to get away from Çanakkale without being sent on a tour of the battlefields. I almost told one tout that I had no interest in seeing places connected with war – but then I remembered I'd just come from Troy! I suppose I prefer my wars to be so distant they're almost legendary. I find the thought of walking around a place where grandparents of my friends could have died too immediate and too harrowing.

In the morning, I walked out to the museum. They seemed slightly surprised to have a visitor. It has a mixure of archaeo-logical objects and later documents and photos connected with the First World War and the modern history of the town. I explained that I didn't speak Turkish, but got a guided tour of the modern section, nevertheless. I nodded my understanding whenever I heard a proper noun that I recognised.

Back in the town, I caught a bus to Karabiga, changing at the more modern town of Biga. Karabiga, my Turkish Tourist Board information leaflet told me, 'was known as Priapus after God, and thus has cult and fertility associations'. I hoped there might be a few standing stones at least!

On the second bus, a pretty little baby girl pointed at the feathers hanging out of my bag. I seized my chance and gave them to her. Her family seemed pleased. Evidently they do not have similar superstitions about them in Turkey.

Karabiga is a pretty village full of old houses with red-tiled roofs. In the Biga bus terminal, I had bought some fast food for my lunch – Turkey's answer to a chicken sandwich: a whole loaf stuffed with the wings of several birds and a couple of sliced tomatoes. After the tomatoes and a wing or two, the rest got the better of me and was chucked to some stray cats as I walked through the village. A cannibalistically inclined chicken came and joined in the feast with relish.

On the horizon I could see the remains of some huge walls. I walked along the shore till I came to them. They seemed to be the massive remains of old fortifications – a medieval castle perhaps. But, in spite of the place's associations, there was not a Priapic statue in sight.

The beaches in between there and the village were deserted. I decided to go for a swim, staying very close to my things. I chose a beach where I'd seen a flock of geese on my way out to the ruins. When I got back there, the geese had gone. The sea was full of little choppy waves caused by the wind, but it felt still enough while I was in it. At Çanakkale, the currents had looked lethally fast.

There's an unwritten law that says when a woman takes her clothes off in the middle of nowhere she will pretty soon have company. The minute I was on the beach, dressing myself again and trying to slide off the wet bikini discreetly, I found myself joined by a shepherd and his boy, a flock of forty sheep and a biker with binoculars.

The sheep and their escorts soon lost interest, but the biker stayed. I have always mistrusted men who bring their binoculars to the beach. As if the biker sensed this, he gave me a look through his at distant Istanbul. I was supposed to believe he'd brought them there just to view a very faint skyline of buildings and squat cushion-like mosques, broken up by minarets sharp as hypodermic needles. It needed imagination to turn it into Istanbul. It might as well have been an oil refinery from that distance.

When the biker had established I didn't want a Coca-Cola or any other drink I was allowed to continue on my way. To get to Lapseki, I took the bus that headed back to Çanakkale. Several kilometres along the road, the bus to Lapseki was flagged down by the driver and I sprinted over to get on it. I had about an hour to look around the town before the next ferry to Gelibolu, known to us as Gallipoli. Lapseki is built on the site of ancient Lampsakos, the town that the cult of Priapus originally spread from. I had heard conflicting reports on whether there were any ruins or a museum there. A Turk from the tourist office at Izmir airport had once told me that there were suitably Priapic remains. A headmaster who makes obscene phone calls to me had said the same. Yet the Çanakkale tourist office completely denied it. I assumed they were covering up, although later the heavy-breathing head-master penitently admitted he'd just been fantasising. Evidently Kaan in the tourist office at Izmir shares the same fantasy. If I find any other men who do, I'll have to call the thing a mass hallucination.

Gelibolu has little to see but a market. It's not a tourist market, in fact it outdoes any British one for the horribleness of its goods. Most of what's on sale is cheap and cheerful plastic kitchen ware. Vilest of all are the carpets – machine-made parodies of traditional patterns done in acrylic fibres. The most prevalent colours are lurid baby pinks and blues. I supposed that this might be where the Kurd loaded up his van before taking off into the villages of Eastern Turkey.

As the crowd gathered to wait for the boat, more and more women came up with those vile carpets in bundles on their heads, or slung across one shoulder. Some women were veiled, some not. One of the women gave me some pumpkin seeds to nibble on.

The journey to Gelibolu took so long that I wondered if I'd got on a boat to Istanbul by mistake. The wind was blowing hard, so I went inside to drink apple tea and run a comb through my hair. The soap shampooed into my hair at Selçuk and the warm winds had tangled and dried it out completely. I had noticed the wind since I came to Çanakkale. It had dropped only in Karabiga, round the corner as it were, on the Sea of Marmara.

Because of the currents, the ferry took a long curving track to the shore opposite. It was sunset by the time we landed. Almost every sunset I've seen in Turkey has been beautiful.

Gelibolu is a fishing town with a pretty waterfront. I booked into a hotel. I thought I might have a last Turkish bath before leaving the country in the morning. The manager of the hotel told me that the local baths were some of the cheapest and oldest in Turkey – in use pretty well continuously since the fourteenth century. That thought proved irresistible. They opened early, he told me, at about six-thirty. That sounded ideal for my plans.

When I came down in the morning, the manager, Mehmet, insisted on accompanying me. My heart began to sink – but they were public baths after all: I couldn't tell him not to go to them. He had been up all night, he explained. A relative had died. Everyone was dying young of heart attacks that summer. He'd lost various friends and acquaintances. I'd heard similar stories the month before in Greece. In Britain, we're more likely to die of the cold.

When we got to the baths, everything was dark and deserted. To my embarrassment, Mehmet went and knocked up the couple who ran them. They came out of a sort of flat built above part of the baths. The man was barefoot and dressed in pyjamas. Behind him, his wife appeared, swathed top to toe in robes with only a slit for the eyes. Her clothes were as bright as an advert for Persil.

The owner went back for his shoes, then came down to let us in. They had a long whispered conversation. When we were left

235

alone, the hotel manager explained that this was the best time to go there before all the soldiers invaded the place. Actually, I think it might have been more fun full of soldiers.

Mehmet was obsessively house-proud. He went down on his knees, his portly form wrapped in striped towels, and started to clean the place. Before he would let me take water from the little basins at the side in the steam room, he scrubbed them all out with soap and water, wiping them clean with towels.

The baths at Gelibolu are small and less well-equipped than others I've been to. Massage is done on the floor rather than on a table or raised area. Mehmet apologised for the place: 'Six hundred years is too old for baths. Two or three hundred years is right.' He obviously fancied his chances. He kept offering to massage me, but I told him I only liked that to be done by professionals. He wouldn't listen and kept starting on my feet and legs. He swore that he had been trained in the arts of Turkish massage. If it was true, he had no talent for it. His hands were thick and coarsely made, lacking in all sensitivity. A man with fingers like chipolatas will never make a good masseur.

About half an hour later, the real masseur joined us. He'd changed the pyjamas for a towel. He was muscular, with a tattoo of a crescent and stars on one arm. When he started to scrub me, Mehmet complained that I wasn't as filthy as the last party of British tourists he'd taken there – and they were nothing to the previous set of Australians . . . I felt I'd let the side down.

When the masseur came to shampoo my hair he built up such an enormous lather that it engulfed my head. I had to keep my eyes tight shut and spit the foam from my mouth to be able to breathe. I gulped and bubbled for air like a fish. At that stage, the masseur swept away the towel that is usually left between a person's legs in a massage. I would have been tempted by the masseur. He was good-looking in a kind of sailorish type of way – but then Mehmet was there too. Besides, I couldn't help remembering the swathed, mummy-like woman upstairs. Yet the thought of an orgy in a Turkish bath was intriguing . . . Would a condom stay on amongst all that soap and water? As I hesitated, blinded by foaming soap and indecision, I felt some chipolata-like fingers attempting to gain entry. I yelped and got away to one of the bowls of water, dowsing my head till I could see who was who again.

Both men promised to be good – or so Mehmet said – the masseur didn't speak much English. I washed more soap off. Did I want the dry massage as well? he asked. I've never had a dry massage in Turkey, so I said yes. But soon, more suds were flying around and more attempts were made. 'Dry massage' must be a euphemism for something else.

When we got back to the hotel, I was half tempted to go on one of the Gallipoli tours – it was still early in the day. I sounded out some Australians in the lobby – they'd been on one the day before. The man was extremely surly – unlike the friendly Australians I'd met in London. Eventually he said: 'I don't know why you'd want to go on one. It's not your lot here!'

'But I'm British,' I said.

'No you're not, you're German,' he told me. Now I know. I must be the only non-German-speaking German in the world.

The buses through to far-away destinations in Greece seemed expensive, so I decided to forget the tour and save the last of my Turkish currency. I might not be able to change more at the weekend. The buses straight to Greece didn't run till the evening, but I could get one within a few minutes to the last main town before the border.

Outside Gelibolu, the country became open and bleak. There were few cars on the road. Once I got to the Keşan terminal, several men came up asking my destination. The next bit of transport over the border proved to be a taxi. Demetrios specialised in cheap border runs and was willing to

237

take me as far as Komotini for a very reasonable sum. The only snag was that I had to wait an hour or so for him to pick up a second fare.

The second fare proved to be a Turkish teacher of mathematics with his arm in a complicated sling that contained a device to separate his fingers. He explained that his hand had been almost severed in an accident. He had to have the seat belt hooked round his shoulders only, to avoid bumping the wounded arm. The conversation in the car was strangely multilingual. The Turk talked Turkish to the driver and a mixture of that and French to me. The driver spoke German to me and I answered in Greek. Although I hadn't learned German, I seemed to understand him thanks to years of singing lessons which included some *Lieder*. I could probably have even strung together a few German sentences – as long as they were about trout playing in streamlets, the Rhine flowing softly, or roses among the heather. But it was time to give in: I realised I must sit down and learn the language everyone swears I know already.

Thasos

*T*he country grew more and more desolate as we approached the border. At last, our taxi stopped at a square of new buildings – offices and duty-free shops. Demetrios processed our passports quickly at the Turkish office. A Greek woman at the next department asked the statutory question, accompanied by a stony glare: 'What is purpose of your visit?'

There seemed to be no customs control as such – nobody asked me if I was importing anything. There were no red or green channels, although this was months before the Common Market did away with such things. While I stood around waiting for the Turk to return from the duty-free shop, I read a notice on the wall forbidding the import of dairy produce. I dutifully downed my carton of *ayran* (a buttermilk drink) at a gulp, before we crossed over into Greece. I didn't want to be dropped into a Greek gaol for importing buttermilk. If I ever go into crime it'll have to be for something bigger than that.

The Turk came back laden with cartons of Turkish

cigarettes. We were joined at that stage by a German who needed to take the taxi across the bridge that marks the official border. He was being met by friends a couple of hundred yards on. He told me it was illegal to cross that bridge on foot – trained marksmen were standing by with orders to shoot. I'd always assumed that border controls between countries that weren't at war could be walked through, simply by showing the necessary documents.

The Turk undid one of his cartons and offered packs of cigarettes to some customs officers and workmen by the bridge. Most refused, saying they weren't allowed to take them, but one workman turned out to be an old acquaintance.

As we were about to go on our way, two Greek customs officers came up to the car. The man was still in uniform, the woman had changed. They seemed to be a couple. They demanded a free ride in the taxi to the next town. The girlfriend was extremely fat and sat down heavily on me without apologies. It was a tight squeeze with four of us in the back. The German's friends were waiting for him on the other side, fortunately – but the car still felt packed until the next town where the customs officers got off.

The countryside was still fairly unattractive, not really like either Greece or Turkey – perhaps nearer in appearance to a desolate part of Albania as seen on some ITV documentary. None of the towns we passed through looked inviting. The Turk had to stop at Alexandropolis. You might expect a city with a name like that to look interesting, but it didn't. We waited outside the place where he worked. It was either a secondary school or a polytechnic – there was no sign by the gates. The few pupils around seemed to be in their late teens. The mathematics teacher told us he'd only be ten minutes, but it turned out to be nearer half an hour. The minute he was out of the car, Demetrios began to slag off the Turks, although he'd been chatting away pleasantly enough with one before. Some

Muslim girls with covered heads came out of the school and Demetrios shook his head in horror. He was a Christian, he explained, so he didn't like Muslims – they were turning up everywhere these days. Well they would, wouldn't they, if you spend your time shuttling across the border into a Muslim country anything up to thirty times in a week?

The Turk came back and we went on our way. I was dropped off at the bus station in Komotini, where I was able to get a bus to Kavala in time for a ferry to Thasos. The country became more lush. It was not a long journey, but the bus stopped at a *pâtisserie* and almost everyone succumbed. I'd only had fruit for lunch, eaten late in the bus terminal while I waited, so I plumped for some tiramisù and an iced coffee.

Kavala is a very attractive port. The bus enters the town under an old Roman viaduct. Most people pass through on their way to the popular island of Thasos, but there's an archaeological museum and other things to see. I looked at the museum briefly on my way back, but it had nothing on my particular speciality.

Thasos is a pleasant island. When you get off the *Flying Dolphin* from Kavala, you see it at its best. The main town, with its waterfront full of restaurants and fishing boats, is backed by hills and mountains. I found a hotel a street or two away from the port. The early evening air was fragrant and warm. My tiredness started to drop away. After I'd changed, I walked along the front to where paths began to lead up to the excavations. I followed the one that led to the Greek theatre. There would have been enough light for another hour, but its self-appointed guardian would not let me in. I got my explanation two days later.

When I got back down to the town, all the lights went out – another Greek strike. A handful of the tourist shops had their own generators and people clustered around them as it grew darker. I had trouble finding my hotel which was through a maze of side streets, none of which had any light at all. Inside, there was one solitary candle burning on the stairs. I placed it on the floor so that it was reflected in a large mirror and would just about light me along the passage to my room. Once inside, I knew I had a couple of torches – at least I'd come prepared for dark Pan caves.

Most of the restaurants were unlit and, unless they cooked by gas, the food would be cold. I decided to forgo dinner and settle for an early night in the dark. I woke up once in the middle of the night to find the lights had come back on.

I was out early and climbed to the acropolis after seeing the theatre. Thasos has two ancient theatres including the smaller one tucked away in the town and a ruined shrine of Dionysos, complete with a wild apricot tree and a long trailing vine, covered in tiny strawberry-flavoured black grapes, that hung right down from a neighbouring house till it touched the stones of the shrine. Thasians must once have had a devotion to the theatre that now has completely vanished. The ancient theatre, halfway up the acropolis, is still complete enough to be used. It can hold around three thousand people. As an experiment, a play in the original Ancient Greek was put on last year. After the first half-hour, Greeks started leaving fast, complaining they couldn't understand a word. Soon, the theatre was clear except for a stalwart few, who were probably English Classics professors.

There are several ways to the acropolis – you can bypass the theatre or continue up from it. There's also a more hidden way from the other side of the town via the Gate of Silenus. There's something strangely sinister and impressive about that route, but I've only followed it back twice, and not gone up that way.

The first area of the acropolis contains ruins of a medieval fortress. You can look out from there into the open country behind the town of Thasos. The lower sections of the ruins are so complete that you can go down steps and out through a gate to the next area, the temple of Athena, which is built in the flat area between two peaks. There's little left of the temple but massive foundations and outer walls. From here, the path reaches the last section. The bottom of this area is solid rock with a niche large enough to sit, or perhaps lie in, carved into it. You can get up into this via two toeholds in the marble.

Inside this area there are several niches for votive reliefs. It looked a possible site for the Pan shrine, but I could see nothing carved on it now. I went on up to the highest point of the acropolis, from which a narrow stair, mostly original, leads down into the town. There's a metal rail to hold. The steps are steep and exhausting to use. Ancient steps always seem steeper than modern ones. The worst I've experienced were those built for Samurai in the Castle of Matsumoto in Japan. But these were a close second, partly because they followed an erratic zigzag down, the way Greek mountain paths do. Eventually, they lead to a path running past old walls. Somewhere on the right there's an ancient inscription on the rock, sprawling upwards. Several ambiguous letters make it indecipherable, like some graffiti. The path then passes under an arch – the Gate of Silenus. An old guidebook at which I'd glanced in the town promised a demon figure on the left of this – but I looked in vain. The path joins the road again by a house with a pomegranate tree. Odhos Acropoleos is the name of the road, so obviously it's a recognised route to the acropolis.

There are a great many other ruins scattered through the town, including various buildings in the Agora and a number of shrines – Herakles has an extremely marshy one. Beside his there's one to Artemis.

I spent the rest of the day as any tourist would – trying to change money, swimming and eating. The banks of Thasos are particularly disobliging. It was Monday and most of them had decided therefore not to change tourists' money. Only the commercial bank showed willing and kept telling us all to return half an hour later when the rates had come in. It was twelve-thirty before they arrived. I wonder if foreign tourists in Britain experience the same look of hatred every time they go to change a traveller's cheque. We're giving a bank about two pounds in commission every time we do it, for a task that takes no more than a couple of minutes, so why are we their least-valued customers?

Thasos is full of bars owned or run by all nationalities from Australian to Dutch. It's easy to get British breakfasts or Irish coffees if those are what you want. There's even a British-style fish and chip shop. Lots of ex-pat proprietors rush out to greet you in your own language, or what they think is your own language.

That night I ate calamari and soon had a feline companion. The cats on Thasos all look adequately fed, at any rate, but that may change when the season's absolutely over. This one had a mouth like a barracuda. When I'd stopped giving her titbits, she put her wide mouth over half my hand and hung on to my wrist with her paws. I had to lift her whole body off the ground to detach her. It happened several times, until she realised that the people at the next table had food and were cat-lovers too.

The next morning I returned to the acropolis early. I stopped on the way to have a lemonade and talk to the man who kept the refreshment tent near the theatre. He turned out to be from Finland. Every year he spent his summer on Thasos sleeping in the woods. He had three cats. The two larger ones had a painted kennel with their names, SEPPO and RITZVA, on it. They were black with bibs and smiles marked in white. One smiled to the left, the other to the right – mirror images of each other. By day, their owner kept them on pieces of string tied to the bramble bushes. The brambles gave a bigger radius for them to run around. There was also a tiny tortoiseshell kitten. The kitten took a shine to me, climbed on my lap, then on my

244

shoulder and round to the back of my neck under my hair. When I stood up to go, she stayed put. I almost forgot and walked off with her.

Before I left, I was made to write in the Finn's visitors' book. He wasn't content with English – it had to be in Greek. I opted for something simple, thinking I couldn't get it wrong if I said: 'Thanks. Thasos is beautiful. I love your cats and the kitten.' Of course I couldn't remember the accents – they're harder to remember than in French, because their change is one of slight emphasis rather than in the actual vowel sound. The Finn decided I had it all wrong and corrected every word, then got me to write it out again. At that stage I realised that his Greek stank even worse than mine. He knew a lot more words, but had no sense of grammar or spelling. He wanted the subject of the sentence put in the accusative and the Greek for beautiful spelt wrongly. The moral is never learn a language from someone who's second or third language it is – however much he thinks he knows.

When I told him my name, the Finn shuddered. It's not the reaction I usually get. Apparently the last Fiona he'd met, ten years or so before, had been raped and murdered while hitch-hiking afterwards on the mainland. He'd seen it in the newspapers and remembered meeting her just before. He stopped people going into the theatre at night, or in the evening, he said, because it had been the scene of several rapes. Stupid women bathed topless on the beach, he said, then came up there with men . . . It didn't exactly sound like rape to me – but then maybe it disturbed his sleep.

The Finn was some use on the Pan shrine, even if his grammar was lousy. He pointed out to me exactly where it was on the skyline. When I got there, I realised I had been right in looking at the semicircular niche. It was between seven-thirty and eight now, and suddenly I saw the carving. The early sun picked it out near the middle. There had once been more, but now there was just a tiny, subtle picture of a horned Pan playing his syrinx. It's impossible to decipher it unless the light picks it out. It's much smaller than the one at St Photini's, but it reminded me of it strongly. You need to know what you are looking for to be able to see either of them. The weather of twenty-five centuries or so has worn both reliefs into something almost invisible – a rough surface on smoother rock. Only the carving of particular details like horns gives the viewer a point to start from in tracing out the whole figure.

I walked down into the town again. The museum has one of those pleasant gardens full of sculpture in front. There's a large Horus-like bird near the door that turns up on all the town postcards. All the exhibits are labelled in French and Greek – most of the excavations have been done by French archaeologists. There was nothing inside the museum from the shrine of Pan – I had hoped there would be and wondered what had happened to the plundered reliefs. There was an unlabelled head with the sort of melted features that sometimes belong to Pan – but it could as easily have been Silenus or a portrait. The labelling by another head which is definitely that of Silenus read: '*Le modèle vigoureux traduit fidèlement la nature démoniaque du personnage.*' It shows the thinking that must have defined the lost carving from the Gate of Silenus as a picture of a demon. Most representations of Silenus just look like sozzled, dirty old men – more pathetic than demoniac. But then, to early Catholic thinking, which may to some extent have continued in France, all gods were demons.

The coffee, catering for tourist tastes, had been vile on Thasos. I got my next fix courtesy of a free-sample stall in the middle of Kavala. I had just enough time for a look around the archaeological museum before catching a bus to Athens.

The mountainous parts of the route near Olympos look beautiful. Perhaps the only beauty left in Greece is in the mountains. Most of the other tracts of land are spoiled with industry or bad modern building. Just outside Athens the coach came to a halt. I could see smoke coming out of the back of a tanker in front of us. There was a warning about dangerous chemicals written on the back, but it didn't stop most of the Greeks on my bus getting out for a closer look. I just lay low waiting for the explosion. After half an hour or so, police let the container continue and the traffic started moving again. We were soon in Athens.

I waited by the bus stop in the terminal. It was a long while before anyone told me that the bus strike was still on. A small, weaselly taxi-man came and offered his services. I noticed soon that he hadn't put the meter on. He refused to, pretending that there was a set charge at night. Then I got all the offers of tours of the sights and so forth. He tried his best to take me to any hotel but the one I'd asked for, but I held my ground. We argued over money finally, of course. I paid him two thirds of what he asked – probably more than I'd have paid had the meter been on. Then we argued some more about the receipt. He pretended he had no forms, so I wrote one for him on paper and got him to sign it. When I got out, he threw my bag hard against the kerb to show his displeasure. I vowed to use taxis as little as possible from then on.

Next day, I made one last, futile search for the Parnes cave before attempting to get a charter flight in the early hours. I had come out on a cheap single to Istanbul, as my travel agent had assured me I'd be able to pick up a cheap flight back from Athens.

Athens airport must be the only one in the world that tells you it's illegal to sell charter flights from there. They would rather send out planes with a few empty seats than take a tourist's money, but encourage you to queue first for several hours before breaking the bad news. Several other travellers were caught in a similar position. We all swore never to return to Athens if we could possibly help it.

Athens airport also has no travel agents' offices and will not make any reductions on stand-by tickets. By the time you've elicited all this information you will probably settle for a full-price ticket rather than risk a ride back into town with a bent taxi-driver on the off chance of there being cheaper tickets for sale there. It's no wonder that Greeks often find the idea of visiting England prohibitively expensive, while we go out there in our millions on cheap return charter flights.

Syracuse

Fresh-water springs come up through bitter brine.

Tennyson: 'If I Were Loved'

*M*y next trip was to Sicily. I hoped that the caves of Pan would be easier to find outside Greece. Italy is better mapped and Italians love their archaeological sites in a way that the Greeks do not.

I landed at Catania on a sunny afternoon. The England I'd left behind was cold in late October. From the moment I left the airport, everything felt easier than it had been in Greece. There was a cheap bus into town. From there I caught a train to Syracuse – my first port of call.

Syracuse has no connections with Pan to my knowledge, but it is a town that worshipped the nymphs. I especially wanted a close look at the Nymphaeum in the high part of the town, Neapolis. I needed to come to some conclusions as to whether the worship of Pan was inseparable from that of the nymphs, or merely something that had been grafted on at a later date.

I've always liked Syracuse, even though the first time I went there I was utterly soaked in the heaviest rain I've experienced and my tights fell down as I walked up the road. If you can forgive a place that, then it proves it's really got something.

This time I was not just on a day trip, so I stayed in a hotel on the edge of the old town, Ortygia. Ortygia is bounded on either side by the sea. It's the most beautiful part of the town, architecturally, with street after street of Baroque buildings mixed with classical remains, and gracious squares linked by a maze of narrow streets lit by curly iron Art Nouveau lamps.

On previous visits I'd failed to get a close look at Arethusa's fountain. It's kept by the owner of an aquarium of tropical fish. He seems to open it for a very short morning only. Arethusa's lover was the river Alpheios, which runs through most of Arcadia. It's said that it pops up again in Syracuse, where Arethusa's spring mingles with the sea. The area in front of the spring is a large pond full of fish and ornamental ducks. The island in the middle of the pond is luxuriantly green with large clumps of rushes. Near the entrance gates there's a fanciful modern metal statue of Arethusa and her lover. From there, steps lead down to a couple of small cave-like apertures where the spring joins the pool.

I made my way slowly along to the fountain. The park benches near the sea were covered with colourful Sicilian graffiti. Newcomers would cap the last wit. If one writer had boasted about having had someone's mother, the next would claim he'd had the father as well. Somewhere, in amongst all of that, an English graffiti artist had summed up his nation's sexuality with: 'Freddie lives in our hearts'.

Shortly after nine, one of the gates of the fountain was left ajar, so I slipped in. When I got down to the pool, I heard someone locking the gate above. There was an old bike propped against the metal statue while the proprietor pottered inside the aquarium. Even if I couldn't raise him, the metal fence looked eminently climbable.

The ducks glared at my proffered bread as if it was poison. I sat and filled my bottle up with the spring water. Perhaps it was a potent love elixir allowing for the romantic story behind it. Not everyone would choose to drink it, though. Fishes have certainly peed in it – there were some in the little caves. It tasted reasonably good. I've always preferred the taste of fishes' pee to chlorine.

The proprietor reappeared soon and let me out. Some old men, watching at the other side of the pool, yelled loudly enough to raise him, even if my knocking on the door had done no good.

I took a brief look at the spring's outlet, down on the beach below. Spots like this where sweet water meets salt are often sacred. There were tiny slimy metal ladders leading down to a two-foot stretch of pebbles where the sea laps the foot of Ortygia. The water was full of tiny fish.

When I climbed to the road again, I found a dying fish in the gutter and threw it back into the sea. For a while, I thought it had been useless – the fish floated vertically, washed in by every tiny wave, but suddenly it righted itself and streamed out to sea against the current. I've always hated gratuitous deaths. Although I eat plenty of fish, I also rescue any I see dropped by careless anglers and return them to the waves.

All the bored old men in Ortygia were watching my activities with great interest. If they'd been Greeks, they'd have demanded an explanation, not to mention my life history.

From Ortygia I went back into the town. There's now a brand-new museum in the centre near the unlovely Sanctuary of the Madonna – a concrete ridged cone visible from most parts of the city. There are no objects from the Nymphaeum in the museum. There are many unusual ancient sculptures, but the layout is too trendy for my liking. A series of arrows directs you over carpeted ramps hemmed in by the odd perspex screen. You have to see everything in the order decided by the designers. If you turned contrary and backtracked, it was easy to collide with a perspex barrier in the low light. I went through their architectural obstacle course as quickly as I could, with little pleasure.

I stopped at the nearby catacombs briefly. Next door, in the Crypt of St Marcian, a wedding was taking place. Underground, in these catacombs, you get a real sense of how much

Syracuse is a city that operates on more than one level – a place of potentially endless discoveries. Water from yesterday's rain dripped in through various apertures above. All the visitors except myself were French.

I went on to the real area of my research, Neapolis. Near the ticket office of the main archaeological site, I was waylaid by a positive herd of jet-black cats who hang out by the ice-cream sellers, waiting for the odd dollop to fall. You can see them summing up toddlers with ice-cream cones – 'That one looks easy to mug.' 'Nah, don't bother, I don't like pistachio. Let's get the next one, he's got vanilla.' I found myself parting with large lumps of mozzarella that I'd intended to keep for a picnic lunch. Amongst the dozen or so black cats, there was one pure grey. He seemed to be the Godfather. The others paid him a sort of nervous deference. He came up and spagged me ungraciously for a larger share of the food.

Once inside the site, I climbed through the Greek theatre to the Nymphaeum. Here, in a site that has no known Pan connections, I could see the form that a nymph shrine took. The central arch concealed a torrential spring that filled a long oblong bath cut in the stone. A hidden outlet took the water away. A masochist could have an ice-cold jacuzzi in it. Perhaps that's precisely what ancient worshippers did. When I'd seen this area years before, one Easter, the stone had been dry. In October, the spring pounded out gallon after gallon and was noisy as a waterfall.

The spring tasted better than Arethusa's so I filled up a bottle from a torrent that was running down the wall outside the main bath. To the right, there were three arches in another cave. Beneath the arches, the stone floor had depressions like double beds. This second cave is not so clearly visible as the central one from the Greek theatre below. The niches for votive offerings are outside. There are a great many of these further along at the beginning of a street that marks the closed part of the excavations.

Before leaving, I went down to the best-known cave in Syracuse – the Ear of Dionysius in the quarries below. Like the Daveli cave below the real Pan cave on Penteli, it's sited in a quarry and has a marvellous echo. There's a legend that it was carved out to make the screams of the tyrant Dionysius's victims ring out, but its true purpose isn't known for certain.

When I left the site, I walked up the main road and veered round hoping to find the source of the spring that thunders down into the Nymphaeum. But all the roads took me too far away. It seems to be on private land. On the way up, I passed an ancient necropolis covered with tiny niches where portraits, tablets and inscriptions must once have recorded the occupants. I've always been puzzled by the Greek and Etruscan habit of elevating cemeteries. It can't be too good for the springs that rise on high ground. Perhaps the spring of the Nymphaeum had worse things in it than fishes' pee.

Back down in the town I took the train to Messina and caught a ferry for Reggio. A man on the boat was avidly devouring a book of modern poems. Although he wasn't trying to get off he showed me his favourite, which turned out to be about a seagull. That sort of thing wouldn't happen in Britain. I was able to boast to him that I had a family of five hungry seagulls coming for food to my kitchen roof.

It was hard to find a room in Reggio. All the hotels seemed to be full, or horrendously expensive. It's a holiday resort for many families from the south of Italy. The only hotel possible was near the station. I had hoped to get one near the museum. I had seen its collection years before and I knew that it contained intriguing exhibits connected with the worship of Pan.

Locri

In caves and grottoes, where the nymphs resort,
And keep with mountain Pan their sylvan court.

Ovid: *Metamorphoses*, translated by Croxall

*P*arts of the museum were closed for restoration. I worried till I found the objects I had come to see. Everything had been moved to different rooms, but they were still there and absolutely different from the terracottas out of the shrines in mainland Greece.

The objects all come from the Caruso grotto in Locri. There were seven pale terracotta plaques – two of which were hollow like some china figurines. Perhaps they were made this way to be stood on end, or to slot on to something. Perhaps they had only been hollowed out for a practical reason by the potter. Clay tends to trap their bubbles, which can cause explosions when an object is fired. That's the reason most statuettes are hollow. There were other items also beside the plaques – Silenuses, Eros, female figures and a mini cave-shaped shrine.

The plaques were the most interesting exhibits. I remembered their strangeness from years ago. The iconography was essentially the same as that on the much larger reliefs in Athens, but the way the imagery had been put together was entirely different. Each plaque showed three nymphs. Because they were lying flat, the impression was of three women in bed. On top of the coverlet, as it were, there was a Pan image. He

255

was standing or seated, in some cases playing his syrinx; in others, he was represented by his animal, the goat. One of the goats was shown on all fours as if it was walking into the picture. Only the front two legs and face had arrived. There had been a similar cut-off image on one of the reliefs in the Athens museum. One plaque contained no representation of Pan – it had his club on it instead. It was almost like a playing or tarot card – the Ace of Clubs or Wands.

The small figurines found with these were slightly more interesting than those I'd seen from Greek museums. They seemed to be individually sculpted rather than made in a mould. A woman reclined on a couch with one hand trailing in front. Silenus was also on a couch. Pan, being less decadent, had a rocky throne. There was also a miniature herm with Hermes' face above stubby arms and a straight pillar, adorned halfway down with an erect prick shown in relief. It looked like a cross or crucifix because of the short, abstract, squared-off arms.

I began to wonder about Locri. It's not thought important enough to be marked on the map these days. Would the sacred cave still be there? Was there a museum? There had obviously once been a theatre. There was a strange exhibit from it – a woman with a frog's head. Perhaps that had something to do with Aristophanes' play *The Frogs*.

The tourist office was shut for repairs so the station was my only hope of information about Locri. It was not on the timetables, but I was told that there was a local train going there in about two minutes. I had just enough time to buy a ticket and run like hell for the train.

It was siesta time when I reached Locri. There was only one shop open. I bought some mineral water and asked the way to the museum. It proved to be several miles away – a long dreary walk along the main road. There was every chance too that it would be shut. Some museums reopen for an hour or two in the late afternoon, but many small ones do not. I should be able to find out the times if I went there, at any rate.

Locri museum looks recently built. It's set on a pleasant stretch of land with classical ruins tucked away in the fields behind. One of the turnings nearby leads to the village of Caruso. Things began to look hopeful for finding the grotto. The museum itself wouldn't be open again for another couple of hours. Could I make the ruins last that long? At that moment a man came up and asked if I wanted to go for a coffee to pass the time. It seemed like a good idea. But once I'd accepted I found that it meant driving back into Locri. Still, my new-found friend was attractive and seemed harmless.

Giancarlo turned out to be a Ferrero Rocher chocolate salesman. I was offered some free samples, but chocolate was the last thing I wanted on a hot sticky day. I was promised a trip to the Caruso grotto in the morning. Giancarlo said he'd seen it and that it was beautiful – but I always take male promises of that kind with a large pinch of salt.

After coffee – at least that promise was genuine – we turned off the road on to a quiet spot by the beach and made love. To my annoyance, Giancarlo wanted to have his cock sucked endlessly. It's a practice that I and a great many other women find extremely boring. I knew that my jaws would be aching next day. I'm not by any standards a chocoholic, but I was beginning to wish I'd settled for a few of his free samples instead.

Eventually, Giancarlo turned to more mutually pleasurable forms of lovemaking. He had fully reclining seats in his car, as do all Italian red-blooded males. When we had sex I realised that, although I'd shed my clothes, my heavy walking boots were still on. Oh well, it didn't seem the right moment to start taking them off.

Giancarlo proved to be one of those men who has endless fucking stamina. I'm inclined to think he should be sent on a chocolate-selling tour of Greece as a sort of government-funded cultural exchange. Greek wives in the remoter tourist-free towns might be surprised to learn that fucking can last a good deal longer than two and a half minutes.

Giancarlo expected more of his favourite activity afterwards. I expressed doubts, saying that the spermicide from the condom might not taste too good. He happily explained that he only used the plain unspermicided sort. These are much harder to obtain in Britain than Italy, it would seem. Our attitudes to sexuality are less free. The British are open about not wanting (or liking) children, but not so open about the possible need to switch from ordinary sex to oral.

Giancarlo begged for condomless sex, telling me how good it felt. Of course, I agree that it feels much better. My generation was brought up on the Pill so we know the difference. But condomless sex with a stranger is out of the question since AIDS. I put this as tactfully as I could in Italian.

There'd have been a lot to be said for Giancarlo's fucking, but for one annoying trait. When he came he sweated from every single pore. When I felt the first drips on my thighs, I thought he'd been sneaky and taken the condom off. But no, it was still safely in place. Soon, the sweat sprang out and dripped on me from every direction. It was like the sweat you see leaping from people in cartoons. I felt as if I was lying under a dishcloth that was being wrung out repeatedly. Some of the sweat got in my eyes. Obviously, I should have been the sort of womanly woman who keeps them closed, but I've always preferred to see what's going on.

It was more than time to return to the museum. I huddled my crumpled sweaty clothes back on to my even sweatier body. Giancarlo dropped me off at the museum. We had arranged to meet at the station next day. It was Saturday and he wouldn't be working then. If he turned up, I had made a mental note to suggest some other sort of position – one in which I wouldn't be sweated on.

The museum opened late, so I wandered round the excavations. A couple of women were scraping away at the earth in a trench near the remains of old streets and temples. The grass amongst the ruins was liberally punctuated with purple mandrakes.

The museum proved to have more of the tiny Pan plaques. Most of these were broken – Reggio had taken the best ones. They were displayed upended on tiny perspex plinths and were labelled as reliefs with the heads of nymphs. There were also Silenuses from the nearby theatre. Silenus and the frog-faced lady of Reggio – ancient theatre was a lot more colourful than it is today.

The keepers of the museum didn't know exactly where the cave was. However, there was a rough map by the door of all the ruins and excavations in the area. The cave seemed to be near the actual village of Caruso. I decided to walk on up there. There was a hotel. If it wasn't too expensive, I could stay there rather than walking back to Locri.

The King Hotel proved to be the least expensive place to stay in Italy. Perhaps they haven't paid Mafia dues, but it was rated in a very low bracket although it had good clean rooms with bathrooms and absolutely nothing wrong with them. Having spent so little on my night's lodging, I thought I'd have dinner there as well. I had time first to wash all the sweat off – mine and his – and also to go for a walk before the light went. I followed the road on up the hill until it ran out. The villagers all looked curious but did not grill me for information. It's an ordinary little village – a scatter of houses amongst fields. Perhaps the singer Caruso's family originally came from the area. He himself was born in Naples.

I seemed to be the only person staying in the hotel that night. I was interested to see what dinner would be. Old travel books tend to scoff at the food of Calabria. Besides, I was a sudden guest. There would have been no time to get in anything special. I'd be eating whatever the family had. This turned out to be spaghetti followed by a plate of salamis, Parma ham, tiny whole mozzarellas and pickled vegetables. I'd opted for this eccentric but pleasant main course instead of the bistecca. Bistecca – an imitation of our steak – can be as tough as old boots. It's the one Italian dish I avoid like the plague. I finished with a plate of fruit – a small whole bunch of grapes and two large red apples. I managed to get through everything – I even almost finished the pottery jugful of local wine. Calabrian wines are a little like retsina but heavier in texture.

I watched Italian television and talked to the family after this. They were riveted by a game show where various contestants were making prats of themselves. Needless to say, the caricature-like primadonna with a clapped-out coloratura won. It wasn't for the beauty of her voice, but she had the talent of breaking glasses whenever she sang at them.

The owners of the hotel had two children, and a friend had dropped by. They were all slim, in spite of Mamma's spaghetti. I wondered how they had got the surname King. The father only owned up to one short trip to Oxford. Not being a Greek, I didn't enquire further. Instead, I told him a little about my researches and the book I was writing. He produced a huge map of Calabria. It was a much more detailed one than I've ever seen in this country. He recommended umpteen classical sites, not to mention Baroque churches – far more than I could see in a few days. As I looked at the map, I noticed a ring in the centre, drawn in ballpoint, marking a section of the hills as 'a sequestrated zone'. I asked him about this. The Mafia, he explained, had taken possession of a section of the land as a sort of stronghold – a place they could retreat to if necessary. It had obviously been marked as a sort of no-go area for local people. The ballpoint ring curved to a point only a few miles from Caruso. The area seemed to be off the main and even the small roads, accessible only by hilly footpaths. I was rather glad that I'd turned back that evening when the road ran out.

First thing in the morning I decided to look for the cave in case Giancarlo failed to keep his promise. I paid my dues and left my bag at the hotel. I was given vague directions and discouraged from seeing the cave because it was not beautiful – slightly different from Giancarlo's tale.

I took the first turning on the right opposite the hotel, then a first left. This took me up to a farmhouse. I asked the way of a girl who was setting off for school. She returned to ask her grandparents. She said the old people would be more likely to know. Her grandmother came out and I was directed back a little to a small path. I had passed it on the left as I came up. It seemed to peter out across the fields at the foot of a small hill. By the time I got to the hill the ground was squelching mud. It seemed to be the only wet soil left in Calabria. The view from the train had been completely arid. The fields here looked considerably more fertile than those in other parts. The path became tiny and bore round the hill. The ground was drier now and more walkable. It was then that I came on the series of caves that make up the sacred grotto. The first was a sharply cut canal into the rock. The feature of all these grottoes is that they are obviously man-made, unlike many Pan caves where a natural feature has been worked on and improved. The sides of the walls in these were peppered with chisel marks.

The first water-channel vanishes in a curve into the rock. I wondered if anyone has ever followed it into the hill to see how far it goes. It wouldn't be a pleasant task wading and stooping up the channel, but the rock is so sharply and cleanly cut that it would probably be a safe enough one. I wondered also how the original stone-masons managed to chisel away in that narrow space. The fertility of the land around was explained once I saw this water. The spring was led away via a modern addition of a hose-pipe and valve plumbed into the ancient stone channel.

There was something in this narrow, sharply cut water-channel that reminded me of a totally different site – one that had nothing to do with Pan. I once visited Chiusi. While I waited for a tour of the catacombs, the woman in the book-stall of the cathedral told me that Lars Porsenna's labyrinth had been found under the city. It is not yet open to the public, but will be eventually. The only sight I got of it that day was by putting my eye to a small hole in a wooden door down behind the cathedral. This was one of its many entrances. There was an electric light on a cable inside so I could see a narrow passage with a slight curve leading under the city away from my line of vision. I hadn't seen anything of the same shape until I saw the water-channel at Caruso. There is something about that particular architectural formation that is both profoundly annoying and curiosity-provoking. This stems, of course, from the fact that the eye of the observer is led into any passage, then stopped from seeing its end by that slight curve.

The next two caves had more pronounced chisel marks. The water in the other had left deposits on the walls. The second and third caves were dry. The floors were covered with several years' worth of autumn leaves. The second cave was like three rooms with more of the bed-like depressions I'd seen in Syracuse. The third cave had two entrances. Perhaps going in by one and leaving by another was part of the ritual. There were five bed-like depressions there, one of which was only child-size. One of the entrances was hard to get through until I moved away some of the silt of leaves and earth.

The whole set-up here seemed to be like that of Syracuse in miniature. Even allowing for the silt-up of the floor levels, worshippers would have only just enough room to stand, providing they were short. In Syracuse, the ceilings were higher and the water source more magnificent. That of Caruso was obviously not spacious enough for bathing. But it was good to see that it still gives fertility to the fields. I drank deeply and filled my bottle from the water before leaving Caruso.

As I had expected, Giancarlo did not make our appointment that morning at the station. Most probably he was married and his wife had noticed that he had sweated all over and guessed the rest. Perhaps, also, she had noticed the footprints on the inside of the roof of his car – the point where my feet had come to rest.

I planned my journey in a haphazard way. If I took the next train north and changed I could get to Crotona. I had heard that there was a good museum there. Perhaps there were more caves and more exhibits to be found in this little-known stretch of Calabria. I got talking to the man opposite me. He was carrying a ghetto-blaster in one hand and his bag in the other. There was a bottle of wine, swaddled in some of his clothes, lying across the top of the open hold-all. The wine, he explained, was a vintage one, many years old. He'd just been to a wine festival and was taking it back as a present. He poised it delicately in the luggage rack opposite. He was also going to Crotona and encouraged me in my vague idea of looking at the museum.

The countryside got more and more dried up as we travelled north. I began to realise that Locri was the only really green area in Calabria, late in the year. We were entering one of the ugliest areas of Italy. If the weather had not still been reasonably warm I'd have called it bleak. There didn't seem to be much industry, but the tiny hills reminded me of slag-heaps. I imagined that the wind outside would be full of dark grit.

Giovanni said that he was being met by a friend and that they would be able to give me a lift to the museum. He phoned his friend from the station. As we sat waiting and talking, I found out that it was his girlfriend who was to give us a lift. I began to feel very embarrassed, imagining just how she would love such a chore. When she arrived, she glared at me, just as much as I had expected she would, and we drove to the museum in sulky silence.

It was early afternoon and Crotona was dead as a dodo. Everything was shut and there were few cars on the street. When we reached the museum it was closed for the weekend. Giovanni banged on the door loudly and the curator emerged and agreed to open up. The three of us toured the museum. I thanked the curator for his kindness, explaining I'd come a long way. Soon there were other tourists looking round the museum. The curator didn't seem to mind working overtime. He was full of pride for the town's collection. Like most museums in small Italian towns, it's carefully put together and labelled. The Italians have great civic pride in their archaeological remains, unlike the Greeks. But, unfortunately, there were no Pan remains to justify my journey. The local cults seemed to have been more interested in Hera.

When I left the museum I had a long dusty walk back to the station, through the empty town. I was glad not to be offered a lift back. I'd soured the couple's relationship enough for one weekend.

Perhaps Crotona is attractive when the churches are open and when the wind drops and the dust is allayed by rain – but I shan't rush to return there. The only sight I enjoyed that day was the dried-up riverbed near the station where a herd of goats was engaged in polishing off whatever remained of the few scrubby plants they could find poking up through the stones.

From Crotona I zigzagged across the wilds of Calabria by train, making for the port at Villa San Giovanni. I hate going back on my tracks, although it would have been much simpler to return to Reggio. When I arrived, it was late at night and I found the only room I could, horribly near the sound and light of the all-night ferries. I was told that I had the best room in the hotel, which didn't say a lot for the others. The shutters were slightly rotten and the shower dripped all night. I had to make a fuss to get a towel. The man who brought it had a slight squint. Was there anything else he could do for me? he asked.

I woke up in the morning at eight. I wanted to pop out and get some breakfast before taking a ferry across to Messina. When I got downstairs, the doors of the hotel were locked fast. A fat man lay snoring on the sofa. I walked to and fro, tried the door and said good morning in Italian a few times – all to no avail. I banged on the front door a few times and my '*Buon giorno*' got louder, but the snoring was louder still. I drew the line at shaking a stranger. Eventually I found a cleaner upstairs, awake in a little room watching television with his family. I explained to him that I wanted to leave for Sicily.

In every other hotel at which I've stayed in Italy, people have been up bright and early. Here we were all locked in for the morning with an unrousable, snoring guard. The proprietor, I learned, had gone to his other establishment, taking all our passports. The man did not know when he would be back. I insisted he rang him, explaining that I had to go to Sicily.

I hate making a fuss, but I knew that if I only got to Messina by late morning, by the time I'd walked to the museum it would be closed for the rest of the day. The cleaner at least had a key to the front door. I was allowed out and told to go to a café nearby. The man in the café was not actually the manager, but he did have charge of the passports. He slightly undercharged me for the room, but I didn't let him know. It had been overpriced anyway. Besides, proprietors who leave you locked in should be ripped off.

I eventually got my ferry. Messina was up and ready for action on the other side. None of the men on the street were the slightest bit sleepy. In the mile or two to the museum I was propositioned seven times by kerb-crawlers. Three of them had their cocks out so that I should not be under any delusions as to the size and shape of their offers.

While I was waiting for the train to Cefalù, the next town of importance along the coast, I met Paolo. He was tall, dark and twenty-three. We were soon kissing. Single men usually have places of their own, but Paolo was still living with his grandmother, so we had nowhere to go. The station area of Messina is not stocked with parks or beaches for alfresco sex, so the locals use the trains. There's one section of the vast station where trains are parked for twenty-four hours before being brought back into operation – or so I was told. We found ourselves a train. This was the second time I was to have sex with my boots on in Italy. Paolo wanted me on top of him in his lap, although there would have been space for a more recumbent position. He would have been a good lover if he had not had one annoying habit. Thirty seconds into a bout of fucking he would tell me he felt sure that the condom had slipped or broken. That meant that he had to have cock and condom out of me to make sure. Every time he had it out, all was intact, so back it went in again. Perhaps Jiffy could take out an advert to the effect that they are so realistic that nine out of ten Sicilians don't know they're wearing one.

Apart from the *coitus interruptus*, I had another worry. Was the train as stationary as it seemed? Just as I'd done up the last of my buttons, the train gave a lurch as if it was being coupled on to an engine. We grabbed my bag and ran for the door. We were just off the last step as it slid away. So much for the twenty-four-hour parking lot. Paolo left me with a romantic memento – a machine photo that looked so unlike himself that I could have sworn it was someone else.

From the museum at Messina through Cefalù to Palermo I was to see nothing directly relevant to Pan. Though he was once worshipped along the Straits of Messina, there are no visible remains or objects related to his cults left – or they've not been discovered yet. The museum at Messina is an art gallery. The handful of antiquities are kept in a closed building used for restoration. The museum at Cefalù is mostly pictures again, though a few Silenuses have made it to the display cases. The huge collection of Sicilian and other antiquities at Palermo yielded nothing of Pan, nor did the smaller collection above a bank.

The wonderful, little-known puppet museum in Palermo was the only place to contain anything that reminded me of the cult of Pan. Most of the wooden puppets were of traditional form and had an eighteenth-century feel to their design – although many had been made as late as the beginning of this century. Amongst the displays of Sicilian wooden puppets there was one set up in a totally dark room. Most of the puppets are kept in semi-darkness to preserve the delicate colours of the backdrops and the old fabrics of their clothes. As you pass into a room, a sensor beam turns on the lights temporarily. But in one of the rooms the light is kept so low that the objects are barely visible. I could just make out the figures in the Garden of Alcina, the enchantress, an anti-heroine in the Charlemagne legends. In amongst the flying fish, a centaur, a pterodactyl-like dragon and a two-tailed serpent-woman, there were several devils. One in particular – a figure from the west of Sicily – had goat-like horns, fur round his bottom and strong curved thighs carved to look as hairy as an animal's. In folk art, at any rate, the semblance of Pan lived on.

Banyas

When I tread the verge of Jordan,
Bid my anxious fears subside.

William Williams of Pantycelyn:
Guide Me O Thou Great Jehovah

*B*ack in the spring, I had been on a press trip to Israel. At that stage I found out that Pan had made it to the edge of the Golan Heights and that there were remains to be seen. I returned to Israel in the autumn.

I had found on my first trip that El Al views with suspicion any woman travelling alone. I don't have the physical appearance of an Arab terrorist, but I could look pretty much like the gullible girlfriend of one, cajoled into carrying explosives inside a tape recorder.

I have a life theory that single women, like the lone magpie, are considered objects of ill omen everywhere. In many countries I'm pitied for having no father, no brother, no husband to protect me. In Greece, I'd been thought disgusting for not living with my mother, because of the Greek paranoia about living alone. Most Greeks have dreadfully extended families including aunts, uncles, cousins, grandparents and great-grandparents, all living within spying distance of each other. I try to point out to everyone I meet the joys of being on your own. You can get up when you like, eat what you like, go where you like and fuck whom you like.

El Al suspicions were eventually allayed when I gave them the phone number of a friend in Tel Aviv. While they telephoned him, I had a terrible thought. He has a good sense of humour. What if, for a joke, he were to say: 'Fiona Pitt-Kethley? Who's she?' I needn't have worried. Nobody jokes with El Al.

Once on the plane, I realised I was a lone pagan amongst a host of Christians on a Biblical package tour. Most of the Christian ladies had come with lesbian friends. A great many of them were embroiderers. The man next to me, an American pastor, seemed to be the leader of this flock. He spent part of the flight playing with a Biblical Concordance computer. The rest of the time he was reading a paperback on Antichrist. Every now and again he stopped, shook his head and ripped out a page. Presumably he was rendering the book into a fit state for his wife to read. My Plymouth Brethren grandfather had a similar habit of crossing out all the 'damns' in paperbacks so that the next reader should not be corrupted by them. I let the pastor and his wife leave first, so that I could retrieve the torn pages. Most of them turned out to contain paragraphs against nuclear weaponry. There was one page, also, that said that a great many men in the church were receiving psychiatric treatment.

When I reached Israel, my travel couldn't have been simpler. The maps were accurate, buses went everywhere and Israelis know and care about their archaeological sites. Next day I took a bus north to Qiryat-Shemona – the nearest main town to Banyas, the site where Pan was once worshipped. Banyas is a corruption of the earlier name 'Paneas'. 'P' is a letter that Arabs find difficult to cope with – it's as difficult as rolling an 'r' is to the English – not that I'd know about that problem with my Celtic blood.

For part of the way, I sat next to a girl soldier on the bus. She talked about life in the army – she liked it so much she'd even signed on for more. While army life makes all the men and women look enviably fit and muscular, I'm still disturbed by the sight of guns, guns and more guns when I'm in Israel. On my earlier visit I'd even seen teenage kids fooling around with them. I have yet to be convinced that visible weapons deter rather than create violence. It's a point I've argued with Israelis, but I've been unable to convince anyone. It's a point on which half of the human race will have to agree to differ from the other half.

Qiryat-Shemona is an ordinary modern town. There was nothing there for me to look at. By luck I caught the local Banyas bus which was just about to leave. Otherwise, I would probably have had to see the site next day. The country of the central north had been flat and dull. When the bus turned slightly to the east and headed towards the Golan Heights, everything became lush. Banyas is now an archaeological park – the Nahal Ramon Reserve.

I bought my ticket from the hut at the entrance and was handed a map of the area marked with minefields – it could only happen in Israel. I determined to look at my map at all times – luckily it bore a much more exact relation to what was before me than the average Greek map. I had two or three hours of light left before the site closed. There were one or two school parties around. I noted with relief that the minefields were well-covered with an impenetrable mass of foxgloves and brambles. There was little chance that the children would frolic on them, except in the blackberry season . . .

The Pan remains are a short walk from the main entrance. When I got there, I found that they were closed for archaeological restoration. A high fence, not to mention the possibility of further Israeli security, kept me from any attempts at illegal entry. There wasn't an archaeologist around to ask for admission, but I was close enough to photograph. All

271

the niches in the rock were clearly visible. There are five in all. At one time there were inscriptions to Echo, Pan and Galerius, his priest. Whether these are still visible I shall never know because of the closure of the area. Beside the niches there is the entrance to the cave-like shrine, with a broken pillar lying on the ground. There was once a spring inside the cave, but now it flows from its foot. Water collects inside. Rock doves and, occasionally, other birds like the rare Neumayer's rock nuthatch nest there. Probably, with the combination of water and birds, the archaeologists are up to the tops of their wellies in guano.

In spring the rock around the cave is carpeted with flowers. Most importantly the hyacinth squill grows here. Squill is mentioned in some of the stories about Pan's cult – it was used to beat his image.

The other sacred spot that this shrine most resembles is the Kastalian fountain. I had not seen it under the corrugated-iron sheeting, but a postcard showed me what it looked like. The warm, reddish coloration of the rock and the empty niches bear a definite similarity to the Banyas shrine.

The Kastalian's makeshift roof may, with a bit of luck, be off next season, but it seems unlikely that the cave at Banyas will be seen by the public for years to come. Archaeologists are digging in the temple area and a lot of the earth in front of the cave and its niches has been scraped away to reveal old foundations. In several years' time it will be well worth visiting, when all the finds have been recorded. Perhaps there will be a small on-site museum.

Eusebius, the third-century church historian, gives a few interesting details about the area in his time. He doesn't mention Pan, but refers, as any good Christian writer would, to 'the demon'. There was a sacrificial cult here of an unusual kind. Victims were thrown into the source of the Jordan on a certain feast day. The bodies sank and disappeared without trace, seemingly by a miracle. The cult was stopped when a Christian called Astyrius prayed publicly to his God to refute 'the demon'. A body reappeared on the surface, thus disillusioning the pagan worshippers. Nothing more in the way of a miracle has happened there since – or if it did, Christian historians made very sure they didn't record it. These days, the sole reminder of the former drownings is the proliferation of 'No Swimming' notices. It seems unlikely that these sacrifices took place near the cave, where the water is shallow. Presumably they were done by the waterfall. It would be quite natural for the body of an animal or human – whichever the sacrifice consisted of – to sink without trace in a pool like that.

The area has Christian as well as pagan connections – it is supposed to be the spot where Jesus gave the keys of heaven to St Peter. In the Bible, it's referred to as Caesarea Philippi. I had been offered Christian tours of the spot as it rates a biblical mention. I preferred to go alone.

Eusebius also connects the town that once existed here with the woman who was healed of 'an issue', as the Authorised Version puts it – a haemorrhage, presumably, perhaps one connected to cervical cancer. In Eusebius' time her house had become a place of pilgrimage. There were two bronze statues at its gates – one of her, one of Jesus. Caesarea Philippi was largely a Gentile city in those days, so there'd have been no objection to statuary – Judaism, like Islam, prefers to keep its art to abstracts and religious symbols.

Eusebius himself went to see the two statues. Jesus had a bronze cloak. There was a plant growing from the statue's stone pedestal, about Jesus' feet, and up to the hem of the cloak. Needless to say, it was picked by every pilgrim for use in miraculous cures. Eusebius doesn't specify what plant it was, but I'd like to imagine it was lady's mantle – something that would grow in a rocky crack quite well and has a suitable sort of name, not to mention an important role in herbal gynaecological medicine.

Not far above the cave there are other remains. A white building marks the traditional site of Elijah's grave. Here, as on the Greek mountain tops, Elijah is again associated with Pan. There are ruins beneath belonging to a palace built by Herod. Herod got everywhere. A great many of the small museums I've visited in several countries have had a 'Herod's Palace' section.

I turned back down the path and followed a marked route through the park to the famous waterfall of the area. The routes are signposted by the time taken to walk the distance rather than by miles or kilometres. At first I misread the 'h' standing for hour as a slightly misdrawn 'k'. It felt like the longest two kilometres of my life. The Jordan has one of its sources quite near the Pan shrine. This part of the river is known as the Nahal Hermon. The water was shallow there. I drank some and filled my water bottles with it. It was icy and good. A slightly unrealistic notice prohibited swimming there – only a frog or a fish could have managed it. The water was only about a foot deep. I followed the river round its tortuous bends.

The Jordan became a potent symbol for Christians after Christ was baptised by the slightly Pan-like figure of John the Baptist. Anyone who stays out in the wilderness, dressed in camel hair, and lives on a diet of locusts and wild honey has something of the roughness of Pan. Christ's baptism, and that of subsequent generations of Christians, is a kind of antidote to the darker sacrifices where the victim never reappeared. The Jordan seems to have lost all its pagan connections these days. It has become instead a river to be crossed before the soul reaches heaven. It is written of in this sense in scores of hymns.

At Banyas, the Nahal Hermon is little more than a rushing stream. Along the way, there are various small falls and rapids leading on to the big one. Various ruins are marked, including an old mill and a Crusader tower. Eventually, miles away from the site, it merges with another river to become the Jordan. The trees by the water have strong shapes. Their roots, where they are exposed, are washed clean from the earth. The planes, poplars and willows that are natural to the area were supplemented by the trees introduced by cultivators – figs, citruses, walnuts, eucalyptus, laurels, date palms and mulberries. The fig trees are in the greatest profusion. The gentle upward tilt of their branches provides an extreme but interesting contrast to the shape of a willow. You are conscious also here of all the different varieties of greens and grey-greens produced by trees. It's the sort of contrast we find more easily in a herb garden in Britain. The area reminded me strongly of one of the great Japanese gardens. The Japanese have a greater consciousness of the beauty and difference of colour and texture amongst trees than you find anywhere in Europe.

Banyas is, quite simply, one of the most beautiful places on earth. The air along the path is made cool by the shadow of the trees and the rushing water. At every turn and twist, you become conscious of new views. Part of the way along the course there's an old Roman bridge. The path is paved with timber here. The strong low span of the bridge reminded me of a cave. Its masonry is overgrown with fig trees and creepers. Inside, the stone is heavily encrusted with lime deposits from the water.

Eventually, after many climbs and dips, the path culminates amongst trees with a view of the waterfall. It's ten metres high and almost as noisy as bigger falls like Niagara. The water has tremendous force. It has already fallen one hundred and ninety metres from the ridges of hills at the foot of Mount Hermon and this gives it a driving power. The notices about not swimming are in abundance here.

There is another way out, or an entrance, depending on how you view things, a short walk away from the falls. From the observation point nearby you can see the distant remains of 'Nimrod's Fortress'. There is a long trail leading there, but more visitors opt for the shorter walk to the falls.

My biblical encyclopaedia tells me that 'Nimrod's Fortress' is mainly of Crusader origins but that there are Phoenician remains up there also. Presumably there's nothing quite old enough to belong to Nimrod himself. It's natural, though, that Pan and Nimrod should have remains within sight of each other. Nimrod, like Pan, was a 'mighty hunter'. Even the Babel myth reminds me of the panic caused in war by Pan and his worshippers – confusion created by noise. On Parnassus, not far from Pan's cave, the soldiers suddenly suffered a similar inability to understand each others' words.

There was a bus back to Qiryat-Shemona in half an hour or so. As I waited, a salesman offered me a lift. I had thought of staying at one of the kibbutzim nearby, but it was hardly necessary now. If I clocked up a few more museums in northern Israel I might use my time more usefully. I was able to get a bus from Qiryat-Shemona to Tiberias where I decided to spend that night. The next day was Friday – by the evening I would be into the Jewish Sabbath, a difficult time for travellers.

I did the usual tourist thing in Tiberias and ate St Peter's fish by the Sea of Galilee. Several wild cats moved in for the kill. The one I had at first taken for Siamese turned out to be an albino – totally white but for a brownish tip to the tail. His eyes were a brilliant flaming red. The waiter came up to watch the cats. 'I like that one,' he said about a tortoiseshell, 'but, oh no, I don't like that one.' He pointed to my red-eyed friend. I mentioned the cat's red eyes to him, but he simply did not believe the truth that was staring at him malevolently. 'Cats have green eyes,' he countered stupidly. Of course, a large percentage of men are colourblind. An even larger percentage – men and women both – believe only what they have been told, distrusting the evidence of their own senses.

While I sat finishing my meal, surrounded by cats, an Arab came up and started talking to me. I'd been warned against Arabs by almost every Israeli I'd met so far, so I was tempted to see what he had to offer. Since my early school days, I've been tempted to side with the outsider – 'them' not 'us'. The Arab was young and handsome and told me he had an interesting life story. It seemed like a good opportunity of finding out what the despised half of the population in Israel thinks. Thirty minutes later, the interesting life story had not emerged. His idea of a good story seemed to be a whinge or two about how he'd gone down in the world, from a medium-sized to a smaller business. His chat-up line, too, was atrocious. He was using the patronising 'we fancy each other' routine. It's a kind of mock sophistication, the admission of a status quo, that might pull someone in their teens, but not their thirties. These days, it's a line that makes me go off a man fast. I'm much more drawn to those who take a risk and admit that they want me.

Waled went fuckless to bed. I got back to my hostel minutes before it closed for the night. Tiberias seems to have little or no middle-range accommodation – nothing in between basic hostels and first-class hotels.

The next morning I went to visit old Tiberias. The hot springs, so loved by the Romans, are still popular with modern Israelis. If you want the cheap version of the spa treatment you can go and see Hammath Teberias. It's a tiny archaeological park containing impressive mosaics of the zodiac and Jewish emblems and the remnants of one of the original bath places. Everything is explained in the Ernest Lehmann Museum by the gate. One of the hot springs rises on the other side of the park and flows along a narrow channel. It's scalding hot at its source. The curator advised me that I could dip a towel in it and sponge myself when it had cooled off a little. My skin felt soft as silk wherever I'd managed to blanket-bath it under my clothes. I was about to leave the park but the stern curator sent me back for a better look: 'One hour is far too little to look at Hammath Teberias.'

I'm not Jewish, but I was so near the tomb of Rabbi Me'ir Ba'al Ha-nés that I thought I ought to go round the corner and take a look. I have a sort of superstitious interest in all places of pilgrimage – perhaps they contain stored residues of luck; luck is something we can all do with. The wise and witty Rabbi, nicknamed 'Me'ir' – the illuminator – had rescued his sister-in-law from the Romans and thus became known as a miracle-worker. There were about twenty men and women round the edge of the synagogue praying for their own personal miracles. I never miss an opportunity even when it's not my religion. Just as I once left a positive shopping list of requests in the Western Wall in Jerusalem, here I felt moved to ask for a miracle.

What suddenly seemed important to me was that I get some professional respect in my career. I've never been accorded much – and what I once had has been lost. It occurred to me at that point in time that I no longer had a newspaper I could offer ideas for articles to or write regularly for. I had formerly had such a relationship with the *Independent* and then the *Guardian*. Now, those relationships were finished, through no fault of my own. I was also having difficulties with presenting ideas for future books to publishers. I was mainly being offered commissions to write hack books, not those I really want to write. Again, that situation had once been better. Maybe the spirit of the Rabbi, or his religion, will work that miracle for me, maybe not. Maybe things will improve in the due course of time anyway, but maybe not . . .

At the foot of the steps to the synagogue I met an old Rabbi. He was totally globular in shape, like a football with arms. He welcomed me courteously to the site, shook hands and made me promise to return to his office afterwards to hear the place's history.

I took off my head scarf and returned to the Rabbi's office. The minute's lecture contained what I already knew and what was clearly printed in the give-away leaflet from the tourist office. Then, a side door was opened leading on to a boxroom with a rickety fold-away single bed with a foam mattress in a red floral stretch cover. The Rabbi had already established that I was unmarried, without ties and children, so he made his offer, spreading his arms wide, then gesturing to the bed: 'Would you like one minute of loving?' Instead, I gave him the parting kiss he asked for. He deserved that for his truthfulness and recognition of his own limitations. How many older men (or Greeks) would be as honest?

The End of my Journey

My appetite had been whetted by the blanket bath amongst the ruins and I determined to try the spa opposite. It was my birthday the next day, so I decided to treat myself to a swim and a massage. Apart from swimming in the sea at Tel Aviv, all my other attempts had been foiled. The waters at Banyas were labelled as dangerous as were those of the Sea of Galilee. I had just dipped my feet in the edges of the lake. The water had a nasty slimy feel.

The modern spa at Tiberias has two swimming-pools of mineral water, hot as the average bath. I didn't read the small print and get out after a short soak but swam round and round for an hour, occasionally taking my turn at the jets around the edge that bubbled forcibly like a jacuzzi. I loved watching everyone else doing the same. Most people turned their backs to them, or eased a stiff neck down on to one – others took the full force against their stomachs. Old or young, fat or slim, male or female, everyone at a jet soon assumed the wanton, abandoned expression of a cat who is having exactly the right spot on his back tickled. You'd learn a lot about a lover taking him or her to those baths.

The water here is not by any normal standards drinkable – you're best to take it on the body alone. I had tried a drop from a tap on a building across the road. It had been labelled as drinkable spa water by some joker or sadist. I've drunk many other spa waters in my time, so I can stand anything from an eggy sulphur flavour to iron, but these were something else. The water came out cloudy and tasted like a strong cocktail of salt and washing soda. I had to spit it out immediately.

The massage at the spa was not the best I've had – while the technique on various acupressure points on my face was good, that on the body was slightly unnerving. Suddenly, without warning, there'd be a slap and a pummel on a plump area of my body like the thighs. It was particularly worrying when I was on my face and couldn't see when the next blow was coming. I wondered if the masseuse had been trained by El Al.

The Sabbath was approaching fast, so I took the bus to Haifa. The bus driver was one of the best-looking men I've seen. I felt he was wasted on that shuttle service and wished he'd had time to offer me more than the randy Rabbi. It's odd the way we can admire and remember a face and body we see only once, in passing. Nothing is said and the person is probably never aware of the impression they've made. They may even be locked in a relationship where they've been made to lose all belief in their looks and power to attract. I sometimes wonder if life would be easier and happier if we could all spill our erotic thoughts to strangers as soon as they came into our heads.

From Haifa I caught the connection to Akko. Haifa had looked unattractive from the bus and I had no urge to stay there. I could return in the morning to see the museum. The remains at Akko are half Crusader, half Napoleonic. Neither period is really old enough for my tastes – but it's a handsome enough town in the old parts. It's famous for its underground Crusader remains – a large banqueting hall and a maze of rooms beneath the old town. The modern shops in the streets above have a curiously theatrical quality to their wares. The fashions could almost be out of a stage version of a Jacobean tragedy – sombre, full-length silks and velvets with sweeping skirts, beaded bodices and stand-up ruff-like collars.

I stayed in a basic hostel run by Arabs in the old part of

town. When I'd seen the Crusader remains I intended to head out of town. There would be a few buses on the Sabbath. Haifa has a large contingent of irreligious Communist Jews, so shuttle bus services run to its outskirts from the neighbouring towns.

While I waited for the Crusader vaults to open I bought some postcards. The Christian bookshop was happy to do business on the Sabbath. There were postcards of Banyas here unavailable in Banyas itself. I also bought a picture of copulating Caspian terns – quite what a Christian bookshop was doing selling it, I shall never know.

There had been a strong wind and a wild sea at Akko, but the storm really hit in Haifa. We stopped on its outskirts – the main bus station was closed. I worked out a route to the museum. It's a newly established collection of Greek, Roman and other remains, mixed in with art exhibitions and ethnic galleries of costumes, embroideries and jewellery from various Jewish cultures round the world.

I was slightly damp from the rain by the time I reached the museum. A lot of other people had chosen to shelter there too. It had been a long shot, but I was surprised to find that the collection upstairs did contain figures of Pan. According to the labels there were several. I only recognised one figure as Pan, though. The other couple to my mind were flute-players or satyrs – some of the appropriate features were missing. The one definite Pan was well worth a walk through the rain. He was different from any image I'd seen elsewhere. Here was a couch potato of a Pan. His athletic, mountain-climbing goats' legs were stretched supine as he reclined in the position of a Roman at a banquet. He was not even intending to play for his supper. His pipes were missing, as was his hunting club. He was the laziest-looking Pan I've ever seen. The stomach muscles had long given way and the face was monkey-like apart from the horns. Only those horns and the hair and hoofs proved his identity. In every other respect, the small terracotta was that of a blasé Roman intent on wining and dining in a conquered land. Unfortunately the museum did not reveal where the image had come from. I would suppose that it must have been a votive offering from Banyas, unless there are other caves of Pan in Israel that have not yet seen the light of day.

Before leaving, I spotted an irresistible figure of an ancient goddess, thousands of years old. Unlike the Turkish fertility ones, she was not fat all over. The design was as clever as a modern logo. Her hips were huge and rounded, the legs sloping into the floor. The rest of the body was narrow and upright, the arms meeting in a tiny ridge high up, a tiny edge around the head to represent hair. The neck and shoulders were of equal width. The figure was recognisable as a woman and at the same time looked like an erect cock and testicles – a wise ancient statement of the sameness of the human race.

The reclining sybaritic Pan was my birthday surprise of the day. Exactly a year before I'd had a private tour of the Sheila-na-Gigs – ancient stone images of wanking women – in Dublin Museum. It was just coincidence, of course, but from now on I've decided that every birthday shall be celebrated by viewing weird and wonderful images – the more sexual they are, the better.

The rest of my birthday went from bad to worse. Back on the streets of Haifa, the rain had become more torrential than most of that I've experienced in this country. The side streets had rivers pouring down them – they didn't seem to be equipped with regular gratings. I hadn't brought an umbrella. My thick silk tweed jacket will keep out a small amount of rain, as will a silk headscarf, but not this kind of primeval deluge.

One of the worst things about a Jewish Sabbath is that there's nowhere to shelter. Every single shop and café was barred and bolted. I determined to walk to the outskirts and hitch a lift to one of the other sites I wanted to see – Megiddo

284

and Caesarea – the one on the coast. Archaeological sites were open, even if nothing else was. I was utterly soaked as I headed past the town hall. I didn't quite realise it was the town hall – it almost looked like a welcoming museum from the opposite side of the road. A man at the door beckoned me across and I went inside. He turned out to be a Jew who'd converted to Christianity – hence his willingness to caretake on the Sabbath. I was invited to have a coffee and dry out in front of his one-bar electric fire.

It was a long, slow, steamy job. I went and changed my shirt in the Ladies. My skirt steamed dry quickly, but the jacket was another matter. I held it in front of the little fire drying it off seam by seam. It was lunchtime, so I was offered some of the caretaker's snack. He had an electric ring which he'd cooked the potatoes on. He mashed these, peppered them and filled pittas for both of us. Being frozen, wet and greedy, I partook of everything. The only snag to his kindness was the fact that he felt moved to make the odd ineffectual clutch or pinch at my arms and shoulders. On a dry day it would have been enough to make me leave the place quickly. In that torrential weather I was determined to stay there until I was dry. It was a process that took hours. When every last damp seam in my jacket had steamed to a semblance of dryness, I decided to sit it out for another hour or so. It was still raining heavily. About an hour before the Sabbath finished, I left and walked to the bus station. At six o'clock, the bus timetables suddenly appeared on the blank screens as if by magic. Even on the way there, I'd seen people coming out, shops beginning to open, and fruit and vegetables being put outside to tempt the customers in. But it was dark now and I was determined to move on.

I reached Caesarea that evening. I was freshly drenched. The hotel offered me the use of a hairdryer as soon as they saw me. My hair had separated into a series of dripping rats' tails.

The serious rain had abated by the next morning. There was

just a howling wind with the odd spray of rain in it. I was out of Pan's territory now. I had time to see the Roman remains, which look very much like an empty opera lot set against a furious sea. There are some ruins on the beach and even under the waves, but on a day like that it was difficult to get close. I set my face against the wind and made it down to the lower gate of the excavations. The sea had come inside, filling some trenches near the foundations. Outside I could just see fallen pillars through my half-closed eyes, and waves flying thirty feet in the air against a tumble of rocks. I walked through the old Roman theatre. It's a beautiful site – but probably best seen in summer, when you could go down to the beach afterwards and snorkel amongst the remains.

I was offered a lift into Hadera, where I got a bus out to Megiddo. I wanted to see something really ancient by way of contrast. The bus stops by a crossroads, leaving a bleak walk of a kilometre or two through windswept, dusty land. Brochures bill Megiddo as set in the 'lush Jezreel Valley' but, on a windy day, I was only conscious of its exposed, desolate feeling. Megiddo's ruins date back to twenty-seven centuries BC in their earliest part and legend has it that the city will figure again in the last war at the end of the world – Armageddon. It has been uninhibited for two thousand four hundred years, but was the scene of a major battle under Napoleon.

The ruins of Megiddo contain evidence of twenty-five cities. It only became an Israelite city in the time of Solomon. Its whole feeling therefore is of an alien earlier culture. There are biblical connections – you can see the remains of King Ahab's stables and a corn silo from the time of Jeroboam. The most impressive part of the site is the water tunnel from the time of Ahab – the ninth century BC. None of the elderly Christians touring the place went down it the day I was there. Like venturing into a pyramid it involves going up and down a devil of a lot of steps. The passage is three metres high and four hundred metres long from the bottom of the shaft. It leads to the site of a spring outside the city. Cables and light bulbs have been installed as well as a suspended wooden flooring. Yet few choose to visit its dank, dark, ancient emptiness.

When I looked at the ruins of Megiddo I remembered one of the students I'd met at the British School. He was on a brief visit to Athens from Jerusalem. When I told him about my Pan studies he'd joked: 'That's too modern for me. I'm studying the Phoenicians!' Though as yet no remains or mentions of Pan go back much further than twenty-five centuries, I am convinced that there must have been something similar in older cultures – even in the ancient, hardly known times of the earliest settlements at Megiddo. We have need of a nature spirit – something accessible, unlike the jealous God of the Israelites. Just as many ancient civilisations produced gods whose shape revealed partly animal origins, a great many of us need a god who can empathise with the animal state. For those of us who love animals at least as much as humans (if not more), the fact that they are ignored for the most part in the Jewish and Christian systems is a grave defect in those religions.

I returned that evening to Tel Aviv. I completed my researches on the red-light district with the help of a writer friend, Zygmunt Frankel. When it was time to leave, Israeli security didn't seem to want to let me go. At Heathrow I'd suffered three-quarters of an hour of questioning with two officers. This time it was a full hour with five, one after the other.

In the early stages of the interrogation I had to pull out maps and leaflets to show where I'd been. Then came the receipts and museum tickets. Most Israeli site tickets come in the shape of a very faintly printed slip from a cash-till. Just when I needed it most, the one from Banyas had gone missing. The officers also showed surprise I hadn't brought my publishing contract with me, not to mention the half of the book I'd written already. I asked them what was the point of bringing forty thousand words on Greek travel to Israel, when I wanted to travel light in order to walk the odd few miles, where necessary, with my pack. Where were my books on Pan at Banyas, they asked. I told them that there weren't any written, yet. All that could be found was a little information in German and English encyclopaedias of the last century and their own tourist leaflets. I produced photocopies of the encyclopaedia material, which referred to Banyas by its old name, Caesarea Philippi – more cause for suspicion.

In the end it was down to more explanations of the god Pan – stuff about goats' legs and horns – and all of it five times. I could tell by the stony faces in front of me that it was all being written off as a cock-and-bull story.

'So how does this fit into the Hebrew mythology?' the last man asked.

'It doesn't,' I said. 'The worship was brought in with the Romans.' Any modern Israeli with even the faintest interest in national history still hates the Romans, because of all the crucifixions. On my first visit to Israel I had argued with a guide in Masada. He had shown us a Roman pool with no outlet hole, claiming that the Romans were filthy devils who never changed their bath water and spread venereal diseases. I argued forcibly that there were no venereal diseases to spread in those days – lucky old Romans.

To get the topic away from those dreadful Romans I told the El Al officer in front of me that the Pan site was very old, so it had probably been used in ancient times for the worship of Baal. I could see by the Old Testament prophet glare he gave me that mentioning Baal had been a bad mistake.

For a people that have a long history of monotheism, the Jews – the ancient ones at least – went in for an awful lot of idol worship. The Old Testament is full of it. Any chance and they were off dancing round golden calves, and so on, until some

288

prophet pulled them back into line. There are a few things about their religion that make me feel that Pan might not have been such a stranger to them. There's the strange sacrifice of a couple of he-goats on the Day of Atonement. The goat that drew the short straw, as it were, was killed. The other had to bear the sins of the people out into the wilderness. Some say he was consecrated to Azazel, the nearest thing in Judaism to the Christian Devil. In Israel, these goats were sent out into the barren land that belonged to Typhon. Pan had been instrumental in the trapping of that monster in Greek mythology. The scapegoat is a figure analogous to Pan in his nomadic role – Pan's territory is essentially a wilderness where he moves alone and nobody can pin him down. Personally, I'd like to think that the scapegoats were adopted by kindly Bedouins and became stud animals to herds of nannies.

Apart from the scapegoat, there seems to be a curious parallel between several Jewish heroes and Pan. Moses was sometimes compared because a few of the statues of him had horns. I consider this purely a superficial resemblance – the horns came about through a translator's mistake. Moses came down the mountain with rays of light, a glow, or aura – but the Vulgate used a wrong translation of the Hebrew word. The two heroes I see as having a strong overlap with Pan in their functions are Gideon and David.

When we first meet Gideon, he is making the sort of sacrifice that the Greeks made to nymphs – a kid and barley. The angel is standing under an oak – a tree that's significant on Lykaion and elsewhere. The angel burns the offering in the manner of a lightning-strike. From then on several of Gideon's actions have some echo in the tales told of Pan. He uses a fleece prophetic-ally. While this is not exactly like Pan's seduction of the moon, it resembles more closely the procuring of oracular dreams in the Amphiareon in a place near Pan's altar. Gideon then becomes like the military Pan – he obtains his victory by creating panic using three companies blowing trumpets, breaking their pitchers and carrying lamps – not a method recommended by most military tacticians. With only three hundred men he succeeds in killing one hundred and twenty thousand. Afterwards, the men of Succoth refuse to help his army, so he beats them, like the whip-bearing son of Kronos. He uses 'thorns of the wilderness and briers'.

Some of Gideon's fighting tactics mirrored his predecessor Joshua's. Joshua had flattened a city wall with the sound of rams' horns. I have always found him one of the most seriously dislikeable Old Testament heroes. His book is one long catalogue of bloodshed. Although Gideon does his fair share of that, his doings have more of the quality of an eccentric avenger of wrongs in a Western. He retains his likeability. He shows more humanity and sexuality with his quantity of wives and his seventy sons. Although Joshua seems less of a possible Pan figure, I could see some relation between him and the sinister side of Lykaian Zeus. The oddest tale recorded of him concerns the stopping of the sun and the moon for a day. In old age, he appointed cities of sanctuary for those guilty of accidental manslaughter. Both these stories are reminiscent of the sacred enclosure, or *abaton*, on Lykaion, with its lack of shadows and the protection given to animals, or the stoning of victims. Several stories about him concern the moving of stones. Killer hailstones rain down on his enemies. On the day when the sun stood still he had five kings hanged on trees then sealed into a cave.

I see stronger connections between David and Pan. David is the shepherd-king. He turns his hunting abilities to warfare. As Pan fought against the Titans, he matches himself against a giant. He is also a prophet, musician and dancer. His music has the power to cure Saul. David is described as 'ruddy and of a fair countenance'. Though Pan was never fair, his images always bore reddened cheeks. When Saul is out to kill David, his wife, Michal, deceives Saul by using an image and a bolster of goats' hair to represent her husband. One of his victories has a strange element. He smites the Philistines when he hears 'the sound of a gong in the tops of the mulberry trees'. It is after this victory that we see him dancing as a sort of religious rite. It is interesting also, that David in his role as poet, or psalm-writer, coined the one phrase in the Bible that could well refer to Pan – 'the destruction that wasteth at noon-day'.

Even if all this had occurred to me while I was questioned by the men and women from El Al, I would not have spoken of these connections. Monotheists seldom admit the polytheism that lurks beneath their ordered world, any more than those who approve of monogamy are prepared to own up to affairs.

When all the false gods had been disposed of, the officers came to their final questions. Why had my Israeli friend not driven me to the airport? Now the last thing you do to friends, if you want to keep them, is make them drive you to an airport very early in the morning when there's a perfectly good taxi-service. At that moment, one of the women noticed that the envelope I was holding with Zyggy's address on it had something inside.

'So what do you have in here?' she asked in her most inscrutable tones, taking it from me. Out popped the great British weapon – a herbal tea bag.

Eventually, I made it to the check-in desk. The man in front of me was shouting in hysterical tones: 'I must have a seat by the emergency exit!' When he had got the promise of one, he calmed down and added in quiet tones, 'And I'd like ones nearby for my wife and daughter.' Back on board, it was mostly the same Christians again. The embroidery was nearly finished.

Israelis tell me that all the questioning procedures mean that they feel very safe aboard. Personally, I don't feel all that sure that I won't be flying with some other company next time round. Doesn't El Al realise that terrorists never strike in the same fashion twice? Lone women are not to be feared any longer. Next time it'll be a quiet old couple on a Christian package tour. Don't they know that embroidery, like the knitting of the French Revolution *tricoteuses*, can be used as a code to contain a hit list of everyone from the premier down, not to mention military targets?

Afterword

*A*part from my first trip, I completed most of my researches on Pan in the Chinese Year of the Goat.

Early in that year, while recording a video diary of my life – one that was never shown – I had the bizarre experience of spending time in a pen full of nannies under the baleful eye of a camcorder. The farmer's wife had assured me that the animals – her pride and joy – were extremely shy. 'Shy' in goat terms means that they swoon all over you, suck your fingers, butt your backside, undo your flies with their teeth and try to eat your handbag. Much as I like goats, I'm not sure that I could cope with one that was extrovert.

Just after the end of the Year of the Goat, I appeared on *The Naked Chat Show* on television. It was on St Valentine's day – a time of the year that coincides with the old Roman Lupercalia, a festival in honour of the god Faunus, more or less the same as Pan. Nakedness, or at best, a quick cover-up in the shape of a goatskin, was a feature of his worship.

While the time for researching my book may have been astrologically right and the omens in the shape of coincidences good, I was beset with other difficulties. I'm used to lucky finds – serendipity – but this time round everything conspired to block my way. The actual position of many sites had been lost to human knowledge. Where they were known, I had to deal with inaccurate maps and sets of instructions included in guidebooks by editors who'd never actually been to the places.

There is no such thing as a good Greek map, or even a good map of Greece produced by any other country. I found myself using several at once in order to obtain information about any area. The Michelin map I took with me was okay on the main routes but left out small roads and small places. The Greek one I bought at the airport had all the names of villages but was drawn on the principle that taking half the wiggles out of the roads made things look neater. Worse still, its maker had the annoying and extraordinary habit of drawing a straight line between two towns, and pretending that this was the road. Several kilometres of main road followed by, a few kilometres along, a turning would be shown not by two lines but by one – the third side of the triangle. Consequently, every distance on that map had to be gravely mistrusted.

I backed up these two general maps by a variety of photocopies of plans from guide books and sections of military or admiralty maps. The Greek military maps were about the best I found, being on a very large scale, though even they did not mark all the roads. They also ignored most of the minor archaeological sites. In fact, they seemed to leave out all but the most important ones on principle. Caves of Pan did make it on to these maps, though. Caves are probably of potential use as shelters or stores to the military.

Where a mountain map was needed, the Alpine Club ones were reasonably good – based on the military ones, but enhanced by a set of instructions and hints for possible walks. There was one strange mystery, though. All the copies of the maps of Parnes sold in Stanfords were minus their instructions. You could see the edge where they'd been torn off. The shop checked the whole pile for me. Needless to say, that map, complete or otherwise, was unobtainable in Greece.

When I showed any map to a Greek, it was surveyed with the utmost interest. I believe that map-reading can't be a subject covered in Greek schools. Although local people always wanted to look at my maps to see how their area was delineated, they plainly had no idea which way up to hold them or how to interpret anything. Any distance over a hundred metres was always unwalkable and '*Para polu makria!*' (too far).

To aid my travels I bought a compass. It pointed due south – well, a Greek one would, wouldn't it? Next visit I took an English compass with me which promptly fell to bits on its first day out. My third compass, a Japanese one, continues to serve me admirably.

Apart from a handful of Greek shepherds, almost nobody walks anywhere in Greece these days. Consequently all knowledge of the side roads and footpaths is being lost fast. The shepherds will know one area intimately, but it's usually only the side of a mountain. How that connects with the outside world is a very different matter. But shepherds and goatherds are still the best bet for asking the way. While shepherds probably won't know much about archaeology, they may well be able to direct you to a useful path – that is, if you can catch up with them. Often they move so fast across a high level that you've lost the only person you've seen in hours by the time you get to the place where they were. If you do catch one, don't be deterred by his or her loud demonic whoops. All the ones I met were perfectly sane and courteous. The Greek shepherd keeps goats in order by yells that sound like someone declining the definite article in ancient Greek: 'Hoy, Hay, Ta.'

Shepherds are usually accompanied by one or more dogs, sometimes a whole gang. Some walkers are nervous of these dogs. I met one couple who took a tiny electric stun device with them for their mountain walks. But there's no need to be afraid. If the shepherd is there, his dogs will probably fawn on you. If he isn't, after some token barking, the minute you make a friendly gesture, the dogs will faint with fear.

Some of the places I was to visit were so wild that I didn't see even a shepherd for hours. I had to carry quantities of water and some food, because I might not see a shop for two days and I couldn't rely on finding a spring in that time, either.

295

To add to my difficulties there were the Greek strikes. The general bus strike which lasted for months, and may still be lasting for all I know, made the journey to the Parnes cave impossible in the end. Perhaps other minor strikes of the postal service were responsible for my not getting answers to the queries sent to the National Archaeological Museum in Athens.

As I was nearing the end of writing my second draft, other things took place. Some people would think of them as paranormal manifestations. When I added in a few paragraphs about the sacrifices at Banyas, 666 appeared suddenly on my computer screen. The computer broke down after that – it is still in for repair. I have written a very stern letter to Epson. On the same day as the 666 episode, I took a print-out of the last few chapters of the first version to my mother. She likes to act as a sort of unpaid proof-reader. As I cycled, a sudden blast of wind took the manuscript out of the half-zipped pannier. Most of it ended up in Hastings boating lake. I fished sheet after sheet out of the water, but twenty pages sank without trace like the victims at Banyas. The rest I was able to dry out until it was readable. At that stage, I began to feel very nervous about losing the text of those chapters. It was all on a disk that couldn't be read while my computer was in for repair, and now parts of the only print-out were missing. I decided to hire another computer. It worked well for a day and then messages started to appear – not 666 this time, but refusals to recognise its own hard disk, let alone the existence of my floppy ones. The first computer remained beyond repair, so I bought a second-hand one in order to finish the book.

Were all these omens signs of the diabolical nature of Pan, or were they merely coincidences? Had the nosy cat who visits me typed 666? Normally I wouldn't put it past her, but that day I'm sure she was locked out.

I contrasted my feelings of confusion when the computers misbehaved and the manuscript blew away with the sensation of absolute calm I experienced while searching for the actual sites and in many other areas of my life at the time. His worshippers, Christians and scholars have placed as wide a gamut of interpretations on Pan himself.

If you want a semi-human god to pray to, Pan has many roles. In his earliest Arcadian form, Pan was above all a shepherd-god. The earliest inscriptions make his name *Paon* – the pasturer. The later version of his name means 'everything'. That's not surprising, considering the diversity of his roles.

The Greek anthology dedications reveal him to be a god that could be prayed to for hunting, shooting and fishing – an alternative to Artemis if her celibacy is too perfect a role model for you. Depictions of Pan often include a club of the sort used as a throwing-stick to kill hares. He is also sometimes accompanied by dogs. He trained and gave some to Artemis. Presumably that makes him a sort of Barbara Woodhouse among gods. If your sheepdog is not up to scratch, pray to Pan.

Pan is a god of fishermen. He discovered the conch shell and used it as one of his instruments of panic. He also made use of fish as bait to catch Typhon, or, according to other versions, a net and the noise of his syrinx. Ancient fisherman used a strange method of catching bream that must have once been part of a rite. According to Oppian, they dressed in goatskins and wore horns, then threw goat flesh, roast meats and barley meal into the water. There was supposed to be an affinity between bream and goats. Fishermen had to catch the whole shoal – otherwise, any fish that escaped would warn their kind of the trick and spoil future catches. Bream, like Pan, had the reputation of also being unlucky in love.

A proportion of garden produce and crops could be dedicated to him, which shows an overlap in his role with that of Demeter. Pan's relations with Demeter show him to be a sort of intermediary with the other gods. He it was who found her and persuaded her to come back from the depths of a cave in the Neda Gorge when she'd left the surface of the earth and taken all its fertility with her. Pan was also the god of wild, uncultivated nature – the woods and the mountains. Bees were also associated with Pan. Bees turn up in various legends, pagan and Christian. Bee-girls appear in Greek myths. Bees have also been known to create holy architecture for humans. The earliest shrine at Delphi was their work – a creation of wax and feathers – as were various artefacts such as a chapel of wax in medieval Christian legend.

Pan is also a god of athletes. As some of Greece's most ancient games were run in his honour on Mount Lykaion, it's natural that he should appear to Greece's greatest runner, Pheidippides. In the ancient games, poetry and music often went side by side with athletic contests. Pan is also connected with these. The art of prophecy was tricked from Pan by Apollo. Pan retained some skills in this area. In his shrine at Lykosoura he gave oracles through a nymph, Erato.

Pan is known as the instigator of panic terror. Mortals who saw him did not always survive much longer. Pheidippides died after delivering his message which included a caution from the god to revive his worship in Athens. Those who know anything of Pheidippides often misquote or misremember his story. People assume that he dropped dead after a mere twenty-six miles – the distance from Athens to Marathon – not realising that he had also just run to Sparta and back. He had, in fact, clocked up hundreds of miles in a matter of days and was killed by exhaustion. He was the best runner in Greece, so they used and reused him as a messenger until he dropped.

Panic terror is a most interesting phenomenon. Through his ability to produce it Pan became also a god of war. I have found several cases where sudden, inexplicable panic seized the enemy in the vicinity of Pan caves or in areas particularly devoted to his worship. The ancient descriptions of these events all show a combination of bad weather and delusions amongst the men leading to demoralisation on one side. More recent writers often ignore these details and give Pan a more straightforward role. Browning, for instance, turns him into a sort of soldier at Marathon. But Pan would never have become part of the regular army. Gods would never wear uniforms and take orders. While other gods might give instructions like generals, I'd see him as only interested in guerrilla warfare – frightening invaders of his territory by throwing down rocks or creating loud noises with the echoes of his caves and mountains, then doing battle on a one-to-one survival basis with any that stayed, as the shepherd does for his sheep. His humour and quirkiness could also make him willing to lay on a show of odder effects. Perhaps his worshippers used an unorthodox trick mentioned in Aeneas the Tactician's works. He advises getting goats drunk and hanging bells round their necks, then sending them amongst the enemy. It sounds like the only chance a goat would get of a decent drink.

Pan is curiously absent from the wars in Homer. Perhaps they'd have been over more quickly if he'd interfered. Herodotus states that he was born after the Trojan Wars. But this must be a different Pan from the one who was the son of Kronos and fought against the Titans at the beginning of time.

Pan is also a god of music. Midas is punished for preferring his melodies to Apollo's and gets the asses' ears that many satyrs seem to wear. Hermes, like Apollo, took Pan's ideas. The first lyre came from him. In the end, Pan only kept his syrinx. But was Midas entirely wrong to prefer Pan's melodies? He was probably just old-fashioned. Pan was thought by the Egyptians to be one of the eight original gods that came before the twelve Olympians. Apollo was probably more an improver than an inventor. The inhabitants of Arcadia, Pan's main area, were thought to use a different kind of metre in their poetry. It's probable that Pan's music and poetry are earlier, more primitive forms, that only survive in tiny snatches.

Pan and Echo are also inextricably linked. Caves and mountains – his territory – are places of strange echoes. Echoes can also be used for musical or poetic effects. When Pan is lumped with the nymphs he is also a god of dancing. When the name of Asklepios is added as a divinity in dedications, these nymph shrines were obviously used for healing. All these caves once contained water sources; some still do. Probably these streams had medicinal properties. I drank from all those I could find. Some caves also contain bed-like depressions and may have been used for worshippers to dream their own cures or prophecies. The cave near the Pharsalus battlefield was also dedicated to Cheiron, the centaur – another being known for his medical skills.

Perhaps Pan's cures were sometimes psychosexual ones. He was seen in this light both in ancient and Edwardian times. One of the world's earliest novels, Longus's *Daphnis and Chloe*, involves Pan and the nymphs in a sex-therapy scene. The older woman, who wants to initiate the young goatherd, Daphnis (who, by coincidence, has the same name as Pan's only male lover), asks him to go and find her goose 'for Pan's sake'. It's a trick to get him into the wood, where she has her way with him. She claims that the nymphs had instructed her to do this in a dream. Daphnis had been impotent through inexperience before, but afterwards he knows enough to be able to have sex with his real love, Chloe. In the much earlier *Lysistrata* of Aristophanes, Pan's cave on the Acropolis is suggested as a place to have sex in.

In Edwardian times, Pan was revived as a figure representing raw sex and the subconscious in all its power. Aleister Crowley, poet and magician, raised this Pan, and his friend went mad after the experience. Arthur Machen, a devout Christian, made him the epitome of evil. Dion Fortune, who had more than the average interest in psychology, made him a benign figure that represented the integration of conscious and subconscious powers. He is the catalyst that brings a pair of rather unlikely, unlovable and elderly lovers together. This sort of interpretation of Pan continued until well into this century. The sound of his pipes in early French films precedes the intrusion of sex and nature and a general unhinging of bourgeois morals.

Pan is also a god for comics. He was often paired with Dionysos, the god of theatre as well as wine. When Pan was born all the other gods took to him at first because he made them laugh. There's a line in one of the Marx brothers' films that compares Harpo, the musical, slightly idiotic one who never speaks, with Pan. Groucho says that his mother was a goat 'and that was the best half'. I couldn't help noting it down, as I share a birthday with Harpo Marx.

Pan's two known children – though he may have had a host of others by Maenads – are the dog-headed Man in the Moon and Iynx. Iynx is the name of the wry-neck bird. It was also a device used in love spells – a wheel to draw your lover to you. A pottery one was found in the Korykian cave. Pan's children belong to the twilight world of magic.

On a more jokey level, Pan is easily assimilated into popular culture because of his comic qualities. He figures on the modern Greek equivalent of a McGill postcard chasing a girl in tennis shorts. He was also mentioned in an early episode of *Star Trek* when Apollo, no less, was attempting to subdue all the good honest Americans aboard the *Enterprise*. He took an instant dislike to Spock because he reminded him of Pan 'and Pan always bored me'. My mother, who has not visited Greece or researched that particular god, thinks the same way. Those who were educated in the early decades of this century frequently do, seeing Pan as a desexed nature god of the most insipid kind.

Pan is not always desexed and innocent, though. A journalist who spoke to me over the phone recently shuddered at the mention of his name. In his early years he had fallen victim to a slightly disturbed female teacher in the Hebrides who had made all her children learn and practise rites of Pan. The experience had made such an impression on him that he wouldn't even describe what those celebrations were. They remain as secret as the original ceremonies in the caves at Vari and elsewhere.

I believe that most mysteries in life cannot be solved. The best one can hope to do is view the evidence and present it in some kind of order, drawing parallels and making connections where one can. As I drew to the end of my researches I came to conclusions, not so much about the past worship of Pan as about the present. I found that Pan was dead in most of Greece. I became increasingly disgusted with the pollution and the self-created problems of that country. I only felt that he was alive on Mount Lykaion and perhaps in some more secret way on Parnes in the cave I was never able to find. Pan is also alive in many other countries – for the time being, at any rate.

Anatole France once said that no civilised people offer hospitality to strangers. I think that's putting it too strongly. I still feel grateful for the hospitality that was offered to me. On the other hand, he does have a certain point. Taking in strangers does show naïvety. Although I don't take the offering of hospitality as proof, it is a fact that the Greeks are now an uncivilised people. There is a huge gap between what they are and what they think they are. The tourist brochures present a friendly Greece with fat cats, but the reality is very different. Many Greeks are rude and hostile. Beautiful sites are covered with rubbish. Riverbeds and mountainsides are littered with smashed cars. If a Greek can deface a sacred spot with shit, old bedding or used tyres, he will do so.

Greece suffers from a great many problems. Apart from the frightful pollution in Athens, there are strikes of all sorts. There were no buses in Athens during several of my visits. Sometimes there was no postal service. At other times there were wild-cat strikes in museums, in the electricity, and in all the other forms of transport. During one power cut, some unfortunate person was trapped in the lift in my hotel because no one had thought to warn the guests that everything would grind to a halt at eight. Two firemen came and shone a torch around, picked feebly at the lift-doors with a screwdriver, then walked off to leave the person inside to a two-hour wait. In August, the piped water in Athens nearly ran dry, it was rumoured. On that same day, sprinklers were playing on the grass by civic buildings and the underground spring in the Agora continued to pound out unused gallons of water every minute. If Greece was a person, I'd say it was in the middle of a severe nervous breakdown.

I've often speculated on the reasons why Italy recovered its greatness after the fall of the Roman empire and went on to produce great art, music and literature – things that were as good as what went before. I can't help comparing that success story with the utter demolition of Greek culture – its art and architecture, its literature and philosophy. Yes, I know they've produced the odd Nobel-prize-winning poet. But then, there are hardly any great writers amongst those prize-winners.

I would argue that the spirit of Italy survived because the Romans and their successors, the Italians, were well-earthed. They were gardeners and cultivators – they loved the soil and they did not reject their heritage.

As I wrote the closing pages of this book, the postman delivered a postcard covered with ithyphallic satyrs. Its sender, an unnamed reader of the *London Review of Books*, reassured me that Pan was alive and well and living on a mountain slope outside Malang in Indonesia. He signed his card with the Greek letters of the name *Eros*.

Select Bibliography

General

The Cult of Pan in Ancient Greece, P. Borgeaud, translated by Kathleen Atlass and James Redfield, University of Chicago Press, 1988.

Pan the Goat-God, Patricia Merivale, Harvard University Press, 1969.

Greek Votive Reliefs to Pan and the Nymphs, C. M. Edwards, Dissertation NY University, University Microfilms, 1987.

The Archaeology and History of Cave Use in Attica, J. M. Wickens, Dissertation Indiana University, University Microfilms, 1986.

Encyclopedias

Kitto's Biblical Encyclopaedia (for spots in Israel).

Every encyclopaedia devoted to mythology, religion or archaeology will yield some useful information on Pan. The most useful of these on Pan, the Nymphs, Lykaon and Priapus is that in German by Pauly-Wissowa.

Ancient Literary Sources

Pausanias' Guides to Southern and Central Greece (2 vols.), translated and annotated by Peter Levi, Penguin Classics.

Pan is also mentioned by a great many classical authors in their works. Chief amongst these are the Greek Anthology, Menander's and Aristophanes' Plays, Plato's Dialogues, Herodotus' and Plutarch's Works, Daphnis and Chloe by Longus and the Homeric Hymns. Most of these are available in the dual versions (original text plus translation) published by Loeb, or in translation only by Penguin

Classics. There are many other editions also, available from libraries.

Guides and travel literature

Baedeker's Greece, 1909. (I would only recommend old Baedeker guides as the modern versions do not have enough archaeological detail).

The Blue Guide (current edition).

Various editions of John Murray's Guide from several decades ago.

Portrait of Southern Greece, Brian Dicks, Robert Hale, 1982.

Accounts of specific excavations and their finds

Parnes:

Das Nymphaion auf dem Parnes, H. G. Lolling, Mitteilungen des deutschen Archäologischen Instituts, Vol. V, p. 291.

Inschriften von der Grotte des Pan und Nymphen bei Phyle, A. Wilhelm, Jahreshafte des österreichischen archäologischen Instituts, 1929, Vol. XXV, p. 54.

Archaiologike Ephemeris, 1919, pp. 48–53.

Athens and Attica:

Pan am Ilissos, G. Rodenwaldt, Mitteilungen des deutschen archäologischen Instituts, Vol. 37, pp. 141–150.

Bildlexicon zur Topographie des antiken Attica, John Travlos (Tübingen, 1988).

Pictorial Dictionary of Ancient Athens, John Travlos (New York, Praeger, 1971). This contains some of the material in the German title above by John Travlos.

Parnassus:

Archaiologike Ephemeris, 1906, p. 109.

L'Antro Corycien II, Bulletin de Correspondence Hellénique, Supplement IX, 1984.

Penteli:

E Spelia tes Penteles, Syllektes I, pp. 137 on.

E Spelia ton Nymphon tes Penteles, P. Zorides, Archaeologike
   Ephemeris, 1977, pp. 4–11.

Pharsala:
L'Antro delle Ninfe e di Pan a Farsala in Tessaglia, Annuario
   della Scuola Archaelogica di Atene, 1923–1924, pp. 6–7 and
   21–22.

Daphne:
Archaiologike Ephemeris, 1937, pp. 391–408.

Index